To Live Another Day

A true story of the Holocaust

Sylvia Epstein

Dedication

My deepest desire for this book is to carry forward truths that will teach and remind us, so we may never forget. Together we can prevent history from repeating itself. I dedicate this book first and foremost, to the bravest heart I know, my loving and dedicated mother. I dedicate this book to my husband and my two pride and joys; my sons and to my grandchildren who fill my soul to overflowing.

Boryslaw, Poland 1939
"The quieter you become, the more you can hear."
-Baba Ram Dass

Our Precious Noah

Every day at noontime, sisters Louisa and Fania stood at the window huddled together, shoulder to shoulder, like immovable statues molded into one shape and cemented to the floor. Their eyes were fixated on the nursery school directly across the street from Louisa's house. Ever since four-year-old Noah was enrolled at that nursery school across the street, Louisa and her older sister, Fania assumed their position at the family's second-floor window and waited for the teachers to dismiss all the preschoolers. Fania's four-year-old son Noah was Louisa's nephew and was among them.

"Louisa, Moiya Cochona," Fania murmured in Polish. "Every day since the rumors started, I'm so afraid it's going to really happen," said Fania as a choking fear was making her swallow the last syllables. Her trembling body began to shake like a lonely leaf hanging on for dear life, desperately clinging to an almost barren tree branch.

Louisa whispered, "Don't be silly, Fania. It's only a rumor. Don't believe everything people say. They tend to always believe the worst. Things like this can't possibly happen. Anyone in his right mind would never imagine doing such things to innocent children. People still have a sense of decency. Never you mind. It's just mass hysteria taking over," she promised. "Nothing bad will happen," Louisa reassured her sister, while her own words were unconvincing to herself. As Louisa continued to speak, her body stiffened involuntarily. She began to withdraw several inches away from Fania's shoulder, for fear that her sister would feel her tension.

4

Louisa continued, "Try to think positive. We'll do as we always do. We will wait for dismissal to be over. Then, as soon as the students are all lined up, we'll run downstairs, cross the street and go get our beautiful little Noah."

Fania turned to face Louisa as hot tears started to flood the corners of her eyes. "I'll tell you right now, if something happens to Noah, I will kill myself. I will not live on this earth without my son," she cried as rivulets of tears began streaming down both cheeks. Fania turned to face the window and began her protective watch on the playground as they waited for the children to line up for dismissal.

For the past few weeks, Louisa and Fania overheard many rumors from several non-Jewish neighbors and townspeople alike. People whispered about the planned Nazi abductions of children, fearing that they might be taken away by force and never to be seen again. Could such preposterous stories ever turn out to be true? Was it merely malicious gossip? Why would the Nazis target a nursery school? Would they stoop so low?

"There is no way any of it is true," Louisa continued. No sane person could ever imagine the Nazis would roundup and abduct nursery school children. Something so inhumane could never materialize! Families and the rest of the townspeople are good, righteous people. They respect our community and everyone in it. They nurture their loved ones. Many of us in our town have always lived here. Neighbors live amidst the warmth and protection of our town government. We have never done anything to deserve such unseen stirrings of evil. It would never happen here."

Louisa and Fania stared straight ahead in rapt attention, believing in the protective power of their watchful eyes. Somehow, they deluded themselves into thinking that keeping a close guard on the situation might provide an extra safety net. Considering the circulating rumors, they would try anything to provide added protection.

Finally, they breathed a sigh of relief as the children were ushered out of the nursery school. They watched as the children were lined up in three queues of ten, standing obediently just as their teachers had trained them, demonstrating they were ready to be picked up by an assigned adult.

Ordinarily, once the children were ready for pick up, Louisa and Fania would race down the stairs and stop to kiss the mezuzah nailed to the side of the massive wood-carved front door leading to the cobblestoned street. Then, they would cautiously check both ways before crossing the busy street. Their hearts were filled with joyful anticipation. They loved to see their little Noah's face light up the moment he spotted them. He'd give them a wide smile, and his precious little voice would say, "Mammale! Tante! I'm ready to go home!" They would run towards each other, taking turns to scoop him up and smother him with hugs and kisses.

After that, they would all take a short walk towards Fania's house, located several blocks down the street, to have a deliciously prepared lunch made by Fania's gentile housekeeper. For the rest of the afternoon they would have fun together, play games, or maybe take a long stroll in the neighborhood. Then tired Noah would take a nap before Fania's husband would come home from work in the late afternoon. Sometimes Louisa ate dinner and chitchatted with them until later in the evening before walking back to her family home. That was the typical day for them.

"Okay, Fania darling, calm down," Louisa tried to calm her sister while silently attempting to manage her own nervousness. "It's all going to be ok, Noah is having another uneventful morning at school. Be calm because nothing is going to happen. You see, they are lining up exactly as usual. We will go downstairs in a second. You know how they frown

6

upon us for trying to take the kids out earlier than usual, unless it is an emergency."

Fania's worries began clamoring like a police siren. "Louisa, I am so petrified! I just know something horrible is about to happen. I have a terrible feeling. I know that every day I feel like this, but today I can't stop shaking. I am petrified that something bad will happen and the Nazis will take away my Noah! If that ever happens, I will die. I cannot breathe. Oh my God, I may faint. Hold me, Louisa so I don't fall."

Suddenly, Fania's words became barely audible. She was losing her composure, swaying off balance, as her knees weakened and began to give way. Louisa grabbed her shoulders and helped her regain her balance. "Stand up, Fania! Get a hold of yourself! You must be strong. You are overreacting! Think positive. Nothing will happen. Noah is safe. We are going downstairs right now! Come on, grab my hand and move quickly. We are going down to get him, NOW!" They grasped each other's hand and proceeded to turn away from the window.

But then, somehow, instinctively, both of them looked back. Suddenly, in a split-second, it happened. The dreaded prophesy. The rumors proved to be true. As if abruptly awakened from a frightful dream, they could hear the approach of a speeding vehicle. A bullet-colored van going at top speed rounded the corner of the street. Disguised as a messenger of death, a large Swastika emblem was posted on the side doors. The van continued to race forward, pulling right up to the playground! They heard the grating sounds of grinding and screeching brakes before stopping abruptly on the gravelly playground area. Groaning blasts of exhaust blared loudly in earshot, as an uncontrollable fear and gripping panic ensued. It was as if a tsunami was about to engulf everything in its path. This earth-shattering nightmare was about to become the new reality.

The petrified teachers positioned themselves close to the lines of innocent children as if zapped by a stun gun, and they remained steadfast while they glared at the van. Within a matter of seconds, all the children knew that something terrible was happening. Many began to wail, calling for their mommies. Others attempted to run away and were instantly caught by one of the three Nazi officers who jumped out of the van. With one quick reflex, an officer managed to catch a little girl, pulling on her delicate long hair, ripping her backwards towards him. "Oh no you don't, you pitiful Jew baby. You will get back with the rest of the vermin babies! Don't worry your little head. We promise to call your mother later." The officer lied with a smirk on his face. Every time a student tried to run, one of the officers grabbed the child, often wrenching arms from the socket, tugging on ears, or pulling hair so hard that the child would have no choice but to give up the fight and obey the instructions to board the awaiting van.

One of the teachers shrieked. "Oy mine gott, please have mercy! What are you doing to us? Where are you taking our children? You have no right!" Her fresh, young face that was beautifully framed with two bouncing, blonde pigtails were now streaked with a continuous stream of frustrated and angry tears. In better times, it would be fair to say that she was the teacher who resembled the main character, Heidi from the Swiss Alps fairytale by Heiner. Now she looked frantic, like someone whose children were viciously being ripped away from her.

Just then, the other young and petite, dark-haired teacher joined in. "We beg you to leave us alone! We have done nothing to deserve this horrific intrusion!" She dropped to her knees and said, "We will pay you to go away. May God have mercy on what you are doing!" Despite her small frame and

8

slender body, her voice sounded as strong as a heavyweight fighter.

Fania and Louisa stood at the window and stared in help-less disbelief, both realizing what was about to happen, both trapped in a silent earthquake. Cold-blooded fear began coursing through their veins as they saw exactly what they had dreaded. Fania turned away from the window and began to make animalistic sounds. As saliva foamed around her mouth like a mad dog, she declared, "I'm going down there. They are NOT taking my son!"

Louisa lurched forward, grabbed Fania's sleeve with all her might, as if to keep her from falling off the side of a cliff. "Oh no, you are not! It's a suicide mission! You can't! You will be captured in a second! That's what they want, for us to come out! They'd lock you up with the rest or worse, they'd shoot you in front of the others just to make an example! We WILL find out where they took him. We will bring him home. Please, Fania, be smart. Come back here!"

Both sisters were frozen in a catatonic state, pressed to-gether at the window as they helplessly watched in paralyz-ing disbelief. Wracking emotions blurred their vision as their gaping mouths hung open, neither able to utter a sound as they watched the children being forced to board the van. Suddenly, their throats gave way to a primitive moaning be-fore turning into growling noises, sounding like ferocious dogs about to attack their prey. The prey was the children.

An invisible sledgehammer pounded at their temples, cracked open their skulls, blinding their eyes, their faces cov-ered with their own spurting blood. Desperation took over. They were trapped in a frozen solid glacier, no way to thaw out of the deep freeze. Yet they had no choice but to endure the torture, watching helplessly from the window and listen-ing to the haunting sounds of screaming children, their cries deepening into pitiful weeping. This was the day, the signal

9

of doom. This was the day that fate crossed the street before they had a chance. This was the day that their whole world began to fall apart, breaking up families and destroying lives beyond repair, like fine crystal goblets intentionally dropped to the floor; fragments of shattered glass and sharp crystal shards unable to be mended.

In a second's time, Fania and Louisa became living zombies, drained of their blood, hearts ripped from their chests. Neither of the sisters could hear, see, or feel anything at all, not even a scream could escape from their motionless lips. All that remained was a profound helplessness. Lives burning up into smoke, dissipating into the air like snuffed out candles and vanishing into thin air along with youthful hopes and dreams. The new, unconscionable reality was taking over. The children were gone because the unthinkable happened. All that remained was the loud, pounding drums of a deafening silence.

God is closest to those with broken hearts.- Jewish Proverb

Can there be life after Noah?

Hours must have passed by that afternoon, yet it felt like time stood still for them. Everything happened within minutes. There was no semblance of balance, everything upturned, everything ruined. Shattered lives scattered about; old lives became history.

The sisters remained at the window like statues frozen in time, unable to move, ravaged by sheer horror. Fania's concentrated stare drilled holes through the window glass. Louisa's tears continued to fall uncontrollably down her cheeks. Noah, their precious child, had been stolen out from under them, right in front of their eyes! The sisters were left helpless, emotions left to marinate in bitterness and despair. They could do nothing to save him. Both stood paralyzed, choked by a strangling guilt; an invisible vise tightly wrapped around their necks, making it unable for them to breathe.

It was impossible for the sisters to accept the reality of what just happened. The devastating loss was beyond words, a double blow for both. Fania's precious boy was gone, lost into oblivion. If he was still alive, he was somewhere all alone to face the unthinkable cruelty that lay ahead. How could it be true? Their thoughts were fueled by delusions of hope, wishing the Nazis might change their minds and bring them all back. Louisa wished silently: Maybe the van will turn around. My prayers will be answered. A miracle will happen and soon we will celebrate the return of Noah.

Just a few minutes ago, Noah was a happy and innocent four-year-old child standing in line on the playground, routinely waiting for his mother and his Aunt Louisa to pick him up. Then, suddenly, Noah and his peers were marched straight into the hands of the enemy, whisked away to places

11

unknown; swiped away by the Nazi's as if removed by a toxic-soaked rag leaving no trace left on the surface.

It was hard to believe that the Nazi commandants started out as regular men or women with families of their own. Prior to their pledged Nazi allegiance, these men and women may have been righteous people who believed in doing good deeds. Maybe they shared decent virtues and values. Perhaps they were people who believed in the integrity of fairness and justice towards fellow men. Yet, it was shocking how quickly they were able to change gears, abandon former beliefs, and help turn the world upside down. They were brain-washed people following each other down the evil path of Nazism. Their goal was to target the Jews as well as other designated scapegoats, wrongly thinking that they might ultimately improve the condition of their own downtrodden lives. Being a Jew, trying to survive in Nazi-controlled Europe was like being a victim in a game of Russian Roulette. It was like living with the cold metal of a loaded handgun constantly pushing into the temple of your forehead, day and night, painfully awaiting the firing of a bullet.

Many ordinary townspeople readily joined the Nazi movement. Many were uninformed, misguided of its evil doctrines, and unaware of the drastic requirements that lay ahead for them. Yet, the Nazi influence left them with a twisted sense of morality. How could they welcome such blatant bigotry and prejudice? It required that they abandon all sense of humanistic conscience and compassion. So many people merely followed out their orders. unspeakable acts that supported the Nazi mania. How could they go back to their loving families and pretend like nothing happened that day? Only the deranged or the mentally ill might be able to comprehend how the supporters of the Nazi regime could demonstrate or condone such heinous acts. Characteristically, many of them exhibited nonchalant behaviors and a sheer lack of empathy, along with no compassion or signs of hesitation or remorse. They were uncaring people who

12

simply followed orders and who committed despicable acts frequently witnessed by others who could do nothing to stop them. They could only stand and watch in horror.

Somehow Fania's mind began to clear, though her thoughts began racing in all directions. She turned to Louisa and as if her soul could scream aloud, she cried incredulously, "What just happened?" Monsters that were sent by the devil himself came to do his job. How easily they just lifted up the hysterical children, one by one, and recklessly toss them onto the vans as if they were inanimate objects, like stuffed rag dolls! They have no hearts, no souls! They just drove them away without a care about them or for those they left behind. No act could be more heinous!

Louisa's grief-stricken eyes continued to tear. Torturous thoughts continued to plague her emotions, thinking: Noah, where are you, my little nephew? I hope you are not cold. My heart breaks for you! I hope you are not thirsty or hungry. I hope there is a bathroom where you are! You are too young to take care of yourself! You must grow up fast! Maybe there is a nice person there to comfort you when you are sobbing for mama. I cannot take the pain in my heart, my darling child! Louisa tried to find some sort of rationale to soothe the raw pain in her heart, wondering if it was better not to know where they took him so they might cling to the hope they might miraculously meet again.

Deeply embedded in the desperate grips of their embrace, Louisa tried to find the courage to look up, though fearful of seeing the pain on Fania's despairing face. Through her bloodshot eyes, her vision was blurred by the raw, salty tears stinging and burning in her eye sockets. She was hesitant to meet eyes with Fania, selfishly fearing it would only heighten her own intolerable pain, enveloped in the same torture.

Both were helplessly vulnerable to the unspeakable pain. At that moment, Fania made the first move to detach herself from Louisa's desperate embrace. She allowed herself to slowly sink into the make-believe comfort of denial. She made a conscious decision not to face the torture but to pretend that what they just witnessed never happened. She never lifted her face to look up at Louisa. Instead, she focused her gaze downward towards the floor. Despite her unsteadiness, she managed to stand up and wipe away her bitter tears and run towards the landing that led towards the stairs. She moved swiftly as a mouse scurrying away from immediate danger, urgently seeking the shelter of its home. When Fania reached the bottom of the steps, she traversed past the well-stocked shelves, accidentally knocking over several grocery items blocking her way towards the exit door of the family store.

Louisa heard the frantic opening and slamming of the front door. Still peering through the upstairs window, Louisa continued to watch Fania in clear view as she ran down the street erratically in an awkward gait, resembling the reckless abandon of a drunken woman. Within seconds, Fania disappeared from Louisa's sight.

Confused and angry, Fania kept running through the streets, soon forgetting which direction to take home. Suddenly her once familiar surroundings were foreign, almost unrecognizable. She moved through the alleyways that were littered with discarded trash and hungry stray cats. She was lost and alone without Noah. In the faint distance, she thought she heard the mocking jeers of ghostly apparitions. So desperate to run away from herself, from her empty life, from all the devastation, that she wasn't sure if she could still breathe. Her stone heart seemed no longer able to beat.

As a doomed fate took over, Fania was transformed into a grieving mother for which there was no solace. There was nothing left but to suffer from the greatest loss imaginable,

14

when a child is wrenched away from its mother. She was destined to live her remaining days as a broken spirit, forever searching for her lost child. What did the future have in store for all of them?

For the rest of that day, even Louisa's memory became a blur. Her state of mind could have been compared to the story of the frog immersed into a large copper pot of cool water slowly heating on the stove, just a matter of time before being boiled to death. The new street sounds took on a simmering rage as well as the alarming sounds brewing in her head. She wished she could cover her hands over her ears, keep her eyes closed forever, and block out the calamity of this day. Panicky thoughts shook her to the core: How could anyone survive in such darkness? For this to happen was proof that the world went mad. The lunatics overtook the asylum. How could anyone see again when there was no longer a spark of light anywhere? The world was blinded by an abounding evil mist and ruled by ignorance and hate.

Throughout the neighborhood, pathogens of hatred were descending from the sky. People's wails were resonating with tormented sounds that bounced off the houses, even the stone walls. The cobblestone streets seemed to tremble from the brutality in the face of mass hysteria. Its effects left its inhabitants with their lives in shambles. It was an era of human rupture, leaving the remains of shattered hopes and dreams. People were left in the dust to pick up the pieces of their crumbling lives, like an earthquake that destroys and leaves nothing behind except rubble and debris.

Slowly sliding down to the floor, Louisa allowed her back to finally rest against the wall. Impossible to keep from shaking, emotions swirled like a plate that drops to the floor and then wobbles in a shaky spin, trying to settle itself once again. Louisa worried about Fania and where she went. Did she to run back to her home to tell her husband what had just happened? Did she run somewhere else? What was to

15

become of her? Did their parents and younger sister already know about the catastrophe? How was she going to deal with their grief too?

Assuming the posture of defeat, Louisa braced her back to the wall and her head hung low. As tears fell steadily down her face, her mind continued to wander. There is no control over what has happened today. This tragedy will forever make all the saddest songs in the world more heart-wrenching. The volume is too loud for me to bear. I wish I were deaf, it would surely be a welcome solution to dull my senses. Maybe it is better not to feel, not to hear, and not to see. It is the only way to hang on to my sanity. They say that the human mind protects its brain that way. She felt she was rapidly sliding down a black tunnel. She worried constantly about Fania and where she might be. In light of all the cruel things happening around her, she couldn't help but fear that things were going to be getting even worse. This was a mere prelude to what was going to happen next.

If there is a God, he will have to beg for my forgiveness.
– Unknown

Where to Go Now?

Louisa woke up hours later to stone silence. The last thing she remembered doing was sliding down to the carpet on the living room floor. Her body felt numb. Upon waking up to the reality of what had just happened, she found herself gasping for breath. She felt as if she was slowly drowning in a river of sorrow, unable to swim against its strong current. How could anyone sustain one's life and survive such a tragedy?

Paralyzed by profound grief, Louisa realized that she never went downstairs to find out about Fania. The thought hadn't occurred to her to find her mother and father and tell them about the tragedy of losing Noah. Undoubtedly, her parents were working downstairs in the family store. How could they not have seen Fania run away? Maybe they already found out about Noah. But why didn't they come upstairs to find her?

Throughout Louisa's eighteen years of life, nothing like this ever happened before in her small hometown of Boryslaw, which was part of an area of Poland called Galicia. Louisa was the middle sister of the Drimmer family and her brother Karl was ten years older, the eldest child in the family. Louisa, her mother and father, her thirteen-year-old sister Malta and the live-in maid Sophie lived in the upstairs apartment. Fania, eight years older than Louisa, was married and lived down the street with her husband and, until today, their four-year-old son Noah.

The spacious area on the first floor of the Drimmer family two-story house was converted into a general store. Their family's apartment was on the second level. Downstairs, the store was brimming with a huge variety of necessities and household items to suit many of its regular customers. The general store was a well-frequented place to shop, carrying a wide variety of farm fresh vegetables and fruit and an assortment of canned foods. On display was a large glass-covered cabinet replenished daily with freshly baked goods delivered for sale by nearby bakeries. Patrons considered the store to be a convenient, reliable place to shop since it provided for the needs of the immediate neighborhood as well as for the surrounding rural areas.

In the past, anti-Semitism always existed, but the blatant situations were less frequent up until this time. There had been occasional incidents involving narrow-minded people who unfairly judged anyone else from a different culture. Ignorance and bigotry were common characteristics of people who lived outside the ghetto. The same was true for people who were confined to live inside the ghetto.

Before the rise of Hitler's influence, despite the fact that the neighborhood patrons knew their store was owned by Jewish people, it didn't seem to matter. Townspeople shopped there often, considering it to be an impressive showcase to visit, browse, and to buy necessities as well as various specialty items. For the past three decades, the Drimmer family reaped the benefit of a generous income. Their livelihood was built on the accumulation of steady profits from good business practices and management skills, hard work and diligence.

As a bonus feature, there was a back dressing room where a full-time seamstress was employed. Her name was Berta, a Jewish refugee who, along with her family, immigrated to Poland from Hungary. Karl, Louisa's older brother and she were involved in a romantic relationship. People knew her to be an excellent seamstress/couturier. She was also proficient in tailoring men's suits, designing a special dress, custom making a shirt, and replicating the latest fashions straight from Milan or Paris by just looking at a picture.

Clothing was stitched and cut to fit each customer, made exclusively, since the concept of "off the rack" clothing did not yet exist.

The picturesque image of their two-story house was set among a tree-lined street that boasted manicured plots in the small front yards allotted to each homeowner. This house had a charming front courtyard appointed with a wide array of colorful, perennial flowers that bordered the cobblestone path leading to the main entrance door. The house was nestled among two prominent, stately oak trees that promised shade and protection from weather's harsh elements. Carefully balanced to rest against the two stone pillars was a heavy wooden, hand-painted sign. It was scripted in blue and white Polish letters, displaying the store's name, "Drimmer's General Store." Among most Jewish and non-Jewish people in the town, it was indeed a known entity in the town, a charming place to shop. Everyone seemed to enjoy the simple life, the everyday version.

Even the Orthodox Jews in Boryslaw, living together in the Jewish Ghetto, referred to as a "Shtetel," were dictated and regulated by strict laws and guided by a common set of values. Throughout several generations, this was a place where the Jewish people lived amongst each other. They shared the same traditions and beliefs, celebrations and sorrows, joys and pain. Living within the confines of a Ghetto offered a sense of security. Communal living gave them assurance and supported the right to choose how to live their lives. Here, they were able to practice their religion without the judgment of others, all under the pretense of a safe and secure setting. The children of these families were often matched together for marriage shidduch, meaning a match. They lived under the illusion that no other culture or religion could penetrate their heritage bond. They strongly adhered to one another like the adhesive glue that promises to uphold even the heaviest painting, a secure mounting onto the wall. Just like the mounted picture, the inhabitants of the Ghetto never dreamed that the rising power of the hatred in the land could rise to such levels.

Before today, Louisa often wondered why the houses on her street were built so close together. She now realized why the houses were built the way there were, sitting on small tracts of land. She understood the need for close proximity of the houses in the segregated Ghetto. It was a way to create a protective setting for like-minded people of the same heritage, ethnicity, or religion to live together and be able to share their ways and traditions. It was an example of strength in numbers. Unfortunately, the trying times were becoming too difficult to manage. Suddenly, as Louisa stood at the window, hoping for Noah's return, she noticed how a dominant wind was causing a rigorous sway of the tree limbs on the large oak tree. They seemed to whisper the sinister warning that a bad omen was on its way.

For the dead and the living, we must bear witness.
- Elie Wiesel

What is Happening?

It was ten days after Noah's abduction and the Drimmer family was beside themselves with grief. After Noah was taken, savagely ripped away from them, anything was possible. Plus, Fania was missing. Nobody could find her. Louisa thought she may have locked herself away and was refusing to talk or meet with anyone. No one knew what happened to Fania's husband, Josef, either. Did Fania make it home to find Josef, or had he mysteriously disappeared? Were they hiding somewhere together in a secret place other than their home? Louisa and her family worried all the time. All they could do was pray. How could such a thing happen to them? This kind of disaster only happened in books about murder, not to them.

After the abduction of the nursery school students, all their fears materialized into something even worse than imagined. Jews were forced to live this way, plagued by a threatened existence, like a menacing fist of fear that blocked their vision; one that continued to intimate and frighten them both day and night. Since the invasion of Poland, disorder and chaos abounded everywhere. Bad news was spreading rapidly. A barbaric wildness in the streets was happening all around them, plaguing their senses, terrorizing their existence. Stories were rampant. People heard about how the Nazis already had invaded certain neighborhoods during the night, right in her hometown of Boryslav.

At Louisa's high school, she heard about a neighborhood family who were ripped away from their beds in the middle of the night, taken away as prisoners of the state and forced to board the awaiting vans, then taken away to unknown destinations. No one ever saw them again. They were guilty of one thing, the fact that they were Jews. This was the un-imaginable panic that dominated the daily atmosphere in which the Jews lived, like a solid fist threatening a heavy punch, ready to strike hard without warning. Bone-chilling stories and bad news spread rapidly, like a splintered kite heading upwards and downwards, unable to recover its direction, its snapped string following closely behind. This was the atmosphere in Boryslaw.

Louisa's friends whispered about the disturbing rumors. "Louisa, you might be next! They might kill you! Get out of Poland as fast as you can! Look what happened to Noah! Your sister, Fania will never be the same! Be careful! You should try to leave the town! Get out! Go anywhere else but leave Poland altogether!" The persistent warnings were too late. How could they pick up and leave Boryslaw now? It was no longer safe to travel anywhere in Europe.

Louisa was tortured constantly by terrifying thoughts about what happened to Noah and the mystery of Fania's disappearance. She wondered: Could it be that Noah is still alive somewhere? If so, where? Are Fania and Josef together, somewhere safe? All of our lives are doomed. How could this happen? She thought about what her mother said, "The harsh hand of grief takes hold and squeezes your heart when you least expect it."

When Germany invaded Poland on September 1, 1939, the Jewish townspeople throughout Poland became instant victims. Subsequently, all small towns like Boryslaw were caught in the same witches' brew, a Nazi cauldron of perco-lating and loathing aversions. Even though, several days later, European nations like Britain and France responded by declaring war on Germany, sweeping winds of hatred formed a dark, menacing cloud spreading across Europe. It readily covered each targeted country, allowing for Ger-many's easy invasion. The country of Poland was defeated by a combination of German and Soviet forces and strategically partitioned between Nazi Germany and the Soviet Union.

Early morning raids and household attacks were becoming commonplace. It was an easy way for the Nazis to take advantage of vulnerable, sleeping victims. Jewish families continued to live in turmoil and fear. Abhorrent rumors were circulating about how Ukrainian Nationalists, members of the Nazi party, were banding together and invading certain neighborhoods in the middle of the night or in the wee hours of the morning.

Similar attacks on the Jews began to take place not only in Louisa's hometown, but all over Poland. The mania was like a runaway train with no brakes, plowing down the tracks, getting ready to crash and burn. Who was there to help the Jews with no defense against the calamity of the times? There was no authority to call upon, no one to offer protection from the on-coming surge of catastrophe. Where was the rest of the world? Why did no one try to bring a halt to this outbreak of human furor? It was as if Jews were taken aboard the runaway train, unwilling passengers headed for disaster.

That night, Louisa and her family went to bed under a Polish moon, surrounded by an ominous black sky that dominated the darkness that night. An impending doom was descending, like an aircraft sent crashing to the water, waiting to be rescued. Strangely enough, there were no stars, no signs of light, nothing but the hazy lamp posts to light up the way for any pedestrian who might be passing through on the way home that night. The eerie quiet was difficult to tolerate. There were no audible sounds on the street, not even the yelp of a dog or the screech of a bicycle. There was just deafening silence, as a weighted blanket of doom began to fall over the town of Boryslaw.

Say not in grief "he is no more" but in thankfulness say that he was. - Hebrew Proverb

The Siren of a Virgin

The "Aktion," often called a pogrom, started around 4:00 a.m. on the Louisa's Street. Louisa, who was eighteen years old, her thirteen-year-old sister, Marissa, and both of her parents were asleep in their own beds. Suddenly, a horrendous commotion sharply awakened them all from a deep slumber. Within seconds, more explosive sounds pierced through the peaceful night air. Raucous voices of men shouting, banging against and slamming of vehicle doors, and offensive noises were made to disturb the nighttime peace as the Nazi collaborators disembarked from their vans. The noise was intentional, as they were eager to make their presence known to their victims.

Louisa was awakened by the startling sounds and the deliberate, rhythmic thumping of jackboots began ascending the stairs. She sat up in her bed and stared into the pitch blackness of her bedroom, paralyzed by fear. Her spine was so straight that every muscle and nerve ending tightened, squeezing relentlessly against her spinal column. Helpless and afraid to move, she heard the horrendous protests of her parents being roughly awakened, pleading for their lives,

Louisa's blood ran cold and her heart thumped erratically, realizing she was a witness to her family's plight. All she could do was hope that it all was a bad dream. If not a dream then maybe, miraculously, the intruders might take pity on them, change their minds and even spare them. Louisa knew she was next and she began to shiver uncontrollably. The sleepy warmth of her bedroom was being replaced by a gust of frosty wind blowing in from an open window. A chilling awareness enveloped her like ice pellets stinging her senses with battering hail. Her bedroom was still pitch dark, except for the tiniest glints of early morning light trying to peer in through the sides of the heavy damask curtains.

Just then, the door to Louisa's bedroom sprang opened with a powerful thrust. Out of the darkness she saw the barest outline of the tall, young man, most assuredly a Nazi collaborator, looming over her bed like a demonic force about to attack. He looked to be about her age, it was hard to tell in the darkness. Now fully awake in her bed, Louisa backed her ramrod straight spine hard against the adjacent wall. Naturally, her first reaction was to scream for help, but in this case there was no one to call for help. The intruders were part of the police state, all of them participants of the Nazi cause to rid the Jews from the country.

Louisa opened her mouth to scream while expecting to hear the sound of her own voice, but to her dismay, no sound came out. She tried again, but her vocal cords refused to cooperate. Her shallow breathing made her lungs feel deflated and she could feel the involuntary clamoring of her own heart thrashing against her ribcage. Louisa was aghast, knowing full well she was trapped in a horrible situation with no escape, and all alone with this intruder. She couldn't breathe, and the realization made her erratic heart beat out of control. Suddenly, she felt overpowered. A dizzying fear began to take over her senses and the only sound she could hear was the screaming silence of her own terror.

Just then, a strange occurrence happened. Both Louisa and the soldier seemed to freeze into a stupor. Lasting for a mere few seconds, it felt like an eternity before either one of them could even attempt to move. Finally, the young Nazi moved on impulse. He must have regained his courage to carry out his mission and aimed his flashlight at her face, the harsh light blinding her eyes. "Well, just take a look at this beautiful Polish girl!" his voice bellowed in a thundering tone.

Louisa's panic was rising, as she was literally face to face with danger. Like a hammer to the head, she was the nail being pounded down. Conflicted with mass confusion, she tried to gain her composure so she could survive. "Think straight!" she silently told herself. As a Nazi, he must have done terrible things before. How will I be able to get away? I can't allow myself to be trapped here! What can I do? She knew she had to find a way to stall, maybe even reason with him to leave her alone.

There was no time to spare. Was it too late? She managed to remain still, her eyes magnetized to the young Nazi's face, watching as his flashlight's path moved deliberately slow, up and down her face and body. It was like a searchlight looking for a treasure, a high beam of light used to penetrate through the fog of darkness. Suddenly the world took on the intensity of an eerie stillness. Louisa felt caught in the eye of a storm as fierce hurricane-force winds of evil continued to blow, determined to destroy everything in sight.

The guiding light of his flashlight paved the way for him to stop and dwell on the vision in front of him - noticing how the soft, fluffy goose down blanket barely covered her nakedness. He refocused his gaze, attracted to the image of her sitting on her bed in a silky nightdress, how one thin strap slid down off her left shoulder to rest on her slim upper arm. At first, Louisa made no move to adjust the strap back in place. At this point of their encounter, the provocative pose began as an unintentional move, but surely was becoming a sensual pose, perfect for the subject of an artist's canvas: a vision of a striking young beauty posing suggestively. In a split-second, Louisa made a quick decision not to readjust the fallen strap, thinking it best to remain in a suggestive gesture. She would do anything to buy some time, to save her own life. Suddenly, Louisa became the subject of a provocative image; a young woman sitting back against the wall in a silk nightdress, a fallen strap softly caressing her upper

26

arm. It would become a difficult temptation for any young man to ignore.

It happened quickly. The scent of sexual intoxication caused a palpable energy shift in the room. Suddenly, Louisa realized this was the turning point in her life on many levels. If he were to seduce her, did it matter to him that she was Jewish? Of course, he knew she was a Jew. Everyone knew that according to Nazi law, Christians were prohibited to have relations with a Jew. After all, he was the one who barged into to her home, intent on taking her and her family away. He was the dutiful one, the diligent follower obeying his orders. Was he able to ignore his mission and fall prey to his sexual instincts? Was she but a convenient distraction, an opportunity to be seduced by the powerful lure of sexual desire?

Louisa imagined how he might reason with himself. She sat invitingly situated amidst the fresh white bed linens, posing as the purest specimen of a sultry virgin, primed for the taking. Could this be my lucky day? Take this hedonistic gift, enjoy the recklessness! I don't even know her first name and I don't care. No strings attached, just pure body pleasure! Why not? I cannot resist. I can almost feel myself sink into that warm body of flesh like a cold, steel knife surging into a tub of soft, warm butter!

Louisa's confessing thoughts simultaneously abounded, just knowing she was about to lose her virginity. In a mixture of sultry fear, her thoughts scrambled. Under these conditions, who would ever know? My only chance is that he'll succumb to my lure. I'll use my body to barter for my life!

It was decided. She had no choice but to fan the fires of sexual tension. As she sat there, her emotions were conflicted. This in terribly unfair, she thought. I'm only eighteen. How could my life be over when I am so young? What makes me think this man is somehow different than the others? She

27

answered her own question by thinking how the other Nazis came roaring into the house, snarling and growling like wild, hungry animals desperately searching for their prey. Louisa sat in frozen silence on her bed and reflected on the way this young Nazi entered her room. After he saw her, he become quiet; almost shy, and she thought: Maybe he is different, maybe he has a conscience. Maybe he has a heart, not like the others, a bit nicer. Also, he looks around the same age as I am...

Despite the fact that her life might end abruptly, Louisa was able to come up with calming thoughts: No matter what the outcome, either way my life will be changed forever. It won't matter at all. It doesn't matter what we do now, there is no one left to judge us. We share a commonality, our youth! I'll just pretend we are pawns in a chess game.

Logic began to dissolve her panic and crippling tensions. Louisa slowly gained a rational awareness and plotted silently: Maybe I can work out a deal with him. I'll flirt with him and then seduce him. I know how to flirt. I've watched the movie stars at the cinema and how they acted out the art of seduction. After all, he's about my age, maybe not as horrible as the others.

As Louisa's self-esteem rose, she remembered how even as a little girl, she was not only considered to be beautiful, but also a talented singer. Her charisma and flirtatiousness charmed many admirers. Her mother used to say, "Louisa is a little coquette. While her beauty is most alluring, she sings like a songbird!" Ironically, who would imagine watching American Movies with Polish subtitles on Saturday nights might eventually save her life? One of her favorite pastimes was to get lost in the reverie of romance and love stories. Before the world went crazy, teenage girls believed in the dreams; hoping for a wonderful life ahead of them. She was taking a big risk, and what if her plan backfired? There was the distinct possibility he'd not take the bait, or become furious, or maybe shoot her right there in the bed! It didn't matter, though. It was her only hope and she had to try something. What did she have to lose? Louisa plotted: My plan has to work! I know how to bait him; I will pose like the famous actresses did in the American movies! Yes, I'll tease him with my body the way a lion tamer uses his training stick to make it perform according to his demands! I can do this, just like I have practiced in the mirror so many times. Feeling more empowered, a new-found strength prompted her next move.

The sudden movement, the shift in her seated position attracted his attention like a shark to bloody waters. Louisa flinched, for the sudden awareness of her partially covered body exposed to a complete stranger was new and extremely disconcerting. All at once she felt shamed, with an overwhelming sense of modesty. Although she tried desperately to uncover her proverbial blanket of self-consciousness, she knew that nothing must block her intentions.

The danger of her situation brought Louisa quickly to her senses and she demanded of herself: You must do this; it is a matter of life or death! Who cares about morality at a time like this. Let him see your breasts, let him see everything! Pretend you don't know he is looking at them. Act coy and sexy like in the movies. They say men like it when a girl looks vulnerable and inviting. It'll turn him on, and at the same time it might cloud his thinking like a dense shroud over his head. Do it! Be brave! Do anything you can to save yourself!

This was the moment. It was Louisa's last desperate attempt to change her maiden conscience and accept the challenge of what she had to do. As her self-reasoning continued, the icy blood in her veins began to thaw and her heartbeat was becoming more regular. The soldier's eager eyes wandered around the silhouette of her body, admiring the budding freshness of her skin. He eyed the cascading waves of her long brown hair softly sheathing the naked glow of her ivory shoulders, her graceful neck, and the lure of the feminine curve of her upper hip.

As if the flashlight had a mind of its own, it began alternating between both breast mounds, noticing how they pushed up against the translucent gauze nightdress, and stopping to admire the outline of rich brown nipples that pulsated with each rapid breath. His eyes narrowed, his body heat rapidly rising as he became mesmerized, slowly taken in by her voluptuousness. He was unable to refuse her lure, as if it was like the siren call to a sailor lost at sea in the darkest night. The beguiling spell of her seduction drew him in, leading to the place where her youthful breasts were begging for him to rest his head on their silky softness. Lost in a trance, he was totally unaware he was now the object of her seduction.

Louisa watched the bulge in his trousers begin to push against the fabric while he remained fixated at the softness of her round breasts. Her nimble fingers clutched the puffed blanket with a contrived coyness, pulling it up to her neck, and pretending to shield herself against the burning blaze of his sexual desire. Feigning a mistake, she purposefully allowed the blanket to slip from her hands, offering him a shame-faced look of embarrassment, "Oh no, I'm so frightened of what you will do, I can't control myself," she spoke in a soft, sexy whisper. The tone of her voice had the sound of a blues singer pining away, yearning for the blazing touch of a lost love.

Louisa watched the muscles on the side of the young soldier's jaw line twitch and pulse rhythmically with a hint of a masculine force. Their eyes focused on each other. Her glimmering green eyes, now softened, offered the welcoming assurance that there was going to be no resistance for what was to happen next. Without releasing his narrowed gaze, blue eyes of desire seemed to penetrate into every fiber of

30

her flesh. She began to prepare her virginal body for the acting performance, the passionate sexual interlude she had seen in the movies. She allowed her romantic nature to enhance the scene; her facial expression looking as if taunted by the bittersweet heartache a pianist feels playing a Chopin nocturne in a minor key. The power of innocence and youth was the promise for them, to take them both away to a safe harbor, far away from the tumultuous reality of the times.

Intent on feeding his desire, Louisa positioned herself in an alluring pose, gracefully leaning back to rest her head on her right elbow. She slowly raised her knee up, planting her delicate foot down on the bed sheet, carelessly allowing the blanket to fall to the floor. The gleam of passion in his eyes shone through the darkness like the nocturnal eyes of an owl, her semi-nakedness became the beacon of light amidst the darkness of the room. He sank down, kneeling at the side of her bed, as one would worship an idol. Possessively, he put one of his large-knuckled hands on her uplifted hip, while his other hand gently cupped her left buttocks possessively, gently warming her face with his tenderness. Then he slowly tugged the bottom of her sheer nightdress, subtly signaling her to raise up her arms, anxious to remove the last vestige of covering between them.

Struggling against the subtle protestations of self-consciousness, Louisa managed to hide her silent resistance. When the nightdress came off, he kissed it and allowed the silk fabric to drop to the floor. She gasped, trying to manage the wild emotions, becoming enveloped in the confusion; the bittersweet combination of runaway fear and the primitive excitement of experiencing her first sex act. Without a second of hesitation, he bent down to kiss her neck. She dared to boldly reach for his hand and plant it gently on her left breast. She sighed with a feigned pleasure, as if his touch made her long for the next move. He responded by cupping both breasts and began to feel the rise of her nipples.

31

As he met her eyes, the timing seemed right for her to begin the plan of diversion. She lowered her lashes coyly, matched his fervor, one that could be easily translated to a shameful desire. Observing his response, watching him succumb to her feminine wiles, she felt encouraged by her assumed power. She felt as if she had succeeded in trapping a wild animal in a cage. He was hers to do with whatever she wanted.

Just as she did that, she softly spoke to him. Murmuring in a low and sultry voice, as if to sing him to sleep with a lullaby, she said, "Wait, wait please, before we have sex, because I am so attracted to you, I have an important secret to tell you. You must know this before it's too late and we have to go!" Despite his body's growing desire, she could see that she had aroused his interest. "I really like you," she whispered. "You are so handsome, so sexy, and I think I can trust you with what I'm about to tell you. You must know about the precious jewels, crystal, china, and other luxuries that are well hidden upstairs in our attic. No one knows about it. I'm giving them all to you! We've gathered an abundance of valuables here throughout the years. Only my family and I know exactly where these riches are hidden. Go up and take them! We won't be needing them anymore." Then, she dared to say, "Maybe you could just forget me here, let me be, even come to visit me for sex whenever you want?"

She'd say anything to continue the delay, to gain a little bit of time, hoping to weaken and distract him with her body so that she might try to grab something. Noticing the small lamp next to the bed she told herself, I'll grab the lamp and pound the back of his head while he is on top of me!

Thankfully, the hypnotized expression on his face still radiated his physical desire. He was still lost in a sexual frenzy, as if he didn't hear a word she said. She wondered: Was it a good thing to tell him? What about the deal? Did he believe her? Was he able to see through her scheme? Fortunately,

Louisa could see that her words didn't break the mood, for it didn't matter what she said to him at that moment. She continued with her plan, warning herself: You need to have patience and proceed with great caution!

She glanced up at him, searching his face for reassurance. He was still lost in a trance and stubbornly intent on having sex with her. Ever so slowly, like an examining vendor looking to buy a bolt of silk, his hand inched up and down, circling, caressing the soft skin on the straight leg supporting her body. His fingers teased their way towards her most private, sensual place. It was the guarded place where no one before had dared ever to touch. Curiously enough, despite her plan, her body seemed to betray her, for her breath quickened and her pulse raced, the inhibitions of maidenhood were beginning to melt away. As if she was on a runaway horse, Louisa had lost control. Her sexual urges were taking over. She was supposed to be acting! But her body refused to listen, and was readily preparing itself to match his desire.

The theme of destiny and fate, the timing of what happened next could have been played out in any romance novel, yet truth is stranger than fiction. Downstairs in the street, the loading of all the prisoners onto the vans was nearly complete. All the while, the commandant officer who had herded her parents and sister down the stairs, was howling German obscenities, attacking and accusing her family of being worthless. His terrifying voice yelled, "You dirty Jews litter this town, and you must be exterminated like the sweeping plague of black locusts who do nothing but infest and destroy everything in sight!" The feverish, manic screaming was a common example of the characteristically unhinged behaviors of the bigoted Nazi leaders.

The Nazi commandant stood at bottom of the stairs, his face turned upward, as he cupped his hand at the side of his mouth to form half a megaphone. "Hey comrade Waldheim, what is taking so long up there? Get down right now, we are leaving! I order you to hurry down this instant!" After yelling upstairs, the commandant turned around in the doorway and headed back down the front porch stairs to the walkway. As he walked back to the van he tripped over a pebble and injured his ankle. He winced with each step as he hobbled with an unsteady gait to the boarded van of newly captured Jews.

The abrupt, shrill screaming of the commandant startled the young Nazi and awakened him from his aroused, dreamy stupor. Both he and Louisa began to shake. The harsh interruption was as if it had broken a sound barrier, a loud blast to their ear drums. A cold-blooded fear began to permeate the room, quickly vaporizing the sexual mood and bringing them back to an unpalatable slice of reality.

Louisa watched his metamorphosis, the look of horror on the young man's face became fierce, raging with anger. Never bothering to look back at her, the soldier stood upright as if nothing had happened. He readjusted his uniform and took a deep breath, then he left Louisa in the bedroom before readily sprinting down the stairs.

Louisa sat up, stunned, in shocked disbelief. Her thoughts raced as she sat alone on her bed. He just left me here. Was he angry with me? If he gets in trouble, surely, he'll blame me because I am Jewish. What just happened? Is he coming back for me? Did he leave me here on purpose? Did he just forget because he was petrified?

Louisa sat alone in her bedroom, shocked at what had just happened. Her mind swirled in a whirlpool of contemplation. I think he left me here! But how am I left to fend for myself? I have no family now; how can I survive? Was there anything I could have done to save my family? Louisa was all at once completely alone. Was it a fantasy, a dream? Maybe she was destined for a far worse fate? Did the young man purposefully leave her there? Did he pretend to forget her? Why would he do that? What did he want from her?

Louisa sat in a hushed silence as a dreaded chill tore through her body, leaving her to grieve in solitary aloneness. Nobody was there to help. The Nazis were deaf to their pleas. They cared only to complete the mission to remove and exterminate the Jews. The barbaric yowling of the Nazis officers ceased, along with the desperate cries of her parents and the last words of her little sister begging for help. All Louisa knew for sure was that the vicious rumors circulating in the streets were now ringing true, if only for the time being.

Thou shalt not be a victim, thou shalt not be a perpetrator, but, above all, thou shalt not be a bystander. -Yehuda Bauer

What Will Become of Me?

Louisa couldn't move. Shattered by the unspeakable calamity that had just taken place, she was numb. She sat upright in her bed in a stupor for what seemed an eternity. Disturbing thoughts began to weave a complicated web of worry: Will the Nazis come back? Maybe the soldier who almost took my virginity really did just forget me. Maybe he left me intentionally so I would have a chance to survive. I wonder if he really did like me? Or maybe that is a ridiculous notion.

All at once, Louisa heard the rumbling of the motors, the van's heaving engines beginning to pull away. As hot tears streamed down her cheeks, her vision blurred. With tears dripping from her mouth, Louisa screamed in silent terror as she shook uncontrollably. "Oh my God, oh my God! Someone has to help them! Who can stop the vans? They're taking away my family! Where are they taking them?"

The Nazis' mission was accomplished. It was as if someone turned off all the street sounds. Gone were the tortured wailing sounds, the anguished crying of the captured innocents. There were no rolling tires on the street pavement, no occasional barking of a dog. The Nazis created their own sudden earthquake, leaving behind haunting echoes in a seismic silence.

In shattered disbelief, Louisa mumbled out loud: How could they take my family? How could I not have helped them? I have to leave. I can't stay here but I must hide somewhere. Louisa's dizzying mind turned somersaults: What if the head commandant realizes the young Nazi left me? They might come back looking for me! Oh my God, where can I hide? I'm only eighteen, barely an adult, how will I survive against these odds? Louisa wanted to scream outside the bedroom window, but no one would hear her. She wanted to tell the world to stop rotating and please listen to what's going on. She wondered if there were any decent people left out there.

Louisa needed to find a place to hide. She felt like a spider scurrying up the wall, seeking immediate shelter and ready to hide inside any available crevice. Then she remembered the secret she told the young Nazi about the valuables stored in the attic. That was it! The attic was a perfect temporary hiding place.

In an instant, she willed her unyielding legs to swing sideways over the edge of the bed. Unsteady and moving painstakingly slow, she was careful to set each foot down, one at a time, before reaching the wide floorboards. Confused and distracted, she stole a quick glance at the sturdy base of the flowered porcelain lamp set on the white lace doily covering the side table. She remembered her backup plan, to use that base as her weapon against the young Nazi and, if need be, to crush his head.

Swirling thoughts about what could have happened made her shudder with relief, thinking: I'm glad I didn't have to resort to violence, and I am not sure I would have had the nerve to do it. I can't let myself think I might have killed him! I've never had such a vile thought of hurting anyone! Who have I become in just one night? Commit murder? No, I can't think about that now. Quickly re-focusing her thoughts, she knew that time was of the essence. She had to get to the attic and hide.

Still unsteady on her wobbly feet, Louisa stumbled forward trying to regain a semblance of balance. After padding across the room, she managed to flatten herself against the side wall adjacent to the window so she could peek sideways out the window. Assuming the stealthy pose of a stalker wait-ing to make a move, she peeked out the window. Her heart was pounding vigorously against her chest as she thought, what if someone looks up and notices me standing at the bedroom window? She managed to sneak another glance towards the street. As she looked down into the empty street, all she could see was the emptiness of her life. Her family was gone like an evaporated mist vanishing into thin air.

Maybe Karl, her older brother, was still alive. After hear-ing the early rumors about Germany's threat to overtake Po-land, he joined the army and was stationed somewhere in Siberia. Louisa wondered about him. She wished he was there to protect her. She needed to tell him about what hap-pened to their family.

Louisa's restless thoughts turned to the unsolved mystery of her sister's disappearance. She blamed herself and wor-ried: Where did Fania go? After Noah was taken, she ran away and made it worse for us. How selfish! Fania added to the pain of loss, leaving her with only the aftershocks of the Nazi-induced earthquake.

Louisa thought back to how she and her sister Fania sat in horror at the window as they watched their precious little Noah being taken away. They were helpless and could do nothing but watch in disbelief. Barely able to breathe, the harsh realization of her new reality hit Louisa like a blow from an unsuspecting fist to the stomach. Desperately alone, there was no one to turn to for help. What does an eighteen-year-old teenager do after just witnessing the loss of her family? There were no police to call. The police were, in fact, the enemy.

More questions were left unanswered. Louisa was afraid they would come back for her if the commander realized she was left behind. He may think that she was somehow a part of their unfinished business. Dreaded twinges of loneliness and crippling fear began to twist at her lower spine, terrorizing the nerves, racing up and down her spinal column before finally burying itself deep in the marrow of her bones.

All at once, Louisa came to her senses. She knew there was no time to waste. She knew that she had no other choice but to figure it out. I must find a way to survive, hide in the attic, and wait to be saved. A warning intuition that sounded like a chorus of angels rang out in unison, telling her to stay put in the attic. She didn't know where it came from, but she heard the message loud and clear: It is not safe to go downstairs or out into the street for any reason. It's not the time to search for a neighbor. Remain vigilant and never to let down your defenses! Always remember you're not to blame for anything that happens to other people. It is time to just watch out for yourself, that's the only thing that matters now.

Careful not to turn on the bedroom light, Louisa slid through the semi-darkness of the early morning light that was peering through the curtains in her bedroom. Carefully, she pulled open the top bureau drawer, trying not to make the tiniest sound. She chose two hand-knitted sweaters and slipped both over her head for extra warmth. She grabbed a lingerie bag and stuffed some panties inside, along with a warm pair of long cashmere stockings. She needed to prepare herself for the rest of the day, and perhaps several cold nights ahead. She then tiptoed to the closet and chose a long woolen skirt. She slipped it over her hips, and finally pulled on the short leather boots positioned neatly on the floor. She spotted two blankets on the bed, grabbed them and folded them up in her arms. Like a thief in the night, Louisa turned on her heels and made her way up the creaky attic stairs.

When Louisa reached the top of the landing, she began to turn the brass knob of the ancient wooden door. She quickly whisked away mounds of cobwebs framing the old, wormy-holed oak door. Most likely, the doorknob remained undisturbed for years. She peered inside, keenly scanning the attic loft. Her gaze swept over heavy trunks and valises stacked on top of each other. It was difficult to see because the light in the attic was so dim and the suitcases were partially blocking her vision of what lay beyond. Louisa began inching forward, stepping lightly, worrying that the wooden rafters underneath the attic floor might break from the weight of her step. Louisa cast a glance at the multitude of boxes in the far corner, covered with dusty-white muslin cloths. In that corner was where her family valuables were stored; precious heirlooms, including silver and fine china.

Daybreak came and cast a gentle glow on the attic where Louisa was planning to hide. Fingers of sunlight pushed through cracks surrounding the large palladium window facing the street. Soft shafts of filtered light began to rest on old furniture and decorative items strewn about the attic. Louisa had never before seen the attic's collection of odds and ends, faded tapestries, an antique upholstered divan, several Queen Anne chairs without cushions, a chipped wood Mahogany roll-top desk, a broken swivel stool, and several oil paintings of pious Jews resting against the wall opposite the window.

Louisa contemplated: Which corner of the attic should I choose to plant myself? I have to be able to see from all the angles in the loft, just in case someone discovers I am missing and come back up the stairs. Where should I hide? A chorus of supportive voices, like angels in her mind, encouraged her spirit. I am a warrior. I am capable, ready and able to outsmart the enemy. I have no real weapon against danger, but I have the strongest weapon of all, my thoughts. Just as her mother taught her, she would go forward believing in hope.

Louisa carefully unfolded the blankets and spread them out along the attic floor. This would become her temporary hiding place, a blanketed corner situated near the large window. In this strategic spot she would be able to keep watch on the street, possibly giving her moments to prepare for any dangers lurking in the shadows. Suddenly, a strange feeling of relief began to settle around her. She was beginning to relax her muscles, despite the wounds of trauma still fresh in her mind. Her balance was returning, an illusion of safety, right there in the attic.

Now that Louisa was settled in the attic, all she could do was wait. She was alone with her thoughts. What am I waiting for? I might survive this day, but I could die tomorrow. No, she reminded herself. I won't allow myself to think this way! Her determination seemed to bring about a lulling sense of calm and she became sleepy. She leaned her back against the wall and closed her eyes, hoping to finally get some sleep.

Suddenly, just when Louisa was about to doze off, she was startled by a sudden noise in the distance. Her eyes opened wide, her heart began to race and she froze in place. Could it be that she was hearing faint footsteps, the quickened, pitter-patter of a woman's heels tapping onto the sidewalk and heading towards the front door? Was there a pounding downstairs at the front entrance door? Was imagination playing tricks and allowing paranoia to take over her mind? Daring to lift her head just enough to peek through the attic window, she saw it was her missing sister Fania! Could it really be her, or was it just an apparition?

"Oh my God! I must let Fania inside the door!" Louisa whispered to herself. "I must run down and save her!" she thought. But what if I take that chance and someone discovers that I am still here, I will be taken away too! Louisa's anguish created a floating sensation, an out-of-body experience. Just then, she popped her head up. She took another chance, quickly peeking through the window. This time she knew it was Fania, standing there frantically pounding on the door, crying and begging for someone to open it and let her in. I was definitely not a hallucination.

41

Louisa couldn't move. Her body was besieged by a cata-tonic stupor, a rock-solid glacier in a frozen Northern Sea. Her rigid spine galvanized into a steel girder set in stone. Faced with the most devastating decision of her life, Louisa contemplated whether or not she dared to run down the three flights of stairs, open the door for Fania and risk com-promising her hiding place. Were there any witnesses out-side in the early hours of the morning? If so, she might be killed while trying to save her sister.

The bone-chilling screams and relentless pounding seemed to go on for an eternity. Fania's despairing pleas echoed in the stillness of the street, ringing loudly in her na-tive Polish. "Somebody, let me in! Louisa, if you are there, open the door! Let me in, I beg you! Please, in the name of our God in heaven, please!" Fania continued to clamor against the heavy wooden door with both fists. Yet, the painful pummeling didn't stop her determination. Soon her delicate fists were covered with multiple bloody scrapes, yet nothing would stop her pounding.

Fania's hysterical screams reverberated off the cobble-stone street. What should Louisa do? Distraught with fear and trepidation, she found herself in a war of turmoil, like bombs falling and blasting the recesses of her mind. Should she take a chance and open the door? If they were both dis-covered, at least they might be killed together. Unable to de-cide, she was losing the battle against time, yet she could not move. Frozen by fear, Louisa knew she mustn't move, but also knew she should move.

Just then, the distant sound of an approaching van mov-ing at high speed turned the corner and then screeched to a stop in front of the house. Louisa stood helpless, not believ-ing her eyes. The passenger door flew open, then a Nazi sympathizer jumped out and charged towards Fania. As the yellow star pinned to her jacket glowed like a neon light in the semi-darkness of the of the early morning, he grabbed her. Fania's blood-curdling screams resounded in the street and then abruptly stopped when they slammed the door to lock her in the van. Louisa held her breath as they pulled away with her precious sister. All she could do was watch helplessly until the van was out of sight. Fania evaporated into the mist like the rest of her family; just another Jew, one more captured by crazed Nazi hunters. After that moment, to Louisa, everything became a blur.

If we bear all this suffering and if there are still Jews left, when it is over, then Jews, instead of being doomed, will be held up as an example. -Anne Frank

Hiding in the Attic

When the next morning came, a blanket of impending doom hovered over the Boryslaw neighborhood. Louisa awoke from a fitful sleep, slowly opening her eyes to swirling dust particles dancing in the air. Trying to remain half-asleep, she was afraid to face the day ahead, thinking about the morbidity, the haunting nightmare of what happened to Fania. Painfully guilt-ridden, Louisa couldn't block the reverberating echoes of Fania's pleas to open the door. Did anyone in the neighborhood see or hear her yelling? Was Fania gone forever? Her heart sank, thinking she may never see her again.

Louisa sat up in the corner of the attic for hours, afraid to move, with her legs folded like a pretzel under her body. She felt as if she was waiting for a time bomb to explode. Emotionally drained and too exhausted to stand, she shivered uncontrollably on the drafty floor. As the penetrating cold soaked into her bones, the unpleasant dampness and smells of mildew worsened her misery. She felt like a trapped animal, alone and forgotten, held captive in the confines of the attic. Louisa had nothing else to do but think and wait. The harsh reality that her family might be gone forever was sheer agony. The despairing situation felt like the stabbing pain of a knife continuously ripping through the chambers of her broken heart. She had come to know about heartbreak and loss, the types of profound aches for which there is no medicine or healing tonic that can palliate such pain.

As the hours ticked by, Louisa scrutinized the crude, uncomfortable surroundings of the attic. She looked around, and began to wonder if her hiding place was still a safe haven. Gone were the comforts of her former life, the simple pleasures of being snuggled in a goose down blanket and

44

nestled safely in the cozy sheets of her warm bed. Instead, she found herself lying on a scratchy, woolen blanket and resting on uneven floorboards while trying to avoid the pro-truding nails and wood slivers from piercing her skin. This small area of the attic became her comfort zone, where tiny mice scurried about and made scratchy sounds on the creaky floorboards. Strangely enough, she was grateful for their company, her only companions. Exhaustion was her sleeping pill. When early nightfall began to darken the loft, she fell asleep in the make-shift corner of the attic, pretend-ing that the tattered blanket could provide enough warmth throughout the night.

Louisa ruminated constantly about what happened to Noah and her family, and for not opening the door for Fania. She felt overwhelmed by pangs of guilt and plagued with re-lentless blame; a punishment that would stay with her for the rest of her life. There was no choice but to face her crumbling life, like a building with a dangerous crack in its foundation. While the heartbreak of loss darkened Louisa's world, she had no choice but to grow up overnight. Her teenage years were disappearing, and all she had were sweet memories of her former life. She was forced to leave that all behind, like the life cycle of a snake when it becomes time to shed its skin. She knew she had to find a way to survive in a forsaken world bombarded by powerful bombs of hatred. Not knowing what else to do, she began to pray. She tried to make a bar-gain with God, begging for her family to come back. God seemed to not be listening, or maybe he had another plan.

Louisa had no time to wait. The world was swiftly trans-forming from a goblet of fine wine to a glass of vinegar. She was wasting precious moments feeling sorry for herself, and time was of the essence. It was imperative that she find a way out of the attic and discover a new hiding place. Slowly rising from the floor, Louisa began to rub her neck, still aching from the discomfort of sleeping on the unforgiving hard floor. She winced in pain as she pushed aside the crumpled blanket, remembering that she had slept fully clothed. She had forgotten to take off her boots, and her cramped toes were screaming for mercy. Worry distracted her from the pain as she began to wonder. Had Fania's screams and pounding at the door aroused suspicion? What if someone had alerted the police and they were on their way? Louisa had to push the thoughts aside to address a more pressing problem; she had to use the toilet.

Cautiously creeping along the groaning floorboards, Louisa stopped to open the ram-shackled door leading down to the stairs. With a flick of her wrist, she whisked away the new cobwebs surrounding the door frame and she was suddenly comforted by new thought: I am not alone! I am here with the spiders and mice, living creatures who have been working industriously throughout the night. They are living proof that all of God's creatures have a rightful place on this earth. Why couldn't the Nazi's think that way? What made them think they were superior?

Louisa stood silently at the top of the stairs and listened intently for any noises. After several seconds, she deemed it safe to tiptoe down the stairs. She remained cautious, descending each stair as careful as a legally blind person trying to thread a needle. Finally stepping off the last step, she arrived at the door to their second-floor apartment. Pulling up the iron latch of the lock, she went in and softly closed the door behind her. Careful not to turn on a light, she hoped no one would notice an interruption in the stillness of the shadows. She quickly scanned the shaded room, squinted hard, and willed the pupils of her eyes to focus through the veil of darkness blanketing the room. While making her way to the bathroom, she noticed that the apartment was seemingly untouched by tragedy. Choking back angry tears, she thought: Right now, this isn't a safe place to hide.

Louisa hurried along to use the toilet and she washed her face and hands in the white porcelain sink. Then she headed towards the kitchen, opened the icebox and emptied out the food and grabbed some essential supplies from the pantry. She collected and organized necessary items in manageable stacks so she could carry them upstairs. After making many trips up and down the stairs, she was prepared to stay there for at least a few more days. She hoped she wouldn't be there for much longer, praying she wouldn't starve to death.

Three days after the trauma, Louisa followed the same routine of watching the spiders and the mice carry on with their daily activities. Sometimes she played a game, pretending to be a spy who had to guard the strangely deserted streets and remain unnoticed. As Louisa peered outside the attic window, her head bobbed up and down. She watched for any signs of neighbors she might trust, anyone who might help her find a way out. One thing she knew for certain, she could no longer remain in the attic much longer, afraid of dying a slow death while breathing in the acrid scent of impending doom that hung in the air.

The quiet neighborhood street seemed to whisper an eerily soothing lullaby, trying to lull itself back to normalcy. A contrived silence descended over Boryslaw, the pretense that the trauma was to be forgotten. To Louisa, nothing would ever be the same. She remained repeatedly plagued with the same torture: Why didn't I run down the stairs? I am a selfish coward and I am responsible for killing my sister! Why didn't I take the risk and just run down the stairs to open the door; she might have been saved if only I had the courage! Louisa was exhausted and she felt completely lost. Feeling all alone in the world, in deep desperation she whispered, "What am I supposed to do now?"

Suddenly, the wise words of her father arose in her mind. "Louisa, whenever you are faced with a challenge and don't know what to do, look inside yourself. Become still and listen, because the answer lies within. Follow your inner guidance and you will make the right decision for yourself." Somehow, those words encouraged her and gave her hope.

I swore never to be silent whenever and wherever human beings endure suffering and humiliation. We must take sides. Neutrality helps the oppressor, never the victim. Silence encourages the tormentor, never the tormented.
-Elie Wiesel

Change is Coming

As Louisa gazed out of her make-shift prison window of the musty attic, she wondered how long she would have to remain hidden. Trying to find ways to fill the void of monotony and boredom, she spent hours creating new mind games. She occupied her time by identifying and categorizing outside sounds. By playing this game, she tried to appreciate the differences of familiar sounds that otherwise were taken for granted. She spent hours isolating each sound, studying the characteristics; like how the wind rustles through the trees and wraps around the branches. She carefully observed when the birds first announced the sunrise and she tried to figure out the secret conversations of birds chirping back and forth to each other as they sat on the roof.

In the early morning of the fourth day in the attic, Louisa was awakened from yet another restless sleep. She heard the alarming blast of frantic shouting and screams, sharp enough to pierce her eardrums. She froze as cold tendrils of dread began to pinch her spine, sprouting new veins of fear throughout her body. She sat up in shock, helplessly listening to the piteous screaming of newly discovered people being ripped away from their homes. How well she recognized the familiar Nazi voices, the clipped, guttural scrape of their German words. She sat and shivered uncontrollably, her heart going out to the victims, and wondering if they were coming for her next.

This was another early morning round up, another 'Aktion.' It happened so quickly. Her ears buzzed from the prevailing roar of the Nazi's bellowing commands and the haunting cries of petrified victims pleading for their lives before being systematically herded into the awaiting Nazi trucks. As the vans sped away, the neighborhood was left in grave silence, a heavy fog descending over the streets. Once again, more innocent people were torn away from their homes, purged of their belongings, and robbed of their former lives.

Louisa crawled along the floor, getting closer to the attic window. She resumed her daily position and stood watch through the dull haze of the dirt-caked and weathered window. Desperately trying to see through the cloudy glass, a curious thought made her take notice of how the intrinsic pattern of shattered glass was like a microcosm of people's broken lives. As the hours ticked by, she pondered the fragility of life. Many innocent people were so vulnerable and weak; even the strongest ones had no choice but to succumb to the evil forces of merciless men. People's lives could be so easily snuffed out and crushed, like stepping on eggshells. At times, Louisa could barely tell if it was really happening or if it was all just a figment of her imagination.

On the morning of the fifth day in the attic, Louisa woke up to hear markedly different sounds coming from the street. Was it possible that she was hearing the murmurs of voices outside in the near distance? Her first involuntary reaction was to pull the blanket up to her chin, a protective gesture mimicking a shield against danger. She hesitated to move, but strained to hear as she tried to decipher if what she heard was real. She heard the low and controlled rumbling of voices, like real people having conversation. There was no roar, no Nazis shouting commands. It seemed like the voices were right in front of the house! She realized that there were actual people talking outside. Fraught with uncertainly and afraid of what she might witness below, Louisa knew she had to be brave. She wrapped the meager blanket around her body and started the slow crawl back towards the attic window.

Squinting against the rays of morning sunlight, Louisa peered through the foggy glass streaked with lost family history. There she saw a gradual assembling of homeless neighbors who miraculously had not been taken by the Nazis. How courageous they all were, daring to venture out and leave the safety of their hiding places! Together, there were at least twenty of them walking along the street. Suddenly, new throngs of people began to turn the corner onto the street, looking like a lost flock of sheep without a shepherd to guide them. As the muted conversations on the street drifted upward, Louisa heard familiar Yiddish and Polish speaking voices; soothing sounds of comfort, like wearing warm earmuffs on a cold winter's day. Fixed in position, she continued to watch them, trying to grasp the crowd's purpose and to where they were going.

Suddenly, Louisa heard a man's voice, louder than the rest. Like blaring bursts from a large trumpet, he yelled loudly, "Is anyone left up there from the Drimmer family? Answer me if you are there! If you are there, come down now. Don't worry, it is safe now! Join us! Together, we are going to congregate at the Jewish Community Center, the Ghetto at Tarnopol." Louisa tensed, plugging her fist into her open mouth, hoping to push back the throbbing fear gathering at the back of her throat. Louisa gasped. Oh my God!" she thought. What should I do? I have no one to ask and I can't tell if it's a trick or a way for me to expose myself. It might be a ploy! There is no one can I trust. If they are telling the truth, is it wise to risk my life and make change, possibly exposing myself like a stowaway hiding on a cargo ship? Do I stay here and wait to be caught? Am I becoming the last piece of a family puzzle?" Louisa listened to her conflicting thoughts and prayed to make the right decision. She silently wished that her only true companions, the spiders and the mice, could be able to advise her as to what to do.

Contemplative thoughts faded in and out, alternating between turmoil and confusion. Louisa refused to drown in the tumultuous sea of indecision. She made up her mind to force the chaotic emotions aside and decided to trust her instincts: I must take the risk, no matter what! I can't stay here, like living among the remaining bottom dregs of an empty wine glass. This may be my only chance to survive! Summoning up all of her courage, she jumped up and scrambled down the three flights of stairs leading to the street, ready to join the remaining victims, the ones who managed to circumvent the morning's 'Aktion.'

For a few seconds, Louisa stood outside the front door of her house and looked up at the sky. She closed her eyes and took a deep breath. She stood there inhaling deeply and slowly expelling the stale attic stench. She began drinking in the outside air like someone who had stayed under water for too long. Somehow, the fresh air replenished her with the promise of hope and a renewed vitality. Louisa looked back at the door to what was once her safe haven, her family home. She caught her reflection in the glass of the front door. As she peered into the glass, she could barely recognize herself. Louisa was no longer the same person that she was five days ago. Have I undergone a metamorphosis?" she wondered. Voices down the street brought her back to the present moment. "Take one more breath," she whispered to herself. Louisa inhaled, and then exhaled as she turned to rush towards the crowd. "Hey everyone, wait for me!" she shouted.

The powerful echo of her voice sounded eerily different and not her own. It was lower in range, more mature, as if it belonged to someone else. Although it sounded different, it was her new voice; a resolute force coming from somewhere deep within her soul. Louisa quickened her pace to join the masses, then hurried to walk alongside the first group in her path.

There are multitudes of wretched souls for whom it seems the sun of hope has set. -Howard Kershner, director of European relief for the American Friends Service Committee

On the Way to The Ghetto

Pushing her way into the amoeba-shaped mass of people moving forward, Louisa shuffled along while trying to find stability against the crowd's wavering imbalance. She wedged herself between a tall, lanky man and a short, stocky middle-aged woman, both seeming oblivious to her, lost in their own foggy state of delirium. Neither one seemed to care about her joining them, like a stray sheep jamming into a strange flock from an adjacent meadow.

As the hordes of people trudged ahead in like-minded despair, Louisa recognized the voice of a man standing on a low stone ledge surrounded by flowers, megaphone in hand. It was the same man who stood in front of her house searching for any members left from her family while she was hiding in the attic! He kept announcing that they were several miles away from their destination, the Tarnopol Ghetto. He informed them about the establishment of the Jewish Council of Elders at the same ghetto, offering hope that the Jewish Council might possibly be able to help them.

More throngs of grief-stricken people joined the traveling group. Step after step, hushed voices filled with desolation and fear echoed through the crowd. Even though many were strangers, they walked like comrades; huddling together. Nobody seemed to care about keeping a proper distance from each other, as if close human contact was a blanket of comfort. It was obvious that they believed in the collective safety of numbers.

Louisa noticed the numb, vacant stares of the dejected people around her. They all looked straight ahead, leaning against each other, trying to find relief from their discomfort and exhaustion. She felt sorry for an elderly man walking in front of her, noticing his half-open mouth hanging in defeat. As he walked, the man attempted to suck air into his lungs with belabored breaths. Next to him walked an old woman; perhaps his wife, crippled and hunched over, walking with a cane. Her ragged sweater still smelled of moth balls.

While walking among the masses, there were many un-distinguishable and nauseating scents; unpleasant odors that wafted straight into Louisa's nostrils. The mixture of human odors turned her stomach, like the scent of an unsavory stew. As she walked amongst the gathering crowds, Louisa listened to a cacophony of discordant noises: whimpering children, the shrill cry of hungry babies, and the moaning sighs of the sick and elderly. Sad and despairing sounds jolted her memory. She remembered how she felt while listening to a heart-wrenching Chopin Nocturne played by an organ maestro at a concert in the park. To Louisa, music played in a minor key triggered a melancholy longing for someone or something missing from her life, each note a woeful reminder of life's saddest moments.

The despairing people attracted each other like magnets to metal. Louisa thought she may have recognized several of the adults, possibly a few of the children. She wondered if her family might have known them from the temple or the grocery store. Almost immediately, Louisa felt a sense of belonging to the masses, realizing it was because they were all a part of the same tragedy. She understood their pain, anger, and frustration. They shared an invisible shield of under-standing, a stable crutch to hold on to as they moved along into the new realm of their own survival.

As they walked, Louisa listened to the constant chatter and rumors that were spreading quickly. She recalled the day in 1939 when her hometown of Boryslaw and the closest neighboring town, Drohobych, were taken over by the Germans. She remembered hearing about the twisted rumor claiming that many young Jewish men were traitors, that they voluntarily joined forces with the Red Army when war broke out between Germany and Russia. Jew-hating Ukrainians and Poles were able to take advantage of the opportunity, alleging that the Jewish men and the Red Army formed an alliance against Poland. Consequently, the Jews would become known as the enemy: betrayers and double-crossers. Ukrainian and Polish anti-semitic mobs, formerly "normal" neighbors of the Jewish communities, now had the excuse they needed to forge ahead with their plan. It was a perfect time to orchestrate their revenge against the Jews.

Commandeered by German soldiers, a good number of Ukrainian farmers joined together with Ukrainians and Polish locals to form programs, or "Aktions" to infiltrate the towns and villages. Fueled by rage and bigotry, they found it acceptable to rape, pillage, destroy and devastate the lives of Jewish victims. Suddenly mutating into thugs and murderers, they organized the 'Aktions,' giving them permission to raid the homes of innocent Jewish people.

Louisa was barely able to feel her feet as they approached the cold, steely gates of the Tarnopol Ghetto. Although she was exhausted, she was determined to maintain the same stride as her neighboring walkers. Members of the crowd seemed to have lost track of time. What difference did it make if it was morning, noon, or night? There was no place to be, no place where someone was waiting for them, no place to belong. Appearing like lambs being led to slaughter, there was heightened sense of danger as they approached the gates.

Louisa stretched her head upward, trying to see what lay ahead, all the while ignoring the numbness in her toes. Finally arriving at the entrance of the Ghetto's tall arch, she lifted her gaze to the gates. The sign read: The Tarnopol

Ghetto, Established September 1941. City of Lvov, First Ghetto in the Galicia Region. She hoped and prayed that behind these gates were people that would be able to help.

Just then a pock-marked female guard approached the crowd, holding a large threatening bullwhip. She stopped in front of Louisa's group and promptly stood in a powerful stance. She crossed her arms to block them, like a mountain lion on top of a hill looking for its prey. The guard lurched forward and clutched Louisa's sleeve with a vengeance, the way one might be caught red-handedly trying to steal something. The woman began hissing, spitting out words through her clenched front teeth. "HURRY UP, dumb girl, MOVE along and don't delay! What do you think that we are your servants, heh? We don't care about you! Don't care if you drop dead; do us a favor! Our job is to get rid of the filth, the pollution you Jews bring to our town." Her words, like stabbing icicles, pierced Louisa's already frozen heart.

Louisa was in shock and she could barely breathe. What about the Jewish Counsel of Elders that were supposed to be there to help? Had the group walked straight into the jaws of the enemy? Her head was spinning. How did this happen? Should I have stayed in the attic? What if I die here? I'm so scared of death. I haven't experienced enough of life! I haven't had enough kisses. I haven't seen enough sunsets. I haven't spent enough time at the beach. Am I never going to get married and have babies? How about the others? Are they feeling the same way? Wait, maybe there is still time. There is strength in our joining together here. Maybe the song of hope will move us ahead, make us free again. Please God, I beg you. Let us live! Maybe there is still a chance for us to survive.

Suddenly, the German guards began shouting warnings for them to hurry up in German. "Stay together!" they barked. "Mach schnell" (move fast!) The crowd followed orders, knowing that there was no choice but to accept the decree bestowed upon them. Their fate lay in the hands of their captors. Louisa and the rest of them shared the same gripping fear, their unknown fate: Who would be the next victim picked for a human slaughter? Am I strong enough to survive? If so, will staying alive be a lucky thing for me, or will I be destined to endure a fate worse than death? Fighting back bitter tears, Louisa felt like an insect trapped in a web, about to be eaten by a spider. Her only chance was to disentangle herself and escape from the web that promised the cruelest fate. She had to find a way to survive, even if for one more day.

Our scars tell a story but they don't determine our worth
- The Tatooist of Auschwitz

Inside the Ghetto

Louisa ambled along with the rest of them, like lost drifters trapped in the blandness of a somber world; a place with no trace of any color. She heard the insistent cawing of a black crow sitting atop of the building, perched next to an old, brick chimney. As she looked up at the bird, clouds of bulbous smoke and grime billowed out into the gloomy, overcast sky. It felt like a bad omen. Was there a way out of this Ghetto, a secret exit, an unmanned door? If she could escape, where could she go? Cold-blooded fear surged through her veins.

Louisa watched as two guards opened the huge, wrought iron gates of the Tarnopol Ghetto and began roughly pushing people through the gates. The guards displayed an authority that dominated the crowd. They strutted along the sidelines with chests puffed out like enraged bulls that were seeing red, posed in pre-attack mode. Once, when Louisa dared to look up from the ground, she found herself facing a guard. His ferocious expression made her cringe. He resembled the Frankenstein monster, with lines of black streaks embedded into the crevices of his forehead.

Three more guards were leaning against the left wall watching the lines. Alongside each guard was a vicious looking German shepherd dog, baring its teeth and snarling. The dogs were eager to attack, tugging at their leashes and trying to break free. The well-trained dogs were not barking but kept a steady tempo of a low growling rumble; unnerving sounds creating a hostile canine chorus. The dogs were stationed there strategically in order to intimidate and threaten incoming Jews.

Overcome with the unsettling presence of guards and dogs, Louisa trembled. She imagined that the attack dogs were used to maul or kill on command. If a guard decided to release his grip on the leash and order the dog to attack, Louisa was petrified she might be the unlucky one used as an example. Not knowing what to expect, she began pushing the thoughts away: Just keep walking, she told herself. Don't look up. Try to be brave. God is with you. Just do as they say and move forward.

Once inside the Ghetto, they were led into a small, crowded area of the old Jewish Community Center located in a dilapidated neighborhood. The few surrounding houses were in shabby and rundown condition. Feeling dismayed, Louisa looked around and thought: This is a slum! How am I going to live here? After a few moments she rationalized and decided it was best to think positive: If this is going to be my temporary home, I have no choice but to make the best of it. I won't worry about it because it's just for the time being. She remembered her mama's words. "Louisa, always remember that home isn't a place- it's a feeling."

As she entered the center's large auditorium, she saw long wooden tables covered with organized piles of papers and notebooks for the purpose of registering and recording names. Louisa knew that the German authorities considered Jewish victims to be part of the same problem, bonded together under the Nazis' new term "The Jewish Solution." She felt hot tears beginning to collect at the corners of her eyes and felt sorry for herself: How could this happen to me? How could my life change so rapidly? My family is gone and I have no one. I am left alone to fend for myself. How will I survive?

Louisa continued to gaze around the massive room filling up with hordes of people. Among them were doctors, dentists, lawyers, bankers, scientists, professors, musicians and teachers. There were children with parents, there were orphans, elderly, paupers, and chronically ill patients. All of these people suddenly became of equal social rank and status, and there were no special privileges for anybody. Every person was required to wait in endless lines to be registered and granted permission to reside in the poverty and disease-ravaged ghetto.

The Jews were ordered to stand in a straight queue, twenty persons deep, in front of one of the ten-foot-long wooden tables. There were approximately twenty wooden tables horizontally arranged from the front to the back of the enormous room. Behind each table sat two female guards. Their job was to take basic information before registering each person into the ghetto. Louisa thought that the guards resembled ruffians, like the pictures she had seen of prison guards from a remote area in Siberia. Each guard had imposing, stocky bodies; looking like they could lift tons of heavy metal up over their shoulders without even straining.

As Louisa moved up closer to the table, her nostrils caught the wafting scent of the first guard's unwashed hair, co-mingling with the smell of ripe perspiration. She watched as the guard, too lazy to get up, remained seated on her chair. She grasped onto the side arms and struggled against her body weight while trying to drag herself closer towards the desk. Her heavy bottom was spread out and lagging over the sides of the seat, causing the chair's legs to screech while scraping along the wooden floor. When she finally got situated, the guard raised her head with a menacing smirk on her face.

Louisa was taken aback by the ugliness of her swollen face. Her plumped-up cheeks were most likely caused by an overindulgence of Polish sausages, causing her gray eyes to almost disappear into her brow. Her pig-shaped nose was positioned above thin lips that connected one balloon-shaped cheek with the other. Mousy-brown hair was pulled back and tightly barricaded by many black bobby pins.

60

Marked by highly arched eyebrows, her expression was un-questionably the visage of someone harboring malicious in-tent. Her austere appearance was a tell-tale sign that her goal was to intimidate others and to show how proud she was to be a part of the Reich's cause. Louisa thought: She looks like an androgynous creature, a robotic shell without feelings. I wonder what made her join up with the Nazis? What happened in her life that made her neglect herself? What prompted her to join the Nazi cause? Did she ever have a family? Was she ever loved by anyone? Is it true that disappointments and unhappiness can mold someone into being heartless and uncaring?

Just then, the guard removed the worn-down yellow pen-cil resting on her ear, gripped it between two short, stubby fingers, and began to write something in the sign-in roster. In an unpleasant tone and raspy voice, the guard spoke commandingly, "State your first and last name." Louisa was taken aback and stood silently with wide eyes. "We're not here to waste any time," the woman barked. "Open your He-brew trap and speak! Speak, before I come over and club you over the head with my cane, just for the fun of it!" Louisa summoned up the courage to raise her head to answer. She was cautious not to give the guard any reason to have an explosive reaction, afraid of poking a sleeping lion. When their eyes finally met, a flash of fear shot through Louisa's spinal column.

Louisa managed to answer in shallow breaths, fearing that a deeper inhale might draw in the fetid air coming from the guard's malodorous breath. The guard's thin lips turned slightly upward, displaying two discolored incisors. Menac-ingly she said, "You will move over to the next table. You will get to the back of the line." Louisa was confused and didn't move. "Listen, you wretched, filthy swine. If you give me any flack, I'll have you shipped out to the Belzec death camp along with the other cockroaches. While you are here under my command, Jew-whore, you will do as I say. If you are strong enough to live in this filth, you might be able to stay alive longer," she sneered, continuing with more repugnant threats. "Who knows, maybe today will be your last day on earth!" she said with an evil laugh.

Louisa panicked again, thinking: Why the change? What line is that and what does that mean? Will that mean more trouble for me? The guard's unsettling, searing words shot through Louisa like flaming arrows, piercing and scalding the inner chambers of her heart. She thought: No one has ever spoken to me with such cruelty. If I survive this bloody horror, these haunting memories will plague me forever.

Still shaking with uncontrollable fear, Louisa could barely feel her legs move as she managed to shuffle her body over to the next registration table. She felt like an apparition, a spirit without human form, as she found herself standing at the end of a line at the next table. Planting her feet in a parallel position, she started pushing down hard on her toes, rocking back and forth on her heels, trying to grasp a sense of feeling grounded. She yearned for some semblance of stability, trying her best to keep from falling into the black sea of despair.

Finally rooted in her spot, she couldn't help but listen to the crying sounds of hungry, crying babies. It broke her heart to think that these innocent babies were screaming for the attention and care they rightfully deserved. She wondered: What would happen to them? Would they be able to survive the cruelty of the times? Would it be better if they were blessed with a quick death and avoid the terrors to come? Suddenly, Louisa felt the room begin to spin. In a quick reflex, she grabbed the arm of the person in front of her. Steeling herself while gasping for more air, hoping for the feeling to pass, she tried desperately to prevent herself from fainting.

Finally, Louisa was the first person in line. While still looking down at the dusty floor, afraid to look up in fear of seeing the face of another ruthlessness guard, she caught a glimpse of a shadow. Focusing her eyes on the dim reflection, she dared to look upwards to the left. There she saw a young man standing next to the guard. She recognized his face instantly.

The final forming of a person's character lies in his own hands. -Anne Frank

Blue Eyes

Louisa was startled by the silhouette of the young man in the shadows. His unexpected presence sent an electric current straight to her heart. The name embroidered on the Nazi Youth's uniform was Wladik Waldheim. Louisa froze, thinking: How is this possible? Could it really be him, the young Nazi who left me alone in my bedroom? The one to whom I almost lost my virginity in the hopes of saving my own life?

Suddenly, their eyes locked in mutual recognition, both recalling what had happened between them less than a week ago. Louisa felt dizzy and light-headed, and almost lost her balance. She began to swagger, and thought: Just the sight of him makes me lose control. My emotions are running wild. What is happening to me? I must fight against this dizziness and regain my strength. For heaven's sake, I cannot weaken now! My God, I can only rely on myself, on my common sense!

Louisa knew she mustn't forget that Wladik Waldheim was among the Ukrainian and Polish youth sympathizers who took part in the 'Aktion.' He was among the others who barged into her home that night. He was a member of the 'Aktion' who, in the early morning hours, pulled her sleeping family away from their beds, marched them down the stairs, and took them against their will to places unknown. He was part of the Nazi youth gangs, composed of bullies who tortured and captured Jews. He participated in taking them away as prisoners, and sometimes shot them on the spot just to set an example. This man invaded apartments and houses while participating in the hunt for Jews. Naturally, she knew she should hate him. But then again, Wladik Waldheim was the reason she survived. Suddenly, Louisa questioned whether her imagination was playing tricks or was she

64

detecting a slight twinkle in his bright, blue eyes; maybe an unmasked glimmer of good intent?

Louisa's intuition warned: Don't be fooled, how is it that he just happens to show up here in this line? I cannot let my guard down and trust him. What if he puts me in harm's way? In the next moment she felt herself soften and wondered, maybe he is here to help me? After all, he didn't take me before! Louisa was so confused. God help me! She prayed.

Suddenly, Wladik Waldheim spoke up in a loud voice for others to hear. "Well, my little Jewish 'fraulein,' (young lady) What is a beautiful girl like you doing in a place like this?" His joking manner and slight sarcasm sounded a bit threatening. "Seems like we might be able to find a special place for you, heh? You will step out of the line and stand here. You are coming with me," he taunted. The soldier's commanding tone implied that she had no choice but to follow his order.

Mesmerized by his hypnotic gaze, Louisa felt herself succumbing to the lure of his blue eyes. Was she imagining it, or was she detecting a shred of caring; a dose of human compassion? Petrified, she didn't dare answer, while swirling thoughts filled her head with confusion. For a fleeting moment her mind wandered, thinking about how the blue color of his irises reminded her of cornflowers that bloomed in the fields every spring. Flashes of memories came back to her of the springtime walks she used to take in the countryside with her family. Visions of beautiful cornflower blossoms brought the promise of a new harvest in late summer. Thinking of the pastoral scene calmed her momentarily, then she came to her senses and realized the gravity of her current life-or-death situation.

Louisa looked again to make sure it was really the same soldier that had been in her bedroom. She examined his face, his shoulders, the outline of his arms and chest. It had been dark when his silhouette hung over her bed with passion on his breath. She remembered his strong hands on her thighs. She looked at his eyes and thought: Yes, that is definitely him. Those are unquestionably his cornflower blue eyes. I will never forget the feeling I had when I first saw them. The pale blue color took my breath away, yet at the same time spiked fear in my heart.

Walter Waldheim was the one who took part in the 'Aktion' that night, the one who left her behind, alone in the bedroom to suffer in grief and despair. Despite the fact that his sensibilities were weakened by sexual impulses, perhaps he deliberately left her; giving Louisa a chance to survive. Was it possible that he panicked and ran down the stairs when he heard the blaring commands of his superior? He took a great risk by sparing my life, whether intentional or not, she thought. That is the only reason I am standing there today. Although this man was part of the 'Aktion', the group of criminals who took everything from me, maybe he is a good person trapped in a terrible job. I must take that chance and trust that he might help me again. As flickering thoughts of confusion plagued her mind like a lonely lighthouse, its muddled lights glowed through the velvet blackness of the night.

Louisa stepped forward obediently and moved to the side of the front desk to stand next to Wladik Waldheim. With an outstretched arm, he indicated where and exactly how far apart from him she should stand. He pointed to a spot uncomfortably close to him, threw his arm around her, while assuming a too-familiar gesture that suggested they had met before. Immediately beguiled by the warmth of his body so close to her, she dared to look up and observe his perfectly chiseled face, strong, square chin, and the shining lure of the blue eyes. Strangely comforted by his possessive gesture, Louisa felt herself beginning to surrender her suspicions and place her trust in this stranger.

"Come this way, pretty girl," Wladek Waldheim whispered under his breath, his words only meant for her to hear. He placed his hand gently along the back of her waist, and with the politeness of a gentleman about to lead a lady onto the dance floor, began to guide her towards the exit door. Almost immediately, they were noticed by the receptionist guard named Olga Reichsmann. Turning abruptly towards them, she spoke in a low, husky voice. "Waldheim, where are you taking this Jew? Don't get any ideas about using her as your sex slave, comrade. I am the only one who chooses who will stay and who is assigned to work in this ghetto. I'm in charge! Don't forget this. You, comrade, are not allowed to interfere with my duties. If you do, I will report you to the authorities!"

At first, Waldheim did not respond. He continued to look down at the floor, pretending to be complacent with her commands. He sported a bland, non-descript facial expression while masking his true intentions. Waldheim had a different plan for Louisa. Like a rapid change in the weather, he dared to look up at the female guard. His blue eyes glared with a look of defiance, like icebergs threatening the passage of approaching ships in frigid Artic seas. "Listen, Reichsmann, we are all in this together. I have no interest in interfering with your duties. Your duties matter greatly. However, my goal is to put these Jews to work immediately. Their work will help us with our goal, our final solution to ultimately obliterate all of them now and wipe them off the face of the earth! I'm taking this Jew to a special place; I think you know where it is! It's the same place where many high-ranking officers also have a special purpose for her, if you know what I mean," he snickered, sounding like a hissing snake. Then Waldheim repositioned his spine in a soldier's stance, clicked his heels together robotically, and gestured a "Heil Hitler" salute with his right hand. All at once, he shot her a resolute grimace, clearly indicating that his decision was non-negotiable.

By the look on Olga Reichsmann's face, he knew his plan was working. "Well, in that case, you take her," the female guard snickered. She is certainly pretty enough, for a Jew, that is. Surely, this Jew-whore is destined to be used for the sole pleasure of our esteemed officers! It is important to keep our officers happy, in good spirits. Her body will suit them and she will give them great amusement, a much-deserved reward for their hard work. Take her away, comrade Waldheim! Heil Hitler!" she saluted.

Waldheim firmly placed both his hands on Louisa's shoulders and quickly directing her away from the desk. Together, Louisa and Waldheim maneuvered their way through and around the long lines of people. Waldheim was intent on pushing aside any person who blocked their path to the exit. Neither one of them dared say a word, somehow fearing that the strange bond, the spell between them, might be broken. They weaved through the over-crowded room, traveling with great efficiency and skill, snaking their way towards the Jewish Community center's exit. It was as if they had rehearsed this plan before, moving together in sync, joined together as a couple to make a straight getaway.

Amazed that she was somehow no longer afraid, conflicting thoughts continued to flood Louisa's mind. She worried: Am I walking into a dangerous trap? Am I being so naive by putting my trust in this strange man, an enemy of my people? Why is he putting himself at risk to save me anyway? Maybe he plans to kill me after he is done with me. Desperate to come up logical explanations, she could find none that comforted her. There was nothing else to do but give up on rational thinking and just pray for a miracle. Louisa knew she had no choice. Waldheim was in charge; her life was in his hands.

How can you compromise with people who don't want you to exist? They want us to disappear. I can't adapt to death.
- Amy Harmon, From Sand and Ash

Waldheim's Plan

Waldheim kept his large, strong hands clamped securely around Louisa's shoulders, cautiously steering her towards the exit door. They headed in the direction of the ancient stone municipal building in the back of the Ghetto. Twinges of cold-blooded fear continued to shoot up and down Louisa's spine. She worried: Where is he taking me? I should have found a way to stay in the first line and let that witch, Olga Reichsmann, assign me a job. But then again, I had no choice.

Several yards ahead, Waldheim spotted his destination and guided them towards it. They stopped to stand in front of the massive-looking medieval door covered with patches of parched brown and green vines of ivy. He tugged on the rusty iron handles; exerting such force that they both fell backwards, landing on top of each other. They managed to get up quickly, brushing away the dirt and tiny pebbles embedded into their clothes. It seemed to Louisa that Waldheim was in a great hurry, always pushing her, moving them forward without the slightest hesitation, while trying to avoid being noticed by the wrong person who might cause them trouble.

Fortunately, this time Waldheim managed to pull the heavy wooden door of the secret and rarely-used staircase wide open. All at once, they were standing close to the crude, dirt-caked steps descending into a musty-smelling stone cellar. The ceiling beams above them were festooned with weathered strands of dirt and spider webs. The foreboding surroundings were a warning that they were entering into a place reeking of danger. They carefully moved down the crumbling stairs, navigating their way into the darkened cellar while an obnoxious smell of mold and mildew blasted their nostrils. As they sank deeper into what seemed like a cavernous hole, Waldheim tightened his grip around Louisa's shoulders protectively, so as to reassure her not to be afraid. She worried: Is there anyone else down there? Is this where he will be hiding me? There is no way to tell. Could Waldheim be planning to do something horrible to me?

Louisa and Waldheim carefully maneuvered their way down the uneven stone steps of varying heights and depths. Both of them were aware that dark caves and dank cellars were known to be natural habitats for dead rodents or infectious disease transmitting insects. They ducked their heads and contorted their bodies as they moved, trying to avoid the ghastly latticework: webbed patterns of entrapped insects and fossil-like objects covering the walls and ceilings and hiding in crevices.

While moving down the steps, Louisa felt like she was a blind prisoner led by a seeing-eye dog. Despairing thoughts overwhelmed her: Now that I am a prisoner, will I be able to survive after being stripped of my dignity and freedoms? I have lost my right to question. Yet, I must be smart and trust my intuition. Louisa was at Waldheim's mercy. Would fate treat her kindly? Why were they going downstairs? There was one thing she knew for sure, there was evil in the air.

It was difficult to see clearly amidst the dimness of the stairs. In order to avoid tripping and stumbling, they carefully measured the distance between each descending step and planted one foot in front of the other. Louisa could barely breathe as putrid odors wafted upwards and assailed her senses. It became impossible to avoid the foul smells. Louisa took in quick, shallow breaths, hoping her olfactory nerve wouldn't have enough time to register the odors and send the message to her brain. The shallow breathing didn't work and suffocating odors began choking her. Dust and debris drifted through the air, making it even harder to breath and Louisa tried hard to stifle her coughs. Walheim turned sharply and shot her a piecing glance, warning her to be quiet.

Upon reaching the twentieth step of the cavernous cellar, it was like entering the imaginary threshold of hell. There were raucous sounds, the echoes of men's voices reverberating off the walls. They stopped at the hidden doorway to the cellar. For a few seconds, Waldheim seemed hesitant to open the door, leaving his hand to rest on the rusty latch. They both leaned in and placed their ears against the closed door to hear what was happening inside. It was a droning, muffled chorus of high-pitched female voices; a cacophony of whimpering, moaning and loud wails. Unmistakably, these were the soul-screaming sounds of women's terrified voices. What seemed the loudest were the heart-wrenching sounds of the young adolescent and teenage girls. Louisa felt an inferno of red-hot fears beginning to rage inside her.

As they slowly opened the door, Louisa was stupefied as she witnessed the shocking scene. It was a chilling sight that would be etched in her brain, marked in indelible ink for the rest of her life. What she saw were three horizontal lines of about ten to twelve petrified women, varying ages from fourteen to fifty, all standing naked, humiliated, and huddled together in a desperate clutch. These women were placed on an indecent display, a public viewing shown especially for the Nazi officers. The theme of the show could be described as, "Man's Inhumanity to Man." The officers seemed to enjoy the show, considering that they saw no harm in defiling, ravaging, and ultimately raping innocent Jewish women. It was apparent that these women were intentionally debased to the lowest level, systematically stripped of their clothes along with any remaining vestiges of human dignity. Occasionally, one woman would cry aloud in raging despair while others chose to swallow their horror, weeping silent tears of

71

shame and degradation. The intense humiliation and shame in the room was palpable. The common thread of all the helpless and desperate women was wishing to become invisible to the gawking audience.

Suddenly, one officer called out to a tall, lanky Aryan referred to as chief Officer Otto Heinreich. "Hey, Heinreich, what are you doing over there? Hurry over! Just look at these delicious tarts we have here. I bet they are begging for it," he laughed amusedly. Heinreich, a middle-aged man with an over-sized beer-laden belly hanging over his belt, whipped his head around to answer as swiftly as a serpent looking eager to snatch and devour its prey.

As soon as Otto Heinreich drew his attentions to Waldheim and Louisa standing next at the open door, he started making his way towards them. As he got closer, Louisa caught the fetid scent of distinctive body odor that was emphatically announcing his presence. He reeked from the stench of cheap whiskey, stale cigarettes, and pungent perspiration. From where she stood, Louisa spotted the unsightly reflection of Otto Heinreich's oily forehead as it caught the skeleton rays of the afternoon sun peering in through the cracked windows. A greasy film topped his balding scalp and accentuated his prematurely receding hairline. Louisa was disgusted. Her first reaction was that of sheer hatred, thinking: He is a vulgar, loathsome excuse for a human being. I have never had murderous thoughts before this moment, but I wish I could kill this despicable monster along with all the others. How could they disgrace these innocent women like this? Is this why I am here then, to be dishonored too? I'd rather die. I need to find a way out!

Upon seeing Wladik Waldheim with pretty Louisa at his side, Otto Henireich began to laugh excitedly; obviously thrilled with the addition of another new female prospect. As he began to laugh, his eyes disappeared into the sockets. His facial muscles tightened and lifted his doughy cheeks, making the thread-like veins alongside his bulbous nose more apparent. The uneven tinge of his ruddy complexion accentuated an inebriated condition, surely the tell-tale signs of a heavy drinker. With an arrogant swagger, Otto Heinreich moved closer towards them. He stumbled, tripping on a hard chunk of loosened cement trapped under his boot. His upper body lurched forward and almost fell over onto the gravelly cellar floor. As luck would have it, he quickly caught the fall. Stopping two feet in front of them, he was able to regain balance, assume his composure, and pretend as if it never happened. Dutifully intent on showing his Nazi loyalty, he made a serious attempt to stand up at military attention, but unfortunately, lost his balance once again. This time he managed to stand up and lean his shoulder against the support of the crumbling wall directly to the right of the stairs. He grimaced, acting as if he was suffering from a bout of indigestion, burped loudly, and gestured a "Heil Hitler" salute. After regaining control of his awkwardness and gaining a bit of confidence, he proceeded to wink at Waldheim.

Suddenly, Otto Heinreich redirected his attentions towards Louisa, then sneering lasciviously, "What have we here? This wench looks like a tender, young piece of ass, heh? There is nothing that suits my pleasure more than screwing a tasty Jew whore. Surely you exist for the sole purpose of making us happy. You will serve me and obey my commands satisfying my every whim." Otto Heinreich's bloodshot eyes turned to Waldheim, saying, "We love to feed our hungers with reckless abandon. We deserve it, don't you agree, comrade?" He then flung an arm around Waldheim's shoulder, pretending to be good buddies; faithful comrades bonded together in unspeakable crimes, proud to be fighting on the same side against the designated enemy, the Jews.

Louisa began to shake uncontrollably, now fearing her fate was sealed. She cringed with shame as Otto Heinreich recast his gaze upon her body, ogling her like a hungry tiger; circling around in a slow, taunting fashion. He took small steps, laughing and teasing, making lewd sexual movements and trying to touch her in her forbidden, private places. He seemed to enjoy the drama he created, emphasizing his sense of power and ownership, like a slave master who was purchasing a new acquisition. Just then, he positioned his beefy lips and puckered them into the shape of a tight anus. He began whistling the familiar howls of disrespect, like those of a shameless thug passing a lady on the street. Purposefully, he positioned his whistling very near to Louisa's face and immediately released the foul smells of rotten teeth, cigarette smoke, and beer.

Finally, when Otto Heinreich decided to end his bullish mockery, he was ready to take the next step and plunge into action by playing a game. First, he raised both hands up high and grabbed both of Louisa's breasts. Through the fabric of her blouse, he began to squeeze both nipples, turning the flesh around them in a painful, circular motion. The vulgarity and physical violation of her body made Louisa scream out in excruciating pain. Otto Heinreich released his fingers from her breasts and roughly grabbed her chin. "What's the matter, 'Fraulein?' You didn't like that?" he sneered, while specks of spittle dribbled down from his fleshy lips. "Don't worry, we have more in store for you. But can you wait, my sex kitten, or are you already in heat? Oh 'vey,' isn't that what you people say? It seems that my dirty little Jewish whore is very horny today!" he taunted shamelessly and then laughed as his huge, round stomach moved up and down.

Waldheim could not stand by silently any longer. He rearranged his face into a mask of self-control. Fueled with a sense of urgency, his voice grew louder and it began to crack, like an adolescent reaching puberty. He tried to shout with fervor, yet his wavering voice sounded hesitant. Frustration overtook him. His voice was faltering, hinting at the underlying dread of what Otto Heinreich might do next. Once again, he cleared his throat and tried to speak with firm conviction. Acting nonchalantly, Waldheim pretended he wasn't bothered at all by Otto Heinreich's outrageous behavior. Responding calmly and carefully choosing his words, he said, "Oh my, yes! I picked this Jew because I agree that she is a delicious tart! That's why we are going to have fun with this pretty young Fraulein!"

Louisa stood silent with her body stiff as a board, not knowing what to do or think. Her heart was racing like a high-speed train in her chest, and she felt as if she were going to faint. Waldheim continued to speak to Otto. "Actually, it is only fair that since I found her, I have the right to claim her first for my pleasures." Suddenly encouraged, thinking his words appeased Otto Heinreich, he dared to add, "The good news is that when I am tired of her, I will cast her aside and be sure to send her back to you. Then, you can do whatever you please! It's only right to share the goods, right, comrade?" Otto Heinreich nodded in agreement, then smiled; sporting the contented look of a Cheshire cat.

Louisa trembled, feeling helpless and frightened to the bone. She wondered silently: Could it be true that Waldheim meant what he said to Otto Heinreich? Who can I trust? Am I being fooled by one or both of them? Louisa's runaway emotions were trapped in a tug-of-war between trust and panic, leaving her confused about Waldheim's true intentions. It was impossible to know what or who to believe. Her mind panicked. The clamoring of imaginary voices in her mind continued to pull in opposing directions. More dizzying thoughts had her head spinning around in circles. She felt as if she was holding a time bomb, and her time on this earth was ticking away faster and faster.

As she stood in the oven-like room, the heaviness of the sweltering heat heightened her nervousness. Louisa took notice of her own breathing; her constricted chest taking in only shallow breaths. Slow rivulets of sweat began to roll down the back of her neck and disappear into the moist collar of her blouse. Despite the perilousness of her situation,

Louisa decided to do whatever she could to avoid falling into the abyss of negative thinking. She knew that she had to find a way to rally quickly. But how? She had to find a mental defense mechanism, a temporary sanctuary, a way to disassociate her mind from the torturous reality. She had to muster the strength to block out the confusion and release herself from feeling paralyzed by fear. Her life depended on it!

At once, a compelling inner voice spoke: Breathe, Louisa. You will find a way, for you are not alone. Then she remembered her mother's mantra. "Never be afraid of anything, for God is always with you. The power of the human spirit is the strongest power in the world." After a few deep breaths she felt energized and renewed. She needed to stay positive and hold on to hope at all costs. She knew that she must never give up.

Louisa's stomach roared with of hunger. She couldn't remember the last time she had something to eat or even a sip of water. She felt confused, dizzy and light headed. She almost lost her balance, and would have welcomed the prospect of fainting, just to have a break in the living nightmare. At that moment, just before blacking out, her eyes began to roll backwards. Waldheim started to shake her vigorously. He tugged her arms and shook her until he made sure she was fully conscious. Then he turned her around to face the door, placed his hand on her lower spine, and gently pushed her towards the back entrance normally used by the officers. Together, they made it up the stairs that led to the main level of the ghetto. As they reached the top, Waldheim pushed open the heavy wooden door. Once outside on the cobblestoned street, neither one looked back.

While quickening his pace, Waldheim yelled, "Hurry up and keep up with me! You must get back to the registration line before anyone realizes that you are missing. Don't worry. I'll meet you there. I will tell them I took you down to the Hitler Youth Cellar and Otto Heinreich selected you for himself. They will assign you to stay here at the Tarnopol ghetto. My hope is that this trick lets you remain at the ghetto and not be sent away. I will watch out for you, Louisa. Don't fear. I like you and I will do whatever I can to help you," he whispered. "Rest assured that Otto Heinreich will never touch you again."

Louisa sighed in relief. She couldn't describe how fortunate she felt, able to escape the horrors of that hellish environment. Waldheim's kindness and comforting words have been my sustenance thus far, she thought. His interest in me has lasted long enough for me to gain time to live for another day. I feel like a starving woman allotted only one frosted cookie each day. Waldheim's presence is like the icing on the cookie, a thin layer of trust. I am still not sure, but what I do know is that I have no choice but to trust him.

Life is like riding a bicycle; to keep moving you have to keep your balance. -Albert Einstein

Clouds of Fear

It was a normal day in Drohobych, Poland for thirty-six-year-old, Samuel Rosenberg. Samuel was a Polish Jew who was happily married to Danika, the love of his life. Both he and Danika adored their little four-year old son, Josef. At the time, Samuel was working as a hospital administrator in his hometown while taking evening courses to become a doctor.

While the familiar pattern of daily life was vibrating with new tensions and heightening anti-Semitic concerns, no one could speculate the future of Jews living in Drohobych. People in Samuel's neighborhood sensed trouble in the air. Many were unwilling to confront their clawing intuitions, warning that something terrible was about to happen. Choosing to ignore the ominous predictions was like choosing not to believe a soothsayer's ill-fated reading. It was easier to live in denial, as if everything was still ok.

Samuel was aware that the Germans broke the non-aggression pact, and then proceeded to invade small Polish towns like Drohobych. He had heard about the outward persecution of Jews beginning in other towns and continuing to happen in the rest of the Galicia region. They were strategically targeted by zealous Ukrainian and Polish Nationalists Nazi Party supporters. As the frightening rumors abounded, mounting fears gained momentum. Panic drums began to beat wildly, clanging against the chest bones of Jews everywhere in Poland.

This particular morning at 6:00am, Samuel left his home before sunrise in order to be on time for his early morning shift. When he arrived at work, people were nervously flitting around, discussing how Jewish employees were becoming targets. There was talk of dismissing any employee known to be Jewish. Administrators, doctors, nurses, technicians, and all others working in any capacity were in danger of losing their jobs. All hospital employees felt threatened, even the non-Jews were concerned. Such an abrupt change would bring chaos to the well-established hospital organization. All morning, there was collective worry that a meeting would be called and that they would be dismissed from their duties. The entire morning had passed and no such meeting had taken place. Samuel thought: So far, so good. People just panic all the time. Maybe it's sheer speculation. It's usually just unwarranted worry.

Distracted by the familiar rumblings in his stomach, Samuel's internal alarm clock announced that it was time for lunch. His mid-day hunger became a welcomed distraction from the worries of the day. As Samuel made his way back to his office to retrieve his lunchbox, he looked forward to eating a nice, quiet lunch in the park across the street from the hospital. Positioned in the center of the park among large Poplar shade trees was the Gothic-style Drohobych town clock. The familiar timber of twelve sequential chimes to indicate the noon hour gave Samuel a burst of pleasure. The chimes were a welcome reminder that it was time to take a well-deserved break from his daily hospital responsibilities. On his way out, Sam was careful to avoid any conversation about troubling rumors, trying to prevent anything from ruining his plan for a quiet lunch. He exited the hospital through the heavy large-framed entrance doors and ambled down the wide, stone steps before crossing the street towards the Drohobych park in the town center.

Upon entering the park, his favorite bench beckoned to him like the beacon of a lighthouse guiding the way for lost ships in the night. As he plopped down on the wooden bench, he looked forward to savoring the surprise lunch his wife, Danika had lovingly prepared for him. Deftly, Samuel unlatched the metal latch of the aluminum lunchbox, his eager fingers moving like a skilled magician. He pulled back

79

the dome of the lunchbox cover, releasing it backwards to rest upon two twisted and rusty clasps. He took out a large thermos, balancing it carefully beside him on the bench. On that particular day he felt especially grateful for his simple lunchtime indulgence. He remembered the mishap he had on a previous day, when half of his sandwich dropped to the ground. Trying to be more careful, he began removing only half of the sandwich that was wedged in the corner of his lunchbox. Careful not to repeat the same fumble, he made sure to hold it with a steady grip as several loose pumpernickel grains fell away, scattering onto the grassy area beneath his feet.

As if secretly watched by undercover agents, Samuel's bench was instantly surrounded by at least eight hungry pigeons, all exhibiting a corpse-like gray color. Boldly approaching the park bench, the pigeons positioned themselves uncomfortably close to Samuel's work shoes. The unflinching pigeons seemed to be in competition with each other; all perfectly posed, anxiously waiting to snatch more of the meager crumbs that might still fall.

With a quick flick of his left wrist, Samuel signaled the uninvited guests to disperse and go away from his bench. He spoke in a loud voice, "Go away and leave me alone to eat! Don't bother me! Don't even think about taking what belongs to me. This is my lunch, not yours to take! You have no right! Do you hear me?" The pigeons didn't oblige. As a matter of fact, more low-flying, hovering pigeons continued to land nearby, also waiting and watching for more crumbs to appear. He thought: Incorrigible creatures. What pests they are! Nonetheless, Samuel knew full well it was their nature to come back and gather any crumbs they could steal. They always did, because that is the nature of pigeons.

Samuel began to think of the similarities between the intimidating tactics of the aggressive pigeons and the bullying by Nazi sympathizers. Didn't Nazi protagonists gain strength and support by using the same grand design? Both used similar strategies to break down and weaken their victims. They taunted and annoyed them, turned up unexpectedly when people were most vulnerable, and always seemed to create an unwanted disturbance. Always watching and waiting for the right time to make their move, pigeons and the Nazis seemed to show up out of nowhere. The element of surprise was their usual ploy. They appeared, stealthily trying to encroach upon their prey when least expected in order to take possession of what didn't belong to them. One consolation suddenly occurred to Samuel; he could still make the pigeons disappear. As per the Nazis, Samuel wished he could do the same.

Samuel was aware of the imminent problem that prevailed over the changing social climate in eastern Poland. The intolerable bitterness towards the Jews left a souring taste that now rested on the tongues of Nazi sympathizers. A foul-smelling wind began to scatter seeds of blatant Anti-Semitism throughout the streets of Polish cities, towns, and villages. The seeds were quickly taking root, not only posing a great danger to the Jews, but to Gypsies, homosexuals, mentally ill or physically disabled. Rumors of vicious crimes infiltrated all socio-economic levels, ranging from highly prominent citizens of monetary worth to blue collar and menial workers as well. Everyone lived in fear. People tried to quell their dread by hoping the talk was based on untruths; rumors that would never come to fruition. They all sensed the danger that lurked in every corner.

Still remaining under the surveillance of camouflaging pigeons hiding behind two large elm trees, Samuel continued to sit on the park bench. He finished the last bite of his sandwich, took the last sip of hot coffee, and twisted the top back onto his aluminum thermos. As he began to walk back towards the hospital to return to work, he maintained an upward gaze, looking at the sky as if he had never noticed it before.

The accumulation of hulking clouds seemed to gather momentum, beginning to block the sun, while developing a core of descending darkness that often signaled a change in the weather. The winds were picking up. It seemed the ominous clouds were a bad omen, a reflection of trouble ahead. As chilling rumors evolved, the dissonance of hatred directed toward the Jews was like a frostbite to the extremities. Terrifying rumors were heard on the streets and the workplace, warning Jews to stay hidden; hoping they would be safe within their homes. Many people refused to heed the whispered warnings to take immediate action and get out of Europe as quickly as possible.

There was no doubt that a proverbial shroud was well on its way to suffocate the Jews. The rumblings of blame and prejudice gave Nazi sympathizers the impetus to commit unconscionable acts of violence. The Nazi momentum was gaining speed. It was a metaphoric tornado; a dark, looming funnel cloud ready to roll in and upturn everything and everyone in its path. Considered a crime to be born a Jew, the dikes of Europe's dam gave way to floods of hatred. Jews were required to pay for this crime with their very lives and with the lives of their loved ones.

Violence is like a weed; it doesn't die even in the greatest drought. -Weidenfield and Nicolson

A Simmering Pot 1941

It was a glorious summer morning in July 1941. Samuel awoke early, peering outside the open window to witness a beautiful daybreak slowly spreading over the horizon. The cool, fresh air was crisp and sweet. Samuel relished the pine-scented intoxicating fragrances of the mossy green grasses and the soil's earthy-smelling dew. However, something about this morning seemed different. As he gazed over at his wife sleeping peacefully under the thin, white sheet. Little did he know that in the next few hours, without warning, a cruel, cyclonic energy was about to bring disaster.

When Samuel arrived at the hospital that morning, he seemed oddly agitated for no apparent reason, as if he was sensing a bad omen was about to change everything in sight. When he arrived at his office, he sat down at his desk and tried to figure out why he was feeling anxious. He sat, thinking pensively, with his face buried in his hands. A hospital colleague and long-time friend of his wife, Dr. Harriette Charmatsky, knocked at his office door and proceeded to open it without waiting for permission to enter. She plopped down in the chair across from his desk, and promptly leaned in towards him. As if planning to share a secret, she said, "Sam, you have to leave. You must run away from here, NOW! There are urgent warnings for all the Jews to leave. Rumors are flying around, running rampant everywhere." In a shaky voice she managed to continue, "Aktions are targeting whole neighborhoods, both in the day and at night, systematically taking away people from their homes. They are taking Jews to camps or to places unknown, shooting them in the streets, even throwing their corpses into mass graves. They are creating killing grounds!" Then swallowing hard, like something was stuck in her throat, she continued. "Nazis have confiscated property and banned merchandise production. They have been lowering rations and limiting any freedom of movement." Swiftly, with the back of her hand, she wiped off the newly appearing perspiration from her brow, and spoke with more urgency. "I have heard that some survivors managed to evade the 'Aktions.' For weeks, I have heard how surviving Jews have joined orphans trying to dig up people from the mass graves at the killing grounds, searching the piles for lost relatives."

As fresh tears began to stream down her face, she said, "The Germans, Poles, and Ukrainian Nazi sympathizers are said to have a sense of entitlement. They feel free to take over the most beautiful and the best Jewish households." She lifted her head, sported a fierce look of defiance, and said with firm conviction, "We must face this harsh reality with vigilance, Samuel. Wake up! You are a Jew! Hurry up and take your family far away from here, away from the danger that now lurks in all corners! Just leave, Sam! Go! I am begging you!" As Samuel listened to her dagger-sharp words, her terrified voice was sending ripples of fear down his spine.

Dr. Charmatsky leaned in closer, her pallid face looking as if she had just been charred by a burning flame. "Samuel, get out and go home now. Check to see if anything has happened there. I fear for you, and for Danika and Josef! Rumor has it that soon there is going to be another 'Aktion' in your neighborhood. My God, it could already have happened today! Run back to your house immediately. Go and protect them before it's too late! Maybe you will be able to get there in time. Go before all the crazy lunatics escape from the asylum! Please Samuel, Go right NOW!!!"

Samuel had heard the rumors but didn't want to believe them. There was no question that every Jew living in the area heard the vicious and evil threats, but Samuel never could imagine they could become a catastrophic reality. Yet, the rising fever of the times was mounting at an alarmingly rate, and time was of the essence. It was already becoming too late for people to heed the whispered warnings, to leave their homes and belongings behind, and get out of Europe as quickly as possible. Little did Samuel know that it was already too late. He had no idea that three hours earlier that very morning, a team of three Hitler youth and two armed Nazi officers set out on their mission, to seek out or even murder any Jew in sight.

It was hard to imagine and truly ironic that on such a beautiful morning in the small town of Drohobych, something horrific was about to happen. The morning setting was like that of a fairytale illustration. There was a predawn stillness hovering over expansive farms bordering both sides of the quiet main road. The only sounds were morning birds, intermittently flitting about from tree to tree, busily preparing for the new day. A handful of scurrying squirrels were racing up and down large tree trunks and tumbling onto the spongy earth. Old country farmhouses were dotted along the road, spaced wide apart in three-acre lots, respectful allowing sufficient distance to maintain their cherished privacy.

Samuel's parents and four out of five sisters lived in one of the white, pristine-looking farmhouses set back along the outskirts of the main country road in Drohobych. One sister, Helena, was married and lived in another town. His elderly parents, David and Sarah, both octogenarians, lived on the same farm for the duration of their long, married life. Throughout the years, the family had a life together of good fortune. They were righteous people who were grateful for the daily blessings bestowed upon them. A tragedy was about to take place in the same family house in which Sarah had given birth to six healthy children: five daughters and one son. This morning, horrific acts were about to happen to them right in this house that was no longer a sacred space. The illusion of safety was all that it proclaimed to be; nothing but an illusion.

The team of five Ukrainian Nationalists, hell bent on killing Jews, pulled up to the farmhouse. Like wild, hungry animals just released from their cages, one by one, they jumped out of the truck. They began stampeding along the dirt path leading up to the front door, setting out on their mission to target, torture, and kill Jewish families. They had already murdered three other Jewish families who lived in the first three farmhouses along the long, winding farm road. Lost in the frenzy of insanity, these misguided young men seemed to enjoy taking part in the marathon killing spree.

Foreboding sounds of exaggerated movements of jackboots pounded upon the wooden plank steps leading up to the front door. This was a deliberate attempt to make their presence known to the sleeping victims inside. Using Herculean force, the malicious intruders raced up the steps to the front door, and barging in with such ferocity, shattered apart the wooden molding surrounding the doorframe, as the falling wooden splinters collected on the floor. Their brutal faces promised ill-will and brought with them the suffocating stench of fiendish intentions to the once peaceful house.

With guns pointed at their heads, all the family members were raucously aroused from sleep, rounded up and pushed out of their bedrooms, then forced to stand against the wall into the main living room. Sarah and David, alongside their four teenage daughters, stood paralyzed. Praying helplessly, shivers of ice-cold terror shot up and down their spines as they dared not look up from the floor. For this unfortunate family, their surroundings were beginning to fade and the final death shroud was being lowered, ready to extinguish the light of their existence. A funereal silence began to permeate the room, while their quivering bodies trembled beneath the soft material of their bedclothes. They stood waiting, like distressed and corroding bronze statues, for the bullets to take their lives.

All that was left to do was pray to a seemingly absent God. Was he there with a plan to save them? How could he disappear at a time like this? It wasn't fair. They were observant Jews who obeyed and honored God, and respected the laws of their religion. There was nothing else they could do but hope for a miracle. They stood with their backs against the wall in desperation, feeling like they were trying to balance on a sinking raft amidst a raging sea, waiting to fall into the abyss.

As they waited, unanswerable questions continued to plague them: Should they protest? Should they stand up for themselves and order them to get out of their home? Once-normal minds were being replaced with panic and fueled by gut-wrenching emotions. Their souls continued to cry inconsolably, like the demanding, unrelenting cries of a sick or hungry baby.

The youngest daughter, Deborah, dared to whisper in her father's ear, "What do they want with us? Will they shoot us, Papa? Will they take us away? Shouldn't we do something? Why aren't you pleading with them? Please, Papa! Do something! Don't let us die!" Papa continued to stare. He kept his eyes focused straight ahead at the family picture handing on the wall over the stone fireplace. "No, maidele (little girl), it won't help. '*Sha, sha, mein kint,*' (Quiet, my child.) Be still and don't talk. '*Adoshem'* (Hebrew for God) will protect us."

Seething with anger, fear, and frustration, she whispered back under her breath, "I'll kick them in their groins. I'll spit into their ugly eyes. I'll take a knife and cut the noses from these monstrous faces! Oh, Papa, why did they choose us? Why did the angel of death choose to come here? We are good people! Why are you being so still? Do something to save us!"

Minutes later, at point blank range, six shots were fired. Enormous explosions abounded. Human remains were spattered on the wall behind them. Sprayed blood, gray brain matter, parts of skulls, bone fragments and hair flung all over the room; adhering to the ceiling, walls, and floor like the devil's art. It was a three-dimensional abstract of a heinous crime. After leaving the grisly scene of desecrated bodies, the Nazi perpetrators continued to boast about another job well done. They charged out the house, pumped up and ready to hit the next house on the road. The sounds of their laughter reverberated in the neighborhood.

Whoever can stop the members of his household from committing a sin, but does not, is held responsible for the sins of the household. If he can stop the people of his city from sinning, but does not, he is held responsible for the sins of the people of his city. If he can stop the whole world form sinning, and does not, he is held responsible for the sins of the whole world. -Babylonian Talmud: Shabbat 54b

Shocking Times

Struck by the severity of Dr. Charmatsky's insistent warning, Samuel was terrified. Propelled by fear, he knew that a new reality was setting in and he could no longer deny the looming situation. He had no choice but to check on everyone's safety and do exactly what she said. But, understandably, he was very afraid of what he might discover.

Samuel bolted out of the main hospital entrance door, sprinted down the steps and jumped on his bicycle. He pedaled wildly along the narrow streets; past village businesses, restaurants, and storefronts. As he made his way towards the outskirts of Drohobych, the cobblestone streets disappeared into grassy pathways lined with trees that were laden with heavy drooping branches. Hurriedly, he weaved his way along the country lanes, trying to avoid bumping into anyone or anything in his path, and focused on the familiar route towards the countryside where he lived with his wife and child. For some reason, he imagined that the Weeping Willow trees sensed his urgency. He wondered: Are they weeping for me? Do the trees know something I don't know? Are they offering a sign of consolation for what I might discover? No, I will not allow myself to think the worst.

As Samuel bicycled along, he wondered why no one turned around or seemed a bit curious as to why he was pedaling so rapidly through town. Did anybody wonder where he was headed to in such a deliberate rush? They just moved aside and let him pass through, as if they were feeling guilty about something. Did they know something had happened already? He began silently wishing he could make everything go back to the normalcy that existed before, to the life they had unknowingly taken for granted.

Generally speaking, throughout his thirty-six years of life, Samuel had learned a great deal about people and their self-serving qualities. He knew firsthand that they were interested primarily in their own well-being and what benefitted them. As long as their lives were not affected, people remained calm. Sam was sure that in the recent months, people must have felt the boiling heat of evil spilling over the rim of the pot. Despite the blazing fires that continued to heat up their world, many chose to remain oblivious to the horrors that were happening around them. Why did they allow it to happen? Didn't anyone even care? Where were the good people who could have prevented such disaster? Nonetheless, he still prayed for a miracle. Maybe he wasn't too late. As he made his way back to his neighborhood, his heart sank, realizing he could be entering into the aftermath of the latest 'Aktion.'

Without hesitation, Samuel continued to cycle at a feverish pace towards his house, despite the sinking of his heavy heart. Finally, he ran up the front steps to his house, shaking and afraid, all the while praying desperately to find Danika and Josef there, unharmed in any way.

As he opened the front door, a deafening silence pounded in his ears. In a panicked, yet thunderous voice, Sam shouted their names; his broken voice quivering like an injured bird. After each shout, he stopped and strained to listen closely for a response of any kind. To his dismay, there was no response. Suddenly struck by the sheer desolation in the house, he dared to walk in farther, yet the weight of the hard silence was almost unbearable. He began checking every room in the house. Nobody was there. He prayed: Please God, make them be somewhere else. But where could they be at this early morning hour? Maybe they were warned about the 'Aktion.' Maybe someone told them to get out of the house and go somewhere else! Could they have gone to my parents' house? I will not stop until I find them. If I have to sacrifice my own life, I will find them! I must go to the farm and check on the rest of the family. "Please God, make them be safe!" he prayed out loud. Sam's heart was pounding in his chest and he could barely breathe. He took a deep, restorative breath; trying to feel calmer and to keep from panicking. He turned on his heel, slammed the door shut before sprinting down the front steps, and jumped back onto his bicycle like a jockey mounting a racehorse. He made his way onto the country road and headed towards his parents' farm nearby in the country farmlands.

Samuel rode his bicycle at top speed for the two-mile journey to his parent's house. Everything was a blur as his thoughts raced in fear and he gasped for breath. When he finally arrived at his parent's farmhouse, he put his hand on the front doorknob and felt multiple dizzying waves of fear and anxiety. He was too weak to turn the doorknob. Fear had taken over and the dexterity of his fingers seemed to stiffen and resist his brain's commands. Despite his spastic ineptness, he kept trying and was finally able to open the front door. As he pushed it open, he heard the familiar creaking and moaning of the door hinges.

Afraid to enter front hallway, he placed his foot inside with great trepidation, forcing himself to enter the first room on the left. Moving at a snail's pace, he began to inch his body towards the wafting smell of freshly spilled blood, inhaling the scent of death in the air. It was as though he was being magnetized; drawn in by some mysterious sort of supernatural attraction. Samuel wanted to see, but he was afraid to look.

There they were, all six of them; his beloved family, his flesh and blood. They were all lying dead, sprawled out on the farmhouse floor. Samuel froze as he stood there, a witness to the greatest horror he could have ever imagined. Both of his parents and his sisters: Loretta, Deborah, Frieda, and Helena were shot execution-style, mercilessly murdered; slaughtered like cattle. On the carpet were large pools of blood, seeping and collecting around their bodies, while the fresh stains around their heads branched out like red starbursts. As he looked down at the devastating scene, he watched his family's lives being absorbed by the carpet. All of their eyes were open while their facial expressions revealed the terror of the killings. Their clothes were spattered with their own blood. Samuel fell to his knees, crawled to his youngest sister and picked up her lifeless hand. He looked at her delicate face and was struck by the fragility of life.

But where were Danika and Josef, his beloved wife and son? Samuel's body shook uncontrollably as he searched the ransacked house. Furniture had been upturned in fits of violent rage and hatred. Drawers were emptied and left open. Lamps, vases, precious valuables and other personal memorabilia were shattered and destroyed. Remnants of lives that were broken beyond repair.

After searching the house, Samuel didn't find his wife or his son. A silent scream began to rumble deep within his soul, ripping through his heart. The pain of his reality exploded into an outburst of crippling emotions. He fell to the floor in a heap of uncontrollable self-pity. Sobbing uncontrollably, he began to make howling noises, sounding like a distressed animal trapped in a dangerous situation. He cried for what seemed like an eternity; the grief was too much to bear. His wife and child had disappeared and then his parents and four sisters were murdered. Samuel wondered about his fifth married sister, Clara, who lived in another town. He closed his eyes and prayed, hoping that she was somewhere safe and still alive. Samuel's chest was tight and he could not breathe. He tried desperately to regain his composure: I need to find a way to control my rage. I must believe that Danika and Josef are safe and hiding somewhere. What should I do? Time is of the essence, and I need to get back to the hospital quickly! Harriette Charmatsky was right! She needs to know what happened. Maybe she will know what I should do. I need to save myself first so I can find Danika and Josef before it's too late!

Blinded by unstoppable tears, Samuel jumped back on his bike to head back down the winding, countryside road that led back into town. He pedaled hard while trying to maintain his balance on the uneven, rocky road. As soon as he arrived at the hospital, Samuel jumped off his bike and let it fall haphazardly to the ground. He ran up the twenty steps to the front entrance and pulled the heavy wooden door wide open, then ran at top speed down the corridor to find Dr. Harriette Charmatsky. Without hesitation, he barged through the door to her office and was instantly taken aback. Seated on the two high-backed leather chairs positioned directly across from her at her desk were two Nazi uniformed officers.

One of the officers stood up, put his hands on his hips, then eyed Samuel up and down. "And who do we have here, Dr. Charmatsky, an employee?" he sneered in condescending tone. The officer moved closer to Samuel and chuckled. I see that his name tag says Samuel Rosenberg. No doubt a Jew!" he grinned, like a smug detective who just caught his victim. "Well, Mr. Samuel Rosenberg, congratulations on your timing. You are coming with us."

Pray that you will never have to endure all that you are able to suffer. -Folk saying

Taken Away

Within minutes, more Nazi trucks pulled up in front of the hospital. Three armed officers dressed in full Nazi regalia marched up the steps, ready to load their newest captives. Samuel and all of the previously rounded-up Jewish employees were huddled and horrified, knowing they were next to board the waiting trucks. Harriette Charmatsky and several administrators stood by watching helplessly as their Jewish colleagues were being removed from the hospital. When Samuel passed by Harriette, she leaned in and whispered, "If there is anything I can do, you know I will, my friend." Samuel looked at her with tears in his eyes and then hung his head low as he walked. Now that he had been taken prisoner, he had no idea how he was going to find his wife and son.

It was inconceivable how quickly the hospital employees, guilty of nothing but the "crime" of being Jewish, were stolen away and quickly shoved into waiting trucks. Dozens of formerly respected and up-standing citizens who worked in the hospital became prisoners in an instant. The Nazi contingents had accomplished their goal of the day; they were successful in taking away more Jews. According to the Nazi regime, they were regarded as filth, worthless rubbish, less important than alley rats.

Crammed tightly together in the Nazi trucks like sardines in a tin, Samuel and the others were aching in physical discomfort. Some were protesting with grim determination while others displayed a false bravado, pretending not to be afraid. Deep down, they felt the same humiliation, blanketed by the fear of the unknown. They were all slowly suffocating from the intolerable pain of grief, like an iron vise clamped around their hearts. They became lost souls with lost identities. As

94

wards of the Nazi state, their lives no longer belonged to them. They were filled with dread, for no one knew where they were being taken.

In a daze, Samuel stared at the mud-caked floor of the truck as he rubbed the pad of his hand with his thumb. Thoughts of finding Danika and Josef plagued his mind. He remained silent while listening to the agonizing sounds of prisoners jam-packed around him. Some were whispering Polish obscenities that fell on deaf ears, but nothing could drown out the drone of the incessant weeping. Samuel thought: What good will crying do for us now? Praying isn't working. We must face the truth that our lives have been seized by the enemy, and our fate is in their hands. Destiny will decide what will become of us.

A brazen young man was sandwiched in the truck next to Samuel. "Hey, move over glubiec! (imbecile)," said the man as he nudged his elbow roughly into Samuel's rib. "We cannot even breathe here, and you take up too much room. It's people like you who add to our misery!" he growled as he spat on Samuel's shoes. Disgusted by the young man's rudeness, Samuel turned to face him, replying, "I'd gladly move father away if I was able to! Why do you have to be such an ass? We are all in this mess together, and we have more important things to worry about right now. We will be lucky if we stay alive for one more day!" Despite his annoyance, Samuel was only able to move over the width of a hair while trying to remove the glob of spit from his shoe. During these times, families were like cartons of eggs dropped carelessly to the floor. Most of the eggs got broken, but only a few were left intact. While sitting in between the others, Samuel felt like a lonely egg sitting among the broken shells.

As the truck started pulling away, Samuel tried to busy his mind, thinking what to do next. Samuel found himself lost in a daydream, a desperate plea for help in which he was begging for the rest of the world to know about the disaster happening in Poland. The deafening sounds of the bombs could be heard by only the people in Poland. No one else in the world could hear. Samuel worried in disbelief: When did police become the enemy? Why wasn't the rest of the world hearing of the intolerable abuse? Maybe it was easier to pretend not to hear. Samuel knew he was on his own. At this point it was each man for himself. He needed to wake up from the daydream, make a plan, and find a way to face the danger ahead.

Samuel knew he needed to get hold of money, items of value, even liquor, to barter with the Nazis. It was common knowledge that you could bribe enemies for the right price. Money and material goods might be used to buy freedom, sometimes even to save a life. Fortunately for Samuel, he and his family owned and managed a salt business in Drohobycz.

As far back as 1804, Samuel's family came from a line of Jewish families who leased salt mines in the towns of Drohobych, Boryslaw, Dolina, Stryi, and other surrounding areas in Poland. Since the mines did not actually yield pure salt, the mineral had to undergo a refining process. Samuel's father and grandfather were among the Jews of Drohobycz who were granted permission to reside in that town and eventually benefit the town's financial stability. They were quick to learn the technology, how to do a simple extraction of crude salts from their mine, transform it into potash and vodka, and export to Germany and neighboring countries.

Samuel quickly realized it was imperative that his next move was to find a way to smuggle money out of his salt business to where he was being held prisoner. Fully aware of the treacherous risks, one wrong move meant no second chance. He heard the frightful stories and rumors disseminating around the streets as to what happened to bartering negotiators in their dealings with the Nazis. Unknowingly, when a briber dealt with a covert Nazi swindler, it would usually end in a devastating betrayal- he'd be shot to death in the street. Covert swindlers eagerly took bribes, then turned the tables by accusing the briber for attempting to plot against the edicts of the Nazi regime. Rumors circulated about how Nazi tricksters grabbed a bribe, quickly pocketed it, then used the welcomed excuse to brutally attack the briber as punishment for breaking the law. Many Nazi swindlers took exceptional pleasure in this trickery.

To get the bribe money, Sam would have to exploit his existing business and resort to the black market. He worried about the loyalty of the people who worked for his company. Could he trust his Ukrainian and Polish employees, or did they harbor hatred towards him because he was a Jew? Were they brainwashed by the contagious fever of the times? I doubt they would risk their lives or their family's safety to help me. I think my secretary, Mania Krasinsky, might be my only choice. She may be able to help me! Mania was always loyal to him and she could easily siphon money from the business without anybody knowing. Then Sam would have money to pay off guards! He wondered if it was too late. He desperately needed Mania's help; he couldn't do it alone. Samuel knew he had to use whatever means he could to gain some time and not be afraid to take calculated risks. But how could he get in touch with Mania? He'd have to find a way.

When they arrived at their destination, Samuel jumped down from the rear of the truck. As he followed the rest of the prisoners into a building, the only thing on Sam's mind was his plan, and he prayed to find a way to make it make it work. One thing he knew for certain, even if he had to sacrifice his own life, he was determined to survive long enough to find Josef and Danika.

We who have come back, by the aid of many lucky chances or miracles- whatever one may choose to call them, we know: the best of us did not return. -Victor E Frankl

Queues

Terrified and bewildered, Samuel and the others stood in the registration queues at the SOKOL building on Mickewiez Street. Darkness and fear colored their world as they waited in single files, shoulder behind shoulder, dreading their ill-fated destiny. The rich, the middle-class, and the poorest of Jews now shared equal status. Many of them had witnessed families and friends slaughtered before their eyes. Most wanted to live long enough just to see those responsible pay for the inhumanity inflicted on others.

The endless queues (lines) moved excruciatingly slow, silently erasing the seconds, minutes, and hours from their lives. There was no longer any difference between day and night. They had no choice but to wait, now knowing what was ahead. To have patience was no longer a virtue, but a curse. Samuel was thinking: How incredulous it is that innocent people can fall so quickly. How was it possible that prominent members of society could lose rank and be forced to surrender their freedoms? Our jobs are taken away, real estate is confiscated, swept away with all our money and earthly possessions. But I must remember that material things are the least of my concerns. I have come this far and I am still alive. If I can stay alive for one more day, then I am winning. My purpose is to find Danika and Josef.

Despite being determined to find his precious wife and their only child, Samuel was not in the position to take unnecessary risks. He knew the importance of not making waves that could possibly strip away his last hope of finding them. Samuel's thoughts were interrupted by aching sensations in both feet. He had been standing for so long that new blisters had formed and were beginning to burst inside his shoes. His face had the look of a drowning man pushed overboard, gasping for air, struggling to stay afloat.

Slowly, as Samuel's line inched forward, a loud voice from another table disturbed his thoughts. "Hey! Step forward!" yelled a female guard. Samuel turned his weary head to scan the crowded room, shifting his glance to the third line on his left. Standing at the front of the line adjacent to him, he took notice of a man's head, his cap resting on two oversized, elephant-like ears. Samuel said to himself: That must be our neighbor, Sergi Weiss! No one else in Drohobych has such large, distinguishable ears! He felt a surge of comfort, for recognizing a friend was like discovering money in the street.

Just the thought of knowing someone else gave Sam a feeling of solace, the safe feeling of home. Then he had a thought: Maybe Sergi Weiss knows where the people in his neighborhood have been taken, and maybe he even knows the whereabouts of Danika and Josef! His heart was filling with hope. After losing everything else, hope was all that he had left.

The gruff, commanding voice sounded again. "Hey, Jew! Step forward!" barked a guard seated at the front registration table. She lifted her chin and nodded to Sergi Weiss, indicating that he should move to the right, a different line leading towards the exit. Samuel dared to turn around to see which line he was in. Instinctively, he knew he must not lose a connection with Sergi Weiss, deciding: Regardless of where they are taking us, I need to go with Sergi Weiss!

The strangest thing happened next. It was almost as if Samuel felt a forefinger tapping his shoulder. In a split-second, Sergi Weiss turned around and spotted Samuel. Recognizing him immediately, he raised his eyebrows, shrugged his shoulders, and nodded knowingly as if to say, "Who knows what will happen to us next." Then he turned back around to follow the rest of the line through the exit door. There was no logical explanation as to why he turned around at that precise moment. Fate took over, once again.

Suddenly, as Samuel stepped up to the front of the line, he heard the same menacing voice becoming increasingly louder. "Step up! Are you deaf? Pay attention, you idiot!" spat the guard behind the desk. Shaken by her abrasiveness, he turned to see her face. It was a mask molded in bigotry and prejudice. He began staring straight into the small, beady eyes that were nearly buried under crinkly skin. As the guard stared back at him, she sent forth smoldering signals of hatred. Taken aback by her mean-spiritedness, he almost gasped.

It all happened so fast. Samuel hoped he would be assigned to Sergi Weiss's line. He worried: What if the guard sensed my desire to be with Sergi? Did she see me turn around to look after him and perceive the connection? Will she send me to another line, purposefully? In an instant, the guard did exactly what Samuel feared. Sure enough, she focused her gaze to the left, the line parallel to Sergi's. Samuel's heart sank. What was he to do? He knew he wasn't going to accept this fate and allow her to separate him from his friend, because Sergi's presence at least gave him hope. Coming from the same neighborhood, perhaps he heard where Danika and Josef may have been taken.

Suddenly, Samuel had an epiphany. His survivor instinct took charge and breathed courage into his veins. All at once he felt a new strength, a power to take control and it elevated his mood, like air being pumped into a deflated tire. In an instant, he decided to take a new course of action. He carefully watched the guard, and made certain she was sufficiently distracted by the next person stepping up in front of her. He had only a split second to change from one line to the other. As the line pushed forward to wind its way out, Samuel leaped over to the left, quickly planting himself in the back of Sergi's line. Thankfully, no one noticed the change! Not missing a beat, he and the others were herded out and onto the truck headed for the next destination, the Tarnopol forced labor camp.

Sitting on the floor of the crowded truck, Samuel secretly commended himself on his courageous act. A strange satisfaction washed over him, thinking how he got away from the guard's unyielding grasp. Feeling relieved, he was happy for the small victory. Despite the imprisoned conditions, he proved to himself that he still had the power to make choices. In order to survive he would have to trust his intuition. Samuel did what he needed to do, to take the risk and stay close to Sergi. His only purpose was to stay alive long enough to find out what happened to Danika and Josef. Remembering his father's words, "The hands of the almighty are often found at the end of our own arms." As the truck began to move forward, he stared straight ahead and never looked back.

In a place where no one behaves like a human being, you must strive to be human. -Hillel

Mortal Chains

It was a cold, damp and gloomy day in November when they finally arrived at the barren-looking forced labor camp at Tarnopol. Samuel and the others were led through the camp gates into an unwelcoming atmosphere of doom, marching towards a dark abyss. The winds blew about sheets of rain, while trees seemed to moan each time large bunches of shriveling leaves lost their grip and fell noiselessly to the ground.

Just staying alive and keeping themselves strong was each prisoner's main concern. They worried how they would be able to survive the cruel and unsanitary conditions of the camp, the meager food allowance, and the torturous treatment inflicted upon them. They feared being shot to death at point blank, like a deer gunned down by a bragging hunter, who kills for the sport of it. They worried about lost friends and family, wondering if any of them were still alive. They shuttered at the thought of how a cruel fate may have taken their loved ones away, like they never existed. At the camp, prisoner's eyes darted around their new surroundings in hopes of finding any neighbors or family members there. Just knowing they were still alive would give them hope.

Amidst the shouting guards and organized confusion, the rotting smell of decomposing leaves set the stage for a life of wretchedness in this camp. Just around the corner was the taunting promise that misery was waiting patiently for them. While the prisoners were led further into the camp, steady rain made it cumbersome to navigate through the puddles, and the slushy mud covered their shoes.

Inside the camp, they were met by the commanding presence of three Nazi guards. Their primary mission was to fan the embers of fear while systematically deflating any hope for a chance of escape. The mere sight of the Nazi guards who wore intimidating looks on their faces unnerved them, scalding them with paralyzing fear. Standing tall, the guards succeeded in projecting a show of solidarity and authoritative power. Beside each guard stood a growling and menacing-looking German Shepherd dog, ready to attack at any moment.

Riddled with overwhelming dread, Samuel and the others were led to walk in single file. As they passed, the guards spewed loud and insulting comments, often using the worst German profanities commonly directed toward Jews. Though hard to ignore the vicious slurs, the prisoners kept their focus on trying to walk without stumbling or falling, trying desperately not to draw unnecessary attention. No one wanted to become noticed for any reason. It was imperative to avoid becoming the object of ridicule and give a guard any reason to use them as a cruel example.

The guards positioned themselves with their legs spaced apart like tree trunks firmly rooted to the soaked ground, surrounding the in-coming prisoners like caged dogs in an electrified yard. Instinctively, Samuel and the others stayed back, careful to avoid the dangers of getting too near them. Their foreboding presence was a silent warning of what would happen should any prisoner dare cross the invisible boundaries they set.

The expression of the guards' faces posed a threat without them having to say a word. A guard's job was to demean human dignity and reduce the prisoner's psyche to a subhuman category. They were trained to look beyond the prisoners, keep their eyes locked, focused on a distant object, like a twirling dancer trying to maintain a balance. The reason was that if a guard ever mistakenly met with the eyes of a prisoner, the frigid air of superiority might be diminished. If a prisoner might look up from the ground or floor, or even cast a split-second glance in their direction, that action could ignite a combative reaction. Oftentimes, in order to secure a tighter grip of authoritative control, a guard might stage a disturbance among the prisoners by making false accusations. This was a way to demand stricter compliance of their rules. The prisoners could only imagine the worst of what would be in store for them.

Finally, when Samuel and the others reached the assigned barracks number C, they were met by three more stern-faced guards. The guards continued to bark at them. "Hurry up and move along, Jewish swine. You better obey, and get ready to work until your fingers bleed! You will work until you become so exhausted that you drop. If you become useless, we will be happy to be rid of you, maybe even shoot you on the spot!"

Samuel observed the first guard's scowling face. He was an extremely tall, burly man who projected an unnerving presence. His bulging eyes were peering over his small, round spectacles resting on the lower half of his bulbous nose. An unusually small head topped the rest of his overweight, misshapen body. His thin lips were curved slightly upwards into a sneer. The next guard resembled Humpty Dumpty from the popular children's nursery rhyme. His heavy shoulders slumped downward, creating an egg-shaped appearance. His arm lengths were disproportionately short for his body, a perfect specimen for a circus sideshow. The third guard resembled an oversized bulldog. Random wisps of brown hair fell over his wide forehead, a few strands reaching his hanging jowls. His jaw jutted outwards in an under-bite caging his top teeth. Samuel thought he heard the guard making growling sounds, like an imposing animal ready to pounce.

All three guards seemed to be plucked from the same silk; no doubt they were bullies with low self-esteem when they were younger. Their apparent over-indulgence of food and drink stretched the buttons of their shirts against over-grown beer-bellies. All the while, their belts strained to contain protruding stomachs. Not one of them could see his feet. The *Humpty Dumpty* guard led all the prisoners into the small, dank room that housed eight sets of triple bunk beds. He grabbed and shoved each prisoner towards a bed assignment. When Samuel's turn came, the guard lifted his chin to direct him to the middle bunk on the left-hand side of the room. Then he directed Sergi to the top bunk. He said, "Make sure to get your sleep tonight. You will need all of your strength in the morning!" The guards all left, slamming and locking the door behind them.

Samuel and Sergi made eye contact. Despite being trapped in a cruel and unforgiving world, when their eyes met, a bond was forged; under-scoring that all hope was not lost. Samuel believed that meeting Sergi might be a lucky omen for him, at least until he found the whereabouts of Danika and Josef. Fueled by emotion, they reached forward and simultaneously strapped their arms around each other. Tightly secured in a firm hold, they lingered in a friendly embrace, enjoying the warmth of each other, sharing the promise of hope. They stayed like this in silence for what seemed to be an eternity, like star-crossed lovers reunited after a long absence. Finding each other in these circumstances was like being rescued from a secluded life in solitary confinement.

"My God, it's really you, Sergi Weiss, my neighbor!" declared Samuel, like an adolescent child responding with reckless abandon and not caring who might hear or judge his outburst. Sergi's face flushed a deep shade of purple, and as he almost lost his balance he said, "I almost fainted seeing you at the registration line! I am so happy we are here together, assigned to the same barracks!" Samuel was relieved to be with Sergi. He could barely remember that feeling from when life was carefree and predictable. Considering the difficult times in which they were forced to live, few of them would ever feel the soothing comfort of finding a comrade again.

When they finally ended their thankful embrace, Sergi spoke. "Samuel, my pal, how did you manage to get assigned to the same camp? I saw you standing in another line!" Samuel shrugged, leaned in and whispered. "It was a blessing from God; I really had nothing to do with it. Our fate rests in God's hands and we must have faith that everything will eventually turn out alright." Samuel omitted the rest of the story of how it wasn't by chance that they were in the same camp. He decided to keep those details to himself until the time was right.

Just then, a guard entered the barracks shouting, "Attention, *Mach Schnell!* Everyone, take off your clothes immediately. Line up and prepare to go outside. The hoses are ready to delouse you." Samuel and Sergi did as they were told. Without delay, they stripped naked and folded their clothes in a small pile on the floor next to their bunks. Then they stood in a single file line waiting for the next command. The humiliation was intended to further dehumanize the prisoners.

After the delousing, Samuel observed that there was one small window on the front wall that only allowed a minimum amount of sunlight to enter. Otherwise, the room was dim and dingy. As Samuel proceeded to climb into his bunk, he felt a slight tug on his shoulder. Sergi said, "I'm here, on the top bunk. If you need to talk to me, just kick my cot."

It was a miracle that Samuel and Sergi were together in the same camp, the same barracks, and assigned the same bunks. Just then, Sergi swung his upper body to lean halfway over the cot, staring down at Samuel in thankful relief. "My God, Samuel! I'm so happy we are together. You must tell me your story. How did you come to get here? I lost everyone. They shot my family on the street as I watched while hiding behind a large oak tree. The Nazi sympathizers were so intent on the killing spree, they forgot me. I ran away and they didn't bother to look further. I hid alone inside a trash bin, frightened to death. I ate scraps, waiting for a whole day and night until I heard signs of life outside. When I heard people walking on the street, I dared peek out of the cover and saw that they were homeless victims, like me. I got out of the trash can and walked with them. They told me rumors that Jews from our town were sent directly to the Belzec death camp. Germans collected the remaining Jews from nearby villages before the Ukrainians finished the job and murdered the others. I know that many families have tried to build hiding places in remote areas of the forest, like families of mice hiding from their predators. I traveled and hid with the group of survivors until we were discovered by the Nazis and brought here."

Samuel shuttered as he listened and when he began to speak, his voice wavered with emotion. "Sergi, I too have lost my parents and my sisters to the hands of the Nazis. I found them all murdered at home, each of them ripped from their beds and shot in cold blood. I am absolutely devastated. Samuel tried desperately to hold back the floodgates, but the tears burst from his eyes and he was only able to speak one word at a time. "I must find my wife and son, Danika and Josef. You remember Danika. I can't imagine where she is now. When I got home, she and Josef were gone. There is nothing left for me to live for unless I know they are both safe."

Suddenly, a blaring command came from the front door. "Hey, shut up Jews! No talking and go to sleep. You will need all of your strength for a long, hard day of work tomorrow." Sergi moved back onto his cot, pulling his thin blanket over himself. Samuel lay silently with his back on the bed, thinking about the events of the day. He felt a flicker of hope coursing through his veins, reminding him that even in the worst of circumstances, small miracles happen. Samuel believed that

107

Sergi was the only one who would be able to help him find Danika and Josef. Tomorrow, he would ask Sergi to help him find someone who could confirm that Danika and Josef were among those who may have been taken to Belzec. Suddenly, he realized that for the first time in days that there was a real possibility of finding them.

Consumed with thought, Samuel couldn't sleep. What was he going to do? Who would be able to help? Who could he trust? How could he tap into his resources to pay for bribes? Out of the darkness, a coarse whisper called down to him. "Psst! hey Samuel, are you asleep yet? I think I may know who might be able to help us."

When one dog barks, he easily finds others to bark with it.
Midrash: Exodus -Rabbah 31:9

The Power of Friendship

The third night in the barracks of the Drohobycz labor camp was no better than the first or the second. Samuel was restless and couldn't sleep. He was kept awake by the creaking of wooden beams and by the groaning sounds of Sergi's cot above him as he tossed and turned. Neither one of them could sleep soundly. Throughout the night, their nerves were unraveling, both tortured by fear and apprehension. As Samuel lay awake amidst the grayish darkness of the night, he tried to quiet his mind by watching the occasional tiny glimmers of the camp's searchlight peeking through the crumbling cracks of the barrack's walls.

While lying on his left side, Samuel noticed a sudden movement in the shadows. It was the silhouette of Sergi's profile, his neck thrust forward, poking its way out like the protruding head of a turtle jutting out from its shell. Sergi peered down while whispering softly, cautious not to be heard. "I think I know where Danika and Josef are right now." Samuel gasped in the darkness and his heart stopped short. He was instantly paralyzed, in shock from Sergi's words; like an imaginary hand gripping his chest and making it impossible to breathe. As the color drained from his already pale face, Samuel whispered back panicky questions without waiting for any answer. "Where are they? How do you know this? Who told you? When did you hear? Oh my God, what can we do to find them?"

Sergi inched his head farther across the cot's edge, moving himself closer towards Samuel's ear for fear they might be overheard. Clearing the thick, morning hoarseness from the back of his throat, he spoke in a barely audible whisper.

"It all began during this morning's roll call when Tadeusz, the old guy in the bunk next to us, found me. Yesterday morning, he must have overheard us talking. He also said people have told him about my connections in the black-market ammunition business. Anyway, early yesterday morning, remember when we were all standing at attention in the roll call line? Well, when the guard wasn't looking in our direction, Tadeusz pulled tightly at my arm. I had no choice but to sway back towards him while he leaned in towards my ear and whispered, asking me if I had any black-market money in exchange for some useful information. He said that it was crucial information if you and I were even thinking about a plan to escape." "Where did he get the information?" Samuel whispered.

"Apparently, there was a ruckus outside the door the other night when we were sleeping. The guards were very loud when they returned to the barracks. They must have had a night of heavy drinking and carousing with their comrades and they were drunk as skunks. They were all pumped up, boasting how proud they were to be the Ukrainian Nazi Youth officers of the Drohobycz labor camp. They were big-headed and arrogant, and each guard tried to out-speak the other. They obviously didn't care if anybody overheard them. They bragged loudly about how they organized the roundup of Jewish women and children so they could be deported on wagons to the Belzec concentration camp. People say it's actually a death camp known for its systematic extermination of Jews. I think that Danika and Josef might be at that camp! I told Tadeusz I'd find a way to pay him for the information. Sam, what about your salt business? Is there a way to smuggle some money for bartering into this camp?"

Samuel felt his body begin to tremble and his mind clouded over, like a vapor misting over a seaport harbor. He tried to blink away the fog in his mind. He knew he must try to focus on what to do. How was he going to get the money while he was still imprisoned in this camp? At least Sergi and

Tadeusz were willing to work with him as a team and he was not alone. Terror set in as he thought about the dangers of taking such a life-or-death risk. He had to find a way to save his wife and little boy.

Sergi Weiss touched his arm ever so gently, like a mother's loving touch, a simple gesture, instantly redirecting his thoughts. He said, "Hey, Samuel, we'll talk later on when we can find a moment." Sergi's words created a momentary calm, allowing Samuel to relax and come to the realization how, in the midst of despair, a basic human touch can bring about fleeting moments of hope.

Together, the prisoners stopped dutifully in front of the barracks and waited for the guard to give them their daily work assignment. Samuel's daily schedule was grueling. After morning roll call at 6:00 a.m., he and the other prisoners were marched to a large room used for meals, about 100 meters from their barracks. It was a heavily guarded room, where staunch looking officers watched them eat in silence. The officers were clad in full Nazi regalia. Each had a machine gun slung over one shoulder and they were accompanied by trained German Shepherds standing in wait of their next command.

The meals were rationed and always the same; a thick slice of stale bread and a hot mug of a chicory drink, better known as imitation coffee, or an herbal 'tea." Lunch was a liter of a thin, watery potato soup, and if lucky, they might find a potato peel or a piece of a turnip floating around. The evening meal was a chunk of black bread weighing exactly 300 grams, a tiny piece of sausage, marmalade or cheese. The meal was yet another way for the Nazi's to taunt them since most of them were accustomed to eating kosher food. Samuel soon learned that the remaining chunk of black bread was supposed to last them until the morning meal as well. They all had to find ways to hide their bread when they slept, in order to prevent someone else from stealing it. The meager amounts of food served to them were designed to merely keep the prisoners alive for as long as they were needed to work before many of them would be marched to their deaths.

It was late afternoon, around 5:00pm, when Samuel returned from the hard physical labor; his assigned work for that day was to pile up old discarded horseshoes and put them in large boxes. He would then lift and load the heavy boxes onto trucks to be sent to the nearby German ammunition plant for recycling into weapons. Feeling weary and exhausted after a long day's work, Samuel allowed his aching body to sit down slowly on his hard, unforgiving cot. He lifted one foot up at a time and laboriously began to untie his dusty boots, pulling the cloying leather away from his blistery and bloody toes. He actually felt some relief when the cool air kissed his sweaty feet and began the first step in healing his wounds. Then he climbed down to place the boots on the floor next to the bottom cot. At the end of the day, all six boots worn by Samuel, Sergi, and the third guy in the bottom bunk were lined up waiting for their aching feet the next morning. Samuel climbed back up to his middle bunk, trying to ignore shooting pains in his arches and thought: There is no time to worry about my feet; they will be good as new by tomorrow.

Samuel lay down and pulled his battered, old blanket up over his shoulders warming his tired muscles in the cold barracks. He pretended the blanket was his shield against the lurking shadows in all corners of the ice-cold barracks. He thought: Sometimes a false sense of safety is better than no sense at all. I must remember that the concept of safety is just an illusion. I must be grateful for having even a scratchy wool blanket to cover myself. In these times, a blanket is a fortunate gift! I must make the most of this time, since our days are numbered. People are saying that the Nazi's plan is to keep us alive for a certain length of time, just long enough for us to serve the work purpose. Then Samuel closed his eyes, allowing exhaustion to wash over him and fall into the slumber that was coming to his rescue. He was glad he allowed his imagination to serve him, since it offered a meager amount of relief from the discomfort of the day's work effort. He closed his eyes and drifted off to a dog-tired sleep.

At 6:00 pm, Samuel was awakened abruptly. A blaring voice over the loudspeaker was announcing an evening roll call. They were commanded to get up, be dressed and ready. They lined up in single file behind the guard's lead and marched back to the dining hall for the last meal of the day. In a split-second, Sergi jumped down from the upper bunk to stand next to Samuel on the floor. Without delay, they grabbed their already lined up boots and pulled away the jackets that hung on a hook next to the lowest cot. Quickly buttoning up their jackets and managing to pull on their heavy boots, despite the screaming pain of their abused feet, they lined up dutifully behind the guard standing at the exit door, all of them appearing ready to brave the early evening's steadily dropping temperatures.

"*Mach schnell*!" (hurry up!) bellowed the nighttime Ukrainian guard as he began to lead the hungry prisoners towards the food barracks. They were now prisoners moving together into obscurity, the darkening shadows of the cold evening. They walked in deafening silence, a queue shaped like a slithering black snake. They winded along snow-covered paths and weaved through the descending black cloak of dusk's darkening shadows. All the while, the tired and hungry prisoners were constantly wishing for a sign, a glimmer of hope, even a speck of luck that might ignite the dying embers of their souls.

When they arrived at the food barracks, the guard turned around and raised up his gloved hand; indicating for them to halt, while Samuel buried his numb fingers inside his jacket. They were left to stand in wait for what felt like an eternity before being allowed to enter. The final prize was having the privilege of being given the tasteless, oftentimes inedible food that awaited them.

Samuel was seated at the designated bench in front of the long and narrow wooden table. He lifted a spoon from the table and dipped it into the lukewarm soup and noticed a small piece of potato floating around in the thin liquid. He thought about how it resembled a long-dead, faded goldfish. A chunk of stale, hard bread was placed next to the bowl of unappetizing soup. His eyes gazed downward. They flitted around, searching the floor area, before stopping to focus on a corner that held a collection of dust mites and dropped crumbs that escaped from the table. He was secretly hoping to discover an extra morsel of food before it was carried away by an eager, hungry rodent. A crazy thought occurred to him: If I did see such a thing, would I dare try to snatch it away from the rodent and take the risk that might get myself into greater danger? How is it that I am destined to live this way, in the midst of degradation; forced to eat among the wandering rodents and be in competition with them as well? How is it that we take for granted the basic human needs when we have them all around us? We forget how it feels to have the warmth of shelter, the familiarity of our home, or how delicious the meals taste when prepared with loving hands. Oh, my darlings, Danika and Josef, where are you? Please be safe and alive. I will find you before any harm comes to you, I promise. It was then that Samuel decided: No, I will not allow the monotony, the austerity of this life to erode my spirit. I cannot lose my purpose, my will to live, as long as I have the gnawing need to find you.

The trying times felt emotionally raw and unprotected. Just one simple act of kindness made a difference. The mere utterance of offering a positive word or the tiniest hint of implying something nice mattered so much. A kind word offered a smidgen of hope, so powerful it melted the tough exterior of their badly scarred hearts. Warm emotions were a rare event here, as they lived in the midst of the dry and barren ugliness of the camp. An act of kindness or a few encouraging words had the power to change their immediate world. The medicinal value of a tiny dose of empathy or one compassionate embrace was a source for renewed strength, much like the feelings evoked at the conclusion of a clergyman's hopeful sermon.

After a carefully timed fifteen minutes, the prisoners were lined up to head back to the barracks. Soon they would be done with the imposed day and night routine. They would lie down on their cots, pull the blanket up over their shoulders, and allow their overworked bodies to succumb to exhaustion and sink into a dead sleep. If they survived the night, they knew the monotony of the next awaited them.

As Samuel lay in his bunk, he stared up at the intricate pattern of iron springs and straw fillers that supported the above cot upon which that Sergi slept. He listened to the regular night sounds of the prisoners in his barracks, thinking how he was part of a cast of characters; how he was sleeping amongst these strangers. Some were tossing around trying to establish some semblance of comfort on their squeaky cots. Others had nagging coughs, continually spewing their germs around the unventilated room; the habitual clearing of throats developed from newly acquired nervous tics. The worst sound was the intermittent weeping, the haunting sounds emitted from the starving mouths of those who had already given up on this place.

No matter how hard Samuel tried to block the panic that plagued him, terrifying emotions banged against his chest. Who will awaken in the morning or who will die in their cot during the night? Am I strong enough to withstand the punishing effects of each day and night? Besieged with rapidly advancing trepidation, he wondered: What will tomorrow bring for me, for all of us? Will I be able to survive the coldness of the night, the itchiness of this moth-eaten blanket?

Only time would tell. Who among us is strong enough? Will it be me, or Sergi, or Tadeusz in the front? Will I be able to adjust to these backbreaking conditions? What if I don't sleep, how can I work the next day? Put it on the shelf! Don't think about it now, a voice screamed in his head.

Just as Samuel drifted off to sleep, he heard the banter of the night guards as they sat on the ground, leaning comfortably against the barracks front door. He could barely decipher what they were saying, but he thought he heard them say something about tomorrow's round up. There was going to be a selection of prisoners positioned in a line before a firing squad. Each would be shot with such precision that they would fall into a previously prepared ditch, the burial ground for the murdered.

Sam froze in terror. He shook for a long time, not from the cold in the barracks but from his trembling fear. He knew that he must sleep, so he finally closed his mind like a door slammed shut and he refused to think further about it. In his dream-like state, he assured himself that it was entirely possible that he misunderstood the soldier's words because he was so tired. No, he would not let his emotions run away from him, based on what he thought he heard. He must conserve his energy and restore his body in order to work the next day. Worrying about what tragic event might happen to him would serve no purpose but to deplete whatever strength he had left. All at once, Samuel decided to shelve his fears, then he gave himself permission to fall into a fitful sleep.

The hatred of other men destroys your own soul
-Sayings of The Fathers 2:15

Unrelenting Cruelty

The next morning, the barrack's door swung open, allowing a cold blast of air to fill the room. Standing in front of the door was a different guard, a young man sporting a taut physique, standing straight like a rubber band stretched to capacity. He was boisterously shouting with great urgency for them to wake up, dress quickly, and line up outside. He sounded like a firefighter warning of a danger. "*Achtung* (Attention!) "Wake up, you rotten Jew bastards, and dress quickly! Put some clothes on over your wretched bodies! There's work to be done. Who knows, you might even survive another day," the new guard chuckled maliciously. "Line up outside and wait for my direction!"

This was not an ordinary, miserable morning at the camp. Something far worse was about to happen. Judging by terrified facial expressions, prisoners were sensing a new threat of danger, feeling the shadow of death stealthily creeping towards them. Within minutes, they were out of the barracks and lined up. Standing like ducks in a row and trembling in the icy air, they were nervously waiting to hear what was about to happen next.

It was ironic that this change of daily routine happened on the day of Yom Kippur, the holiest day of the year in the Jewish religion. Aware of what day it was, Samuel feared: Could this be my last Yom Kippur on this earth, the day of Atonement? I cannot accept this. I haven't found my Danika and Josef yet. It's too soon to take me, God! I need more time. Please give me one more day to live!

Suddenly Samuel was transported, thinking of the past, recalling how reverent he felt on this holy day. Every Yom Kippur, he would *daven* (pray) in the *Shul* (synagogue) to

117

repent for his sins. He pictured himself standing next to his father, feeling his warmth as their shoulders touched. Pressed up against each other, they both wore *yarmulkes* (skullcaps) to cover their heads, showing devotion to God's sacredness. While praying together in the Shul, they shared a like-minded bond; a mutual demonstration of their faith. They recited the prayers and followed the rituals in the *Siddur* (Hebrew prayer book) while fasting the entire day. They repeated the thousands of years-old Hebrew tropes (chants) along with the other orthodox worshipers. These traditions deepened the feeling of connection and there was a powerful sense of oneness. They followed the same ritual, the practice of bending forward and backward. They prayed that God would hear them repent for their sins and inscribe them in the book of life. Curiously, very little had changed since then. It was always one year at a time. "One day at a time," was a mantra that would become Samuel's plight, a note of encouragement that seemed to buy him more time.

The "rubber-band stretched" guard paced back and forth, strutting up and down the line. He was intent on instigating more fear, hoping that one of the prisoners might step out of line so he would have the opportunity to make an example of him. No prisoner gave him the opportunity and from the corner of his eye, Samuel couldn't help but notice the young guard looked a bit disappointed that no one had challenged him.

While the prisoners were being led towards the area of the food hall, Samuel rationalized his pangs of hunger, thinking that since it was the holy day of Yom Kippur, it was a sacrifice. However, the times were different. Despite trying to ignore his stomach that constantly begged for food, they were starving not just on this day of fasting, but every day. They were victims forced to live in captivity in the cruelest circumstances. These days, he felt he merely existed, constantly trying to avoid being engulfed by the proverbial Nazi-created sink-holes while the rest of the world turned a blind eye.

When they reached the door of the food barracks, they were ordered to stop, wait, and listen for further direction. "Halt!" commanded the young guard. "I will call out five of you. The rest of you will remain watching what we do with Jewish blood. The following five are: Wallberger, Saltzman, Weiner, Weitzfeld, and Rosenberg. Quickly step out of the line and follow me." He raised his club threateningly, making it known he would use it to bludgeon anyone who did not cooperate, and said, "Line up against the side fence with your backs towards me!"

All five of the men chosen were visibly shaken by the sound their names. Beads of perspiration formed on their brows, as they managed to step forward and obey his command. Samuel's heart pounded fiercely against his chest, like the furious beating of a drum. Wallberger and Saltzman were at least twenty, maybe thirty years older. Samuel thought: The others are weaker and in poor health. Having worked with them, I've seen that physical labor was extremely challenging for them. But then why would they choose to kill me? I am in great physical shape and only thirty-six years old. But why would they choose me? I would be an asset to the work force. Facing the fence, Samuel stood shaking uncontrollably, trying to resign himself to the idea he was about take his last breath, yet his mind shifted rapidly to thoughts of Danika and Josef. A flood of memories poured in, quickly turning into a tidal wave of hopes and dreams drowning and disappearing in the vast sea of life. Samuel remembered all of his loved ones, friends, and most of all, Danika and Josef. Then came the battle of mixed emotions, strong enough to unleash the choking resentment and strangulating hatred aimed at his captors.

Desperate to save himself, Samuel's last resort was prayer. With his inner voice screaming incredulously, he prayed: God, how could you take me now? I beg of you. This isn't fair. I am too young. I have led a righteous life. Was that not good enough? I have been a faithful husband and loyal son, and a proud brother. Why would you choose me to be wiped away from this life, discard me like a soiled diaper? After all, this is Yom Kippur, the day of atonement, my heart and soul are pleading with you. Have mercy on my soul!

Upon hearing the rustling of broken, crackling leaves that were breaking one by one under the determined footsteps of Nazi perpetrators, Samuel dared to shift his head to the right. As he stood very still, he overheard the distant conversation of several guards. They appeared already positioned several yards away, yet their voices carried. Samuel's heart skipped and froze, as if he were already dead, listened to the jostling of rifles preparing for the release of bullets. Before the ripping shots were to be fired, there was an eerie silence blanketing them, as all were trapped in a hovering, black cloud of man's inhumanity.

I never really believed in Satan, or that there was pure evil in the world, until I came here. - Gerald Green, <u>Holocaust</u>

Unspeakable Acts

Shots were fired at close range. Two men were left standing and Samuel was one of them. The other three men fell swiftly, their fragile lives snuffed out like a flaming wick pressed between a thumb and forefinger. Their bodies fell, neatly discarded into the awaiting ditch, like the falling rocks of a crumbling earthquake. Samuel was standing, dazed and confused, not certain if he was alive or dead: What just happened? Am I really alive? Did someone just call my name? Then again, he thought he heard the authoritative voice yelling, "Rosenberg! Weitzman! *"Mach schnel!"* You will step away from the fence and come with me. Looks like you *kikes* (derogatory term for a Jewish person) got lucky today. Guess your friends weren't so lucky," he said while screwing up his face into a contemptuous sneer and pointing towards the ditch.

Samuel was paralyzed in shock, living a nightmare and praying it was just a bad dream: Am I hallucinating? Maybe it was all a mistake. Was the shot meant for me? But could it be that the shot missed me intentionally? Desperately trying to come to his senses, he began to recite the *'Schma'* (Hebrew prayer) hoping the distraction might work to shake off his crippling hysteria.

Suddenly, Samuel felt an agitation of air; a movement coming close to him. Shifting his head slightly to the left, out of the corner of his eye, he saw Weitzman still standing next to him, trembling uncontrollably like a badly wounded bird. Fate must have made a last-minute decision to spare both their lives. Who knows for how long fate would be able to stand by that decision.

Despite the momentary relief he was feeling, he feared there might be more bullets to come his way. This was all part of the Nazi assassination plan to kill off the old, frail, and infirm and keep the younger, able-bodied men alive just long enough to use them for labor. The guards viewed these tortuous killing scenes as recreation, savoring the cruelest moments with warped satisfaction. The prisoners, witnessing the vicious demonstrations, were drenched in fear and terrified that they would be the next one to fall lifeless into a ditch.

Samuel heard his name called a second time. He stumbled forward. Despite his blurred vision, he struggled to see through the haze of intense anxiety. He tilted his head sideways, checking to see if the assassins had dropped their guns. An SS Officer named Bender was reading from a clipboard, seemingly unaffected by the merciless execution. He looked up casually as if nothing had happened, and repeated his order without a hint of emotion. "Rosenberg and Weitzman, you will come with me."

Just then, one of the guards blurted out, "Officer Bender, why are they being spared? We should just get rid of all five of them! There is no need to let these two live!" Bender replied nonchalantly, "Shut up. I will take no questions or opinions from an idiot like you. Your only job is to shoot and kill the chosen Jews. Concern yourself with improving your marksmanship skills; that is your only worth. Otherwise, you are nobody to me. You will never voice your dumb opinion to me again."

Bender, appointed by the Nazi party, was in charge of selections for all Jewish deportations and executions in the Galicia region. He worked together with a Commandant SS-Leiderity, the local SS Schultzpolizei and members of the SS Ukrainian in organizing deportation actions. Bender's mission was to target Jews at the Drohobych forced labor camp. He would stand and observe, separating the weaker, sickly laborers from the younger, more able-bodied ones. He was in charge of transporting the old and frail to other forced labor camps, including concentration camps, and oftentimes would see nothing wrong with killing them on the spot; execution style. It was rumored that depending on his mood, Bender would select a few laborers each day to be beat cruelly before being sent back to work.

Suddenly, once again, Bender's commanding voice resounded. "Rosenberg and Weitzman, you cockroaches will walk towards me, then stop three feet to my right." They obeyed in slow motion, forcing their unwilling legs to step away from the fence. Samuel's intense fear prompted him to remain prudent and maintain a distrustful distance of three feet away. Nevertheless, he tried to hurry forward and steady himself while his coat slipped off one shoulder and he swiftly pulled it back up into place. Both prisoners trailed behind Bender as they walked along a gravel path covered by an evening frost. Bender whipped around and said to them, "You two are being transferred to camp Janowska. There is a need for young, able-bodied men to do work there. Work hard, keep your nose down, and who knows? Maybe you'll survive a bit longer. Just keep walking behind me."

It was early April; the weather still crisp and cold. As Samuel and Weitzman followed closely behind, they pushed aside low-lying branches of snow-laden trees hanging over the path. A long whistle caught their attention, indicating to where they should proceed. Then a guard's thin voice echoed, "Officer Bender, we are over here. We have three other Jews here. They are waiting in *the Kugelwagen.*" (The Kugelwagen was a German-made Volkswagon jeep, a light military vehicle used mainly by the Wehrmacht and Waffen-SS.)

Samuel and Weitzman tried to remain calm, not knowing if the next camp would be worse than the first. When the jeep door opened, both of them were shocked and thrilled to see Tadeusz and Sergi already seated inside. They were being transferred with them in the same Kubelwagen! At this point,

Samuel no longer believed in the notion of coincidences. He became a believer that they were all meant to be together; part of fate's plan. While in the back of the wagon, space was limited. Boxes of supplies earmarked for transfer to the next camp were piled up and taking up most of the room. Bender was sitting in the passenger seat. He never turned around once. It was if he forgot about the cramped transports in the back, while engaging in light-hearted banter with the driver.

Although he was thrilled to be with his friends, new questions tormented Samuel's mind: Why are we being moved to another camp? Is it to cause us more heartache, more torture, more humiliation? Why make us move if they are planning to kill us anyway? The bumpy ride over the rough, gravelly roads, the incessant bounce and relentless vibrations of the Kubelwagen's wheels continued to batter their already aching bodies. Each bounce jabbed at Samuel's gut, like a boxer in a ring pinned against the ropes, unable to avoid the punishing blows. Bracing himself, he propped his head to rest on his hands, fighting to steady himself against the strenuous rebound of tires over rugged terrain. Each time the Kubelwagen swung round the road's curves, Samuel's head hit the side window leaving him with a gripping pain. How long will this ride go on? I'm so cold and hungry and nauseous. Where are Danika and Josef? Are we passing right by their camp? I must find them. This is sheer misery.

Finally, after endless discomfort, the Kubelwagen slowed to a complete stop. Samuel could hear outside voices; guards greeting other guards, simultaneously clicking their heels together during the customary *"Heil Hitler"* salute. He listened to people speaking German colloquialisms of the day like, *"Heil Hitler! Gutten tag!* (good day) *Mist!* (damn), *Alles hat in Ende, nur die Wurst hat zwei* (Everything has an end, only the sausage has two). Within minutes, the guards lifted the heavy cartons off their backs before emptying the rest of the supplies from the jeep. It became apparent that the Camp guards at the entrance gate readily gave permission for the Kubelwagen to enter for the purpose of bringing in supplies and a few new workers.

They parked the Kubelwagen jeep in a shady area of the camp, well within the barbed wire fences. SS Bender jumped out first, then he yanked open the jeep's back side door and shouted, "Get out of the jeep! Line up in single file behind me." Despite being squeezed together like sardines in a tin can, each one of the four men were trying to appear unscathed during the grueling ride and they rallied quickly and jumped out.

Samuel glanced around and looked back at the opened entrance gate. The sign above the broad entrance read, Janowska Labor Camp. A menacing Nazi flag was waving proudly, seeming to tease and mock them for what was to come. Samuel's mind was racing, wondering why the change of camps. Was it because the Nazis had something else in mind for him?

Just then, Bender spoke, breaking Samuel's stream of consciousness. "Follow me, Jews. Just know this, you will be living here at the Janowska Labor Camp for as long as you remain cooperative. Otherwise, we will have no use for you. Don't give us trouble. If you work hard, there's a chance we can save you from being transferred to Belzec concentration camp."

Concentration Camp- those were dreaded words that no prisoner wanted to hear. An imaginary fist seized Samuel's heart, fixed like a bolt lock and refusing to relent. He knew he would abide by the rules, knowing he was in no position to even consider an escape. His fate was in the Nazis' hands; he was helplessly trapped in the jaws of ruthless monsters. While Samuel and the others walked dutifully behind SS Officer Bender, their fears were looming larger, like a knitter's spool gathering yarn.

Tread upon thorns while the shoe is on your foot.
-Hebrew proverb

Janowska Camp

Brittle branches snapped loudly under their footsteps as they paved their way through the thorny pathway flanked with lifeless shrubbery. Officer Bender, Samuel, his former bunk mates Tadeusz and Sergi, along with two other prisoners stopped at the arched entryway of the camp. They continued on, entering the main building and then they walked through a wide stone corridor surrounded by gray, stone walls.

"It feels like an icebox in here," Samuel muttered quietly, his body heat trying to adjust to the plunging temperature of the building, coupled with the freezing dread of what lay ahead. Following closely behind Officer Bender, they were led into a spacious room with high ceilings that readily echoed any random sounds. On one side wall, Samuel noticed smoky-colored dark shades that were pulled down over a large bay window. Positioned in front of the window was a long wooden table, where several piles of neatly stacked clothes were placed. Lined up in orderly fashion were numerous pairs of oversized men's boots, all specked with cloying clumps of dried mud.

Seeing the boots placed on the table instantly reminded Samuel of an ancient superstition that declared it taboo to put boots on a table. Sam recalled how his grandmother and mother had passed on the warning to their children, a bad luck omen. Shaking his head he thought: My mother and my grandmother would cry if they knew what was happening here; what was happening to me and to all of us Jews. Things could not be much worse.

126

Officer Bender walked over to the piles of clothes and lines of boots, pointed to the large empty wicker basket on the floor and said, "Jews, take off your clothes, then toss them here in this basket. Each pile of clothes is a complete camp uniform. Pull on work boots when you are finished. After several minutes, Officer Bender urged them to speed up. His impatience was waning and he shouted, "*Mach schnell*! What's taking so long? Are you waiting for a tailor to come and do a private fitting? Believe me, you are not going to be dancing at a wedding!" he chuckled to himself, seemingly satisfied with his jab of sarcasm.

The prisoners wasted no time, earnestly trying to hurry, with fingers fumbling and heads filled with dizzying fears. Quickly disrobing, they discarded their former camp clothes from the Drohobych labor camp into the basket before dressing in the brown-striped pants and tattered, taupe-colored shirts. They pushed their tired feet into rugged, ill-fitting work boots. Now fully clothed in the standard uniforms of the Janowska labor camp, they stood in wait behind Officer Bender, who was about to take them to their assigned barracks for the night. Samuel found out from some other prisoners that Camp Janowska was a forced labor camp in Poland, located on the outskirts of the city of Lvov. It housed two main factories: one for carpentry works and the other for metalworks.

Sunrise came the next morning with the guise of hope, yet instead it proved to be a sign of continued disaster. While the first dangling wisps of quicksilver sunlight began to peek through the crevices of the barracks walls, three guards stormed into the barracks promptly awakening the inmates. Determined to make an explosive entrance, the guards' twisted facial expressions were held tight with taut muscles, their pursed lips set firmly in place as if tightened by screwdrivers. It was a planned ruckus, a scare tactic, meant to rudely awaken the inmates. Samuel sat up in shocked disbelief, surrounded by an eddy of cold fear. While afraid to look up, his peripheral vision reflected the villainous thugs.

127

The guards shouted like barbarians. "Heil Hitler! Time to get up, Jews! Get off your cots, stand up at attention, keep your hands at your sides and eyes towards the floor." One stocky uniformed guard, no more than twenty years old, stepped his right foot forward and planted it noisily on the bare floor in front of Tadeusz's cot; the oldest inmate in the barracks. His left boot reached forward to meet the right boot and like a magnet they clicked together in place. Then he raised the hanging rifle up off his right shoulder and aimed it directly towards Tadeusz's face. The guard nodded to the right, indicating the direction for him to move and said, "You, get over there and begin the line at the front door." Tadeusz's constricted face turned a bluish purple, looking like he was about to have a major stroke as he moved to the door. The same stocky officer marched towards the next cot. He pointed to the next closest man standing beside his cot and repeated this action, signaling him to line up behind Tadeusz. A second guard took care of the western side of the barracks, while a third guard waited at the door.

A deafening silence overtook the barracks as everyone stood in rapt attention, breathing through bated breaths, terrified the guards might take notice; afraid of becoming the next selection. The sounds of their breathing became a matter of life or death; all of them trying desperately to become invisible, not to be heard. Samuel was petrified, fighting against dizzying waves of nausea, feeling the rise of strangling anxiety. Afraid he was to be chosen, he waited while listening to his rapid, shallow breathing; like the softest breaths of a newborn baby. Within minutes, out of the corner of his eye, he could see that his former bunk mate, Tadeusz, and five others were being lined up at the exit door. As the commotion ensued, two shouting guards barged down the center aisle between the cots, their jackboots hammering the wooden floor planks. Samuel tried to control his panic, as the deliberate boot stamping was moving closer to his cot.

Suddenly, another twist of fate. While the pounding of Samuel's heart was making holes into his chest, the clamoring jackboots kept moving on past his cot. Sam thought: Was I just spared? Am I imagining this, or did they pass me by? But they have lined up Tadeusz! What will I do without his connections to the outside? He was going to help me. If he is killed, how will the bribe plan work? At least they haven't chosen Sergi so far. What now?

Samuel struggled in a sea of doubt; lost in a momentary, swirling sense of lightheadedness. Although relieved that the guards had passed him by, he was still not sure it was a reality, not trusting that he was actually awake. After living through so many living nightmares, it was hard to tell what was real. Just then, both stern-faced guards turned quickly on their heels, marched back up the aisle, while the third guard at the exit door helped them to commandeer the six selected inmates to line up outside before being positioned to stand in front of a firing squad.

As the exit door slammed shut behind them, a hushed silence hovered over the barracks like a dust cloud. Samuel and the rest of his bunk mates remained standing, paralyzed in a state of shock and disbelief. Minutes later, outside, they heard explosive rapid gunfire of machine guns, ruthlessly shaking the foundation of the barracks. All six of the chosen bunk mates, their lives wasted. They were the unlucky ones that day, chosen to die by cruel, manic men whose minds were poisoned with lethal doses of hatred and bigotry.

Samuel began to panic. Tadeusz had been his only hope to get information about Danika and Josef, and his life was just brutally ended. Samuel sat there in shock, his mind racing. I must stay alive, at least long enough to save my wife and my son. Maybe Sergi knows about other contacts who could help us find a way to get some 'zlotys' to bribe the guards. Rumor has it that Danika and Josef might have been taken to Belzec after the Aktion in the neighborhood took place. Even if Danika and Josef aren't there, I must know what may have happened to them. But which guards take bribes? Sergi and I will find a way. We won't stop searching until we do.

Samuel awoke the next morning at the Janowska camp engulfed in a sad cloud of smoldering loneliness. The same questions continued to plague him: How long can I exist like this, suffering from a horrible nightmare? Is anyone left in the whole world who still knows, or cares, or even remembers me, maybe even wonders about my whereabouts? In order to maintain his sanity, Samuel had to emotionally distance himself from the horrors at hand, trying to make a conscious effort to bury his misplaced emotions. There was no time to grieve for others, no less time to feel sorry for himself. Instead, he had to focus on finding ways to stay alive, at least for the time being. There was only one empowering thought fueling his energy. It was to do whatever was necessary to stay alive until he could find out the whereabouts and about what might have happened to Danika and Josef.

Suddenly, an abrupt disruption occurred, awakening the rest of the sleeping prisoners in the barracks; a startling uproar that could frighten even a dying man. The deliberate commotion, staged by the two guards, forced the heavy barracks door open, before loudly stomping their jackboots down hard on the wooden floor. The first guard, Frederick Oppenheimer, yelled, "Heil Hitler, Jew rat slaves! Wake up, you've slept enough! This is no time to laze around. No beauty sleep here. Hurry up and get dressed, there's work to be done! You have five minutes to be outside and line up for roll call or maybe I will have the pleasure of shooting you on the spot!"

Upon noticing Samuel and some other new people, he continued. "Well, who do we have here, some new prisoners? I don't recognize your Jew faces. Hey everybody, give them a warm welcome to Work Camp Janowska. We are a camp designed to fulfill all your needs, no worries and no problems, just as long as you do what we say." It was apparent that, during his taunts, Oppenheimer used any opportunity to spew more sarcastic insults.

Fredrick Oppenheimer sported a bullish smirk resembling a bloated frog, his bulging eyes half covered by thinly veined pinkish eyelids. He spoke in a threatening voice that sent chills up their spines, like someone scratching fingernails on a chalkboard. The second guard, Petr Petrovich, was a short, non-descript man, no more than five feet three. He was a mute sidekick for Oppenheimer's tactics, like an exclamation point at the end of a sentence. Oppenheimer proceeded to cough up gobs of loose phlegm, then swallowed it, and with a still gravelly voice said sarcastically, "Prepare yourselves for a delicious breakfast. You will delight in the German sausages and smoked bacon, farm fresh eggs just laid this morning, buckwheat pancakes, freshly baked croissants, sweet jam and freshly churned butter. Breakfast is made especially for you, and, I may add, it is strictly kosher too! A special rabbi was here this morning just to bless it all for you!" No doubt, the malevolent smirk on his face would assuredly spark murderous desires in most men, as he continued to spew the cruelest mockery during his daily taunting rituals.

Within five minutes, the prisoners from Samuel's barracks lined up outside, positioned themselves to stand in two even lines and painstakingly wait in the freezing air for the morning roll call. The same two guards began their agonizingly slow walk up and down the lines of hungry and tired men, purposely moving at a snail's pace to prolong the morning torture. When the guards had their fill of bullying, the prisoners were led into a large mess hall. Here, they had to wait at the mercy of the guards for a meager breakfast of stale bread and tepid, watered-down broth, just enough calories for any healthy human to stay alive and hopefully get through the day. The prisoners were given fifteen minutes for

131

mealtime. Afterwards, they were ushered into select lines designated for slave laborers to perform various tasks in carpentry and metalwork.

Once again, the "talking guard," later known as "Oppenheimer the Toad," got their attention by sounding the bullhorn that hung around his neck. He glanced at Samuel, then lowered the bullhorn down to his side and said, "Hey you. Jew boy. You're a new Jew here. Welcome to the Janowska paradise! We've been waiting for you. Hope your stay is everything you have dreamed it could be! '*Mach Schnell*' and stand in the line for the carpentry factory. You will be assigned to work there every day. That's if you make out it of this camp alive. Of course, that's if you make it for more than one day," chuckled Oppenheimer, his familiar smirk emphasizing the deeply lined, dark grooves beneath his eyes.

Samuel was quick to obey the order. Moving carefully, he turned towards the sign posted on the wall that read, *Carpentry* and hoped to avoid attracting more attention to himself. As he moved closer, he stopped in front of a long reception table that read, *Factory Workers*. Across the room was the same set up, a long reception table. Within minutes, more men began to stand behind him.

Oppenheimer shouted his orders through the bullhorn. "Factory workers must stop at the designated reception desk. Before entering the carpentry factory, all prisoners are required to pick up the large-pocketed carpenter aprons, soon to be laden with hammers, screw drivers, saws, nails, measuring tapes and yard sticks. All tools are recorded and counted when distributed and counted again when returned. You are responsible for every tool."

Later, Samuel learned how the carpentry and metal workers played a major part in German warfare. The finished products contributed to many war projects. Prisoners were often assigned to do plastering, roofing, masonry, and painting. The metal workers frequently helped in the construction of new buildings, bridges, and wharfs. Some of them worked on paving ways for new roads, building parts for new radar identification, aircraft repair, and naval construction. Oftentimes, select prisoners were transported daily to other locations to help build new structures when the Nazis were planning invasions or establishing new base camps.

Samuel was the first person in line. While approaching the long table covered with assortments of carpentry gear, he noticed several young women prisoners, appearing to be in their late teens or early twenties, standing at their assigned posts in back of the table. Their job was to distribute carpentry tools to be used to make parts for the German war effort. Samuel's life changed when he stood in front of the first young woman. The very moment he laid eyes on her, his world lit up; like being struck by a bolt of lightning. He was drawn to her radiant beauty, mesmerized by the glow of her flawless skin and admired how the long chestnut-colored hair framed her lovely face. He couldn't help but think how lucky the women prisoners in this camp never had to have their heads shaved. He imagined that it wouldn't have made a difference for her. No matter what, she would still look stunning.

Suddenly aware of Samuel's long gaze, the young woman piqued his interest even further, purposefully angling her chin toward her right shoulder, posing appraisingly like she was doing a fashion shoot and he was the photographer. In an instant, the twinkle of her youthful eyes captivated him. As her sensuous mouth formed into a flirtatious smile, he noticing her perfect set of glistening, white teeth.

"What's your name, *'moija kochane?'* Samuel chose to ask in their native Polish language, affectionately meaning my sweetheart. The young woman, flattered by his use of such an intimate word choice, replied in a somewhat shy

133

whisper. "My name is Louisa. It is my pleasure to meet you too. I haven't seen you before. You must be new here."

"I came here last night from the Drohobycz camp," Samuel replied. It is a long, difficult story to tell. I was almost executed there. Somehow, I was spared by a miracle. So, I am here. Maybe I was spared just to be able to meet you, beautiful Louisa. I am only thirty-six years old. I feel like my life is like a fading sunset, as the last vestiges of color lower down into the horizon."

"Maybe we were meant to meet," Louisa responded softly, instantly drawn to the warm intensity of his soulful, brown eyes. Samuel felt soothed by the lilting sound of her voice, like a lullaby coaxing a baby to sleep. Both of them seeming to bask in mutual appreciation and in sharing the sweet exchange of kind words.

Louisa was only eighteen years old, much younger than Samuel. Even though he was twice her age, she felt an immediate connection to him. She was anxious to make a new friend, someone whom she could trust enough to share her living tragedy. "I am a prisoner here like you. Starting in the early morning at 6:00am, I work here at the carpentry factory distributing tools and recording what each man takes. Everything must be returned at the end of the day, or the guards will punish you. But at 8:00am, I work at the sewing machines at the west end of the camp until late afternoon. It is tedious and laborious work. Yet, I am so grateful to be alive. I am also alive because of a miracle. I think the Nazis forgot me during the Aktion in my neighborhood. Can you believe that when the Nazi Ukrainian youth barged into my home, they took my family away and forgot about me? By the grace of God, I am still here. All my family is gone. I hear rumors they were taken to Auschwitz. I heard they had to lick their own urine on the train due to such thirst and inhumane conditions," she said as her eyes welled up and large tears began rolling down both cheeks.

Touched by her words, Samuel felt a deeper bond forming, a shared understanding. "I am so sad for your loss, Louisa. I lost my parents and four of my five sisters. I am hoping that maybe one is alive somewhere. We must consider ourselves lucky. We must stay alive and live not only for ourselves but for the memory of our family. We owe it to them."

Samuel's eyes glazed over when he thought about his family, suddenly giving him the desperate look of a starved man. "I am searching for my wife and three-year-old son. I am trying everything in my power to find them; they may even be here. My heart yearns for them every day. You can imagine how not knowing where they are or if they are still alive somewhere is so cruel and tortuous for me. I must stay alive to find them, maybe even rescue them from the horrors. Just the thought of them gives my life a purpose."

Overwhelmed with compassion, Louisa murmured softly, "I sense you are a most admirable and brave man. I have been blessed to make your acquaintance. I cannot express to you my empty loneliness and my fears of what will happen to me. I am only eighteen, left on this earth without a friend. My family is gone. It is just me, left to live on my own, wondering how am I going to survive throughout this lunacy. Poland has gone mad and The Nazis are evil. Where is the rest of the world? Why is no country helping us?"

Louisa took a risk and said, "Please let me help you find your wife and son. We have both been through so much and we can help each other. At times like this, you need someone you can trust. I think we both need someone we can talk to; a confidant. I will count the hours before I see you here again tomorrow morning, my new friend, 'moire kochane.'"

Before Samuel could reply, Louisa felt herself blushing. She felt dizzy and embarrassed by her own words. How could she be so forward? She had never talked to anyone so boldly. All she wanted was a release of the pent-up emotions that were slowly pulling her into a deep depression. The few minutes she had with Samuel were like a welcomed breath of fresh air.

It was clear that the low tides were shifting. A change was taking place, a newfound hope was looming somewhere in the distance. Momentarily elated, Louisa began telling herself: We are two beautiful souls, interconnected by circumstance. Is there such a thing as love at first sight? Was finding each other a gift from God; a sign that we might be able to survive together? Whatever the answer, our encounter will change us. Meeting a man like Samuel is like witnessing a glimmer of light through the darkness.

Samuel was finding it hard to focus on their conversation. He was continuously distracted by other prisoners bumping, pushing against him, and moving around him picking up their carpentry tools. Purposely, Samuel continued to stall for more time, edging slowly along the table, longing to stay and talk with her longer. It seemed like ages since he had a female friend. He was flattered that Louisa seemed genuinely interested to hear about his story. He decided that they were meant to meet. Maybe it was fate's plan, the start of a budding relationship.

Anyone who knew Louisa before the war would describe her as a coquettish, flirty, pretty young woman with a sunshine disposition. She was a singer and a performer, always craving attention and putting on shows for her grandparents, family, and friends. She knew all about Hollywood romance movies. Louisa and her friends could name every famous American movie star from the current era. They were fascinating role models for her. Her favorite pastime was to attend the local cinema to watch love stories with Polish subtitles. She enjoyed watching the glamorous women give beautiful performances, and she admired the handsome ruggedness of American male actors. Every weekend, she and her girl-friends loved watching movies and spent the rest of the week retelling the stories to anyone who would listen. After the theater, she and her friends would stroll down Kasarnick Street, socializing with fellow classmates.

Before the war broke out, Louisa lived a happy life. She was an animated, optimistic young lady who lavished in being a part of a loving family home: brother, sisters, mother, father, as well as many extended family members. It was devastating to think how it was possible that they all could disappear from her world so quickly and dissipate into oblivion. In an instant, her life was shattered and she was left stricken with the enormity of an unconceivable loss.

The chance meeting with Samuel renewed her spirit. Louisa felt a hint of the young woman she used to be, giving her new glimmers of hope. Just thinking about Samuel excited her. She wondered: Am I foolish to imagine that maybe Samuel is "the one" for me? After all, he is married with a son. Would he betray his wife even though he isn't sure if she is alive? If he found them, would he be able to save them? If he found them alive, then what would I do without him?

All Louisa could think about was the soulfulness of his deep set, cognac-colored eyes, the chiseled handsomeness of his high cheekbones, the strength of his muscular physique. Most importantly, she thought about how his very presence exuded an aura of immense kindness. Was her mind playing dangerous games? How could she be so carried away? After all, love at first sight did happen in the American romance movies. Maybe it was happening here, in real life. Only time would tell.

When Louisa was young, she would often wander outside and pick a flower. She would point to the flower petals as she sang, "He loves me, he loves me not." She was a romantic at heart. In that moment after meeting Samuel, she felt like a flower blooming. She felt love in her heart and wondered if he felt the same stirring in his chest. She thought to herself, if he turns back around to look at me, that is a sign that he feels the same way. Just watching him walk down the hall toward the carpentry factory, she felt as if she had known him forever. She couldn't mistake the sight of his beautifully shaped head of dark hair. Just then, Samuel turned around! Their eyes seemed to melt into each other in a silent, unbreakable bond. It was only when he was forced to turn the corner did his eyes have to leave Louisa's face.

If the fire in your heart is strong enough, it will burn away any obstacles that come your way. -Rise Up and Salute the Sun: The Writings of Suzy Kassem

Dueling Emotions

While seated at the carpentry workbench, Samuel pounded away mindlessly at a stubborn nail that refused to cooperate. All he could do was think about his chance meeting with the beautiful young woman at the carpentry supply table. It surprised him to feel such an instant connection with a total stranger. There was an intimacy between them, an immediate bond of affection.

While waves of exhilaration and confusion washed over him, Samuel questioned how she was able to melt his heart so quickly. Was it her youthful aura, or just her welcoming smile? Living as prisoner at the camps, it had been so long since he dared make eye contact with anyone else. Somehow, without hesitation, he was able to meet her eyes and not look away. Before Louisa, no one at the camps had shown any particular interest in him, certainly not in his welfare. But she did. It warmed his soul just picturing the image of her glowing face and how her luminous, green eyes beckoned with compassion and honest empathy as she truly listened to him tell his sad story. All the while, Samuel kept thinking how much he wanted to reach out and touch the silky tresses of her hair and run his hands along the softness of her peach-colored cheeks. He tried rationalizing: How is it possible to be so smitten after just meeting someone for only a few, short minutes? How can I be thinking like this? After all, I am married man. I love my wife. Yet I am helplessly taken away with desire for this young woman. How can I allow myself to live with such betraying thoughts? Instead, I should be feeling crushing guilt and shame for these feelings and I should try to will away such lustful thoughts. I will not allow myself to forget my loyalty and marriage commitment to Danika, I will not let myself become trapped in the midst of mass confusion, like a lovesick teenager. Yet, I can't seem to shake this strong attraction to Louisa. I cannot deny, that for the first time in months, just thinking about her gives me hope, offers me sparks of optimism. Just being in her presence is like a healing tonic, a balm to my soul. I am beginning to feel alive again. Meeting her might just be my lucky omen! Maybe we will be able to create our own team, even survive through this nightmare together. Yes, Louisa will be my muse for as long as it helps me to survive this pure hell.

Desperate to think rationally, Samuel took a deep, cleansing breath. As he slowly released the air from his lungs, he implored his mind to release the relentless longings of his heart. Needing to gain control of his runaway emotions, Samuel attempted to will away his guilt-ridden feelings. But deep within his heart, he knew this burning obsession with Louisa would become a welcome distraction from the gloominess of each day in the camp. Having this small dose of optimism would make him stronger and increase his ability to face the tortures of camp life. But he promised himself he would remember his purpose; to stay alive long enough to find Danika and Josef.

He needed to focus, to think more clearly about a plan of action. He must think about how Sergi promised to help him contact someone in the outside world that might help him acquire money to be used to bribe the guards. Suddenly, Samuel noticed something, a tiny object wedged in the corner of the factory's crumbling walls. As he bent down to look closer, he saw that it was a discarded butt of a pencil, probably used for carpentry mathematical calculations. A tiny scrap paper lay next to it. He couldn't believe his luck! Finding both a nub of a pencil and a piece of scrap paper was like finding nuggets of gold.

Samuel concentrated on what Tadeusz had told Sergi about what he heard from another prisoner. There was an SS officer named Alek Charmatsky who was stationed at the Janowska labor camp and he was rumored to take bribes. What a coincidence it was that he happened to be the brother of Dr. Harriette Charmatsky, Samuel's coworker at the hospital! Sergi said that he knew Alek Charmatsky before the war. He described him as a shrewd opportunist who networked among a group of Nazi youth compatriots who later worked as SS guards. Not only was he rumored to take bribes, Alek Charmatsky was among the SS Officers and guards who also worked at Belzec Concentration Camp. This was the camp where Danika and Josef may be! Samuel's concern was how to get his hands on the bribe money. No matter which way he fashioned a plan, no way was safe. Without a doubt, he was taking the most dangerous chance of his lifetime. The information was like a flipped switch that could change the direction of his life.

Samuel decided he would write a note to Dr. Harriette Charmatsky, his former colleague at the Drohobych hospital, and make a desperate plea for her help. He would ask her to contact the office manager at his salt business and instruct her to withdraw substantial amounts of money. Harriette would be in charge of distributing the money as needed. She would forward the money to her brother to cover the bribes. Since time was of the essence, the first necessary step was the hope that Alek Charmatsky would agree to deliver the note to his sister. It was a far-fetched plan, but he was determined to take that chance. The question was whether or not Harriette and her brother would both agree to take a life-and-death risk to help him.

Despite his lack of dexterity in using a tiny pencil nub, Samuel tried to make his handwriting legible. He diligently worked to scratch out the words on the note. If the plan went as he hoped, Alek Charmatsky would be able to locate the whereabouts of Danika and Josef. He needed to find out whether they were in Janowska, a different camp, or in Belzec. Drenched in sweat, Samuel finished writing the note before shoving it down into his work boot. He was petrified, well aware he was taking the risk of a lifetime.

That night in bed, Samuel was surrounded by familiar echoes of belabored breathing, coughing and mournful moaning of the exhausted prisoners in the barracks. He lay awake, carefully reviewing his bribery plan. He decided that right there, in the middle of the night when nobody was looking, was the right time to talk to Sergi about his plan. He needed Sergi to find Alek Charmatsky and secretly give him the tiny note he had slipped into his boot. Not sure whether Sergi was asleep or not, Samuel was careful not to startle him and disrupt the suppressed night silence of the barracks. Samuel pushed up against Sergi's cot with his feet. He whispered, "Hey Sergi, are you still awake?" Sergi peeked his head over the cot to peer down at Samuel and whispered, "Of course. I never seem to sleep soundly anymore."

Samuel carefully told him his plan. "Listen, my friend," Samuel said and then scanned the dark barracks with his eyes. "I've been thinking about what you and Tadeusz told me about Harriette Charmatsky's brother working at this camp. I don't know what he looks like, but you said that you do; that you know him from being in school together. Alek's sister Harriette has a generous mop of flaming red hair. Maybe her brother is a redhead too. I have been trying to figure out who he is, but I can't be sure, and I need your help. I wrote this note to him, explaining my bribe plan. Please give him this note and beg him to give it to his sister. Assure him he will be paid handsomely. Hopefully, Harriette will take care of everything. I worked with her at the hospital for many years and were not only colleagues, but dear friends. She was good friends with my wife Danika and she adored my son. I am trusting that she will help me. If she agrees, then everyone gets paid, even you, Sergi!"

142

Before taking the note, Sergi turned to look down at Samuel, answering in a barely audible whisper, "If God is willing, this plan will work for you, for all of us. Maybe both the Charmatskys have kept their hearts open with compassion and their minds untarnished from breathing the Nazis' toxic fumes of hatred and antisemitism. I knew him before the war; we were in the same school together. You are correct, he is easily recognizable, with his thick mass of red hair just like his sister. Without a moment of hesitation, he took the note from Samuel's hand and responded in a barely audible whisper, "Trust me. I'll do my part and I will try to find him. Now, get some sleep. Who knows, maybe tomorrow will bring us good luck!"

Although unable to see it through the pitch-dark barracks, Samuel lay back on his cot for a long time, staring upwards in the direction of the invisible ceiling. He thought about the concept of love, comparing it to the invisible ceiling in the darkness: he could not see it, but he knew that it stood there, covering him in safety. Love was something that can't be seen or touched, but can only be felt with the heart.

It was a long time before Samuel fell asleep. He kept thinking about his undying love for Danika and Josef, while feeling conflicted by the overpowering affection he was feeling towards Louisa. Although, while contemplating his swirling emotions, he kept thinking how his love for Louisa was like a comforting blanket, a sheltering promise of optimism for him. As gentle, compassionate tears gathered in his eyes, he rationalized: Don't I deserve to be happy? Why do I think that pain and punishment for being a Jew is my last destiny? Why shouldn't I allow the warm, dizzying waves of love wash over me? Now I am sure that I can love more than one woman with all my heart. That night, Samuel fell asleep thinking about both women, like watching flickering movie clips joined together on a motion picture reel.

143

Although unable to see through the darkness, Samuel lay back on his cot staring upwards at the back of Sergi's upper bunk, proud of himself for having the courage to act. He kept on thinking about his undying love for Danika and Josef. He promised himself that he would always feel the same towards them, no matter what happened. It was a long while until finally, he was able to fall asleep.

For the next few days, Samuel couldn't barricade his mind against the emotional turmoil flooding his mind, like a dam trying to block water from seeping through the flood gates. All he could do was hope that Sergi would find Alek Charmatsky and that he would agree to take the note to his sister. It took an entire week before Sergi found Alek Charmatsky and was able to hand-deliver the note. The first good news was that he accepted it. After that, the wait was torturous. Samuel prayed that Charmatsky would give the note to his sister Harriet, and that she would agree to the plan. After endless days of waiting, there was finally some news.

What soap is for the body, tears are for the soul.
-Jewish Proverb

The Note

One morning, as Samuel was walking towards the factory for work, he spotted an officer with wispy strands of red hair on the sides of his SS cap, looking as if it were fired up in the sunshine. Could it be Alek Charmatsky? Samuel's heart raced. It would be too strange a coincidence that he would be purposefully standing in his path waiting for him. The man was looking straight ahead with a slow smile unraveling, as if he was thinking about some exciting evening plans. Samuel knew it must be him. Within seconds, Alek Charmatsky and Samuel met eyes, a sure connection, both instantly cautious to not acknowledge each other.

As soon as Samuel began to pass him by, Charmatsky reached out and grabbed Samuel's elbow, dragging him closer, like a sly wolf about to overtake his prey. In a split second, he was able to slip his sister's hand-written response into Samuel's palm, winding his fingers tightly around it. In one fell swoop, Samuel bent down, pretending to adjust his pant leg, and pushed the note deep inside his boot. He would read it later in the barracks.

It was sheer jubilation for Samuel; a lost emotion he imagined he would never feel again. He could have jumped for joy. Although he was not yet sure what Harriette's response might be, he worked happily all day with hope in his heart. He prayed that Harriette would agree to help him by contacting Samuel's secretary at his salt business. She would then secretly siphon out enough bribe money to pay the guards or willing officers. It was a note that could change the course of his life, as well as the lives of Danika and Josef. But what if she said no? Samuel felt himself drowning in a paralyzing

145

state of cold fear, extremely nervous to read Harriette's response. He could feel the note patiently waiting in his boot, like an intrusive pebble.

Throughout the rest of the workday, Samuel fought against conflicting thoughts: So far, Charmatsky has done the right thing for me. No matter what the note says, Harriette answered me! Maybe she will help! She is my last hope. The fact that she took the risk to even respond to me is reassuring. Many things could go wrong. I have lived long enough to know that life often presents more than one tragedy at the same time. Sometimes one tragedy is not getting what we want, and the other tragedy is when we get it.

At the end of the day, while Samuel was seated at the workbench, an authoritative voice interrupted his thoughts. A man with an unrecognizable voice began speaking directly into his ear. "Rosenberg, finish up. Put away your tools. Stand in the back of the line-up before leaving work today. I will be walking beside you." Out of the corner of his eye, Samuel took notice of the identification imprinted on his uniform; SS Sondergiest Alek Charmatsky. Samuel turned to face him, looking at his expression and searching for a clue whether or not he was willing to take the huge risk. He couldn't tell if it was a look of compliance or one of annoyance. He did detect an imperceptible smugness, a look of blatant guilt planted on Charmatsky's face, like a lying child trying to cover up a wrongdoing.

Samuel followed his order and stood as the last person in the line-up. Charmatsky walked beside him, speaking low enough so only Samuel could hear. "Here's the latest plan. Don't know if it will work, but we will try. I will be going to Belzec tomorrow. I'll talk to my friends. I know the guards and many officers there. I'll do what I can. Remember, if your wife and boy are there, maybe we can protect them, possibly save their lives. It will depend on which guards are in charge this week. By the way, my sister Harriette is offering cases of good Polish vodka to anyone willing to take bribes as well! By the end of the war, if you make it through alive, you will owe her more money than can ever be counted!"

Samuel smiled inside and his heart exploded with joy. To keep his cover, he contained his bliss and held his face in a stone-cold position. He could not dare having anything noticed by another guard. He looked forward and whispered gratefully to Charmatsky who stood at his side. "How do you repay a person who saves a life? There isn't enough money in the world. What you are doing for me, to risk your reputation and your life is unbelievable, appreciated beyond belief. I pray that what remains is gratitude, that good people still exist in this upside-down world. Your sister is an angel. She brings me hope. Despite the inky darkness of a vast sky, to me, she is a brilliant star who will shine forever." Charmatsky closed his eyes and lifted his head to the heavens, seemingly moved by Samuel's comments. His ruddy face began to match the wisps of red hair hanging out of his Waffen SS-cap. "We are good Christians," he responded. "We always try to do what is right. We keep our word."

Samuel waited his turn to board the transit wagon heading back to the barracks at the Janowska Camp. As he stood there, he felt a tinge of faith, expectation and possibility; like a wistful kiss on the cheek after a lover's quarrel. He silently reminded himself, "Where there is life, there is hope."

That night, Samuel's hands were shaking as he pulled Harriette Charmatsky's note from inside his boot. He carefully unfolded the paper and held it up against the moonlit crevice in the barracks' wall. Samuel slowly read her soulful words. "My dearest Samuel, my heart breaks as I write this note. Every day, we are all living in the greatest human tragedy. It is deplorable that Jewish people have become the chosen victims of such a cruel fate. Of course, I will do my best to help. For me, there is no question. As soon as possible, I'll do whatever I can, and my brother has agreed as well.

147

I cannot wait for this to all end. We miss you here at the hospital. Please try to stay hopeful. Every day matters. I pray I will see your face again alive and well, along with the beautiful faces of your precious Danika and Josef. Sending you prayers and love. Your loyal friend, Harriette.

Tears ran down Samuel's face and he exhaled a deep sigh of relief. He tucked the note carefully back into his boot, planning to rip it into shreds before discarding it. His emotions wavered between joy and fear, worrying about what he would do if his plan somehow backfired. Throughout the night he was kept awake with many gruesome thoughts: What if Danika and Josef were not even sent to Belzec? If they are somewhere else, I will never be able to find them. What if we are too late to save them? There are so many loose ends. How will this end for them, and for me? He silently cried himself to sleep.

The next morning, Samuel was awakened by the startling 'Aufsteben' (wake up calls) from the outside the barracks. He placed both hands in front of his face, stared at the reddened roughness of his fingers, and observed the new blisters beginning to form. Suddenly a strange parallel occurred to him: Blisters are caused by injury to the skin. They are nature's band-aid of protection. Scabs form after the blisters pop so that healing can take place. For me, it's like I'm living inside a painful blister, just waiting for it to pop, for the scab to form, and leave me with a tremendous scar for the rest of my life. If I do survive this blistering world, I will never forget the unspeakable wounds that have been inflected on me.

Days passed with no word from anyone. Samuel tried desperately to manage the intolerable suspense while a looming cloud of doom hovered overhead. At the end of the week, news finally came. One night in the barracks, Samuel was still awake when Sergi leaned over the cot and pretended to cough in order to catch Samuel's attention. He nodded his head as if he just remembered a joke. A slow smile spread into a curved line across his cheeks, conveying a silent message that their plan was a go. He said that all parties were on board with the plan.

Despite the good news, Samuel struggled with great trepidation. He was afraid to let himself trust or be encouraged by the news. All he could feel was the clamoring pangs of intuition that something was about to go wrong, like being on a roller coaster ride but not sure if the strap is pulled tight enough.

Samuel heard nothing more about Danika and Josef for several more days. Finally, one morning, Sergi approached him at the factory and casually whispered into his ear. "Samuel, good news! Danika and Josef are definitely at Belzec! It's for sure they were definitely taken there during the Aktion in your neighborhood that morning. Charmatsky's friend, SS Officer Otto Shuttgarter found out for us, and has accepted the bribe. The names, Danika and Josef Rosenberg, are on the registration list. They were assigned to barracks number 12. The bribes are underway. Charmatsky's sister has already fronted the money, along with the bottles of vodka for all the cooperating guards and officers! Charmatsky will see to it that everyone gets paid. The plan is that one of the guards from barracks Number 12 will find an excuse to first get Danika and Josef to the infirmary. From there, he will help them escape into the woods. Evidently, I'm told he's done this for others before! Now all we have to do is wait and hope it's not too late!"

Samuel froze, speechless. By now, he was getting used to paralyzing fear attacks. Waiting for the shock to pass, all he could do was pray that he would see them again: If it's not too late, hopefully we can get them out of Belzec. Maybe they can hide, live in the woods, just to stay alive long enough until the war is over. But what if we are too late? How will I be able to survive the devastating news? I need to rise above my fears and let faith keep my head above water. So far, fortune has been on my side.

I told him that I did not believe that they could hurt people in our age, that humanity would never tolerate it. -Elie Weisel

Horror in March 1942

Startled by a swift shove to her back, Samuel's young wife Danika and four-year old son Josef were pushed towards the left line consisting of women and children. Josef slowly turned his eyes to look up at her with oversized tears spilling down over his soft, pudgy cheeks. "Mama, I am so frightened here. This is a bad place. Please let us go home. With his pitch rising, Josef cried, "I wanna go home now!" He began to cry out with such pain, such anguish it was as though he could see his entire childhood burn up in a flash. They were about to be enveloped in a terrorizing, impending doom.

On that particular day, known as the "March Aktion," Danika and Josef were among the massive round-up, about five thousand Jews who were taken against their will as prisoners, stripped of their belongings, and transported on wagons and trains to various designations. Many of these wagons also included people from other ghettos that were arriving from two more directions: The Lvov Ghetto in eastern Galicia, and the Lublin Ghetto to the west. The systematic round-up of Jews continued between March until August 1942.

Danika and Josef were part of the first transport of Jews taken from targeted Drohobytch neighborhoods. They were pulled out from their homes with no warning, unable to bring any belongings with them and forced to board uncovered farm wagons. The wagons headed for the train station on the Lubin-Lvov railway line, approximately two hours away. Drowning in mass hysteria, the women and children were crammed into the passenger cars. Their final destination was the Belzec Nazi German Concentration Camp. The

151

camp was built by the SS, and part of a complex of concentration camps located near the village of Belzec. It existed for the purpose of exterminating as many Jews as quickly as possible.

Throughout their frightening journey, the frantic women and children were sardined in place. There was barely enough room to unfold their arms or legs and they were forced to remain in this way, traveling to a place unknown for what seemed to last for an eternity. Finally, the endless journey came to a screeching halt when Danika and Josef arrived at the Belzec station marshaling yard. Both mother and child were indescribably frightened, excruciatingly thirsty, and had no place to relieve themselves. Their mouths were so dry and parched, it was difficult to keep their dry tongues from adhering to the soft tissue inside their cheeks. Danika worried: When will we be allowed some water? Is there a place for us to relieve ourselves? Plagued with mounting concerns, Danika panicked: Are we facing our deaths on this day? What is going to happen to us here? It seemed like an eternity that they were made to stand in what was known as a "spur line," a short off-shoot of a main branch line, so that the SS guards could better maintain a strict order of entry.

Danika's heart sank further as she glanced down to see the wetness, the large urine stain soaking the front of her little boy's pants. She felt her own bladder pounding incessantly, begging for a release. She knew that soon she would have no choice but to do the same and wet herself too. This was no time for shame. There was no choice but to relinquish the basic need to maintain any human dignity at all. From now on, she clearly understood she had to do whatever it took, just to survive for one more day.

Soaked in their own urine, Danika and Josef waited in line while being bombarded by the angry sounds of men shouting. The sound of viciously barking dogs came from all directions. This was all part of the Nazis' plan to unnerve and terrorize incoming groups of prisoners, a way to demonstrate strict conformity to their rules.

The driver of the first wagon in the parade line-up was SS Rudolf Gockel, better known as the German station master of Belzec. In one quick motion he jumped out of the wagon, promptly adjusted the position of his SS cap to sit firmly on top of his head. He then pulled down at the sides of his jacket; rearranging it to fit neatly in place. Seemingly pleased with his neater appearance, he began to smirk, spurring ahead the next wagon in line to move directly into the Belzec Concentration Camp.

Danika's first impression of Rudolf Gockel was that of a loathsome, unapproachable monster. The veins in his neck engorged and bulging, while the coldness of his lifeless eyes etched in his face was like an old shoe frozen in any icy pond. His twisted mouth was contorted into an ugly deformity as he continued to bark out cruel, sadistic obscenities aimed at the incoming women and children. To compliment his ugly appearance, he seemed to aptly enjoy his role; behaving as a schoolyard bully.

As soon as Danika and Josef were offloaded at the Belzec reception yard, there was the blasting sound of a loud gunshot. As Danika turned around to see what was happening, as close as five yards from where they were standing, she saw a motionless young man. He was maybe in his early twenties, lying in a pool of blood oozing from his head, apparently bleeding out. Danika stood there in shock as red blood spurted from his arteries.

They walked forward in straight lines, flanked by SS guards on either side of them. While walking in the line, Danika began to witness atrocities she could never before even imagine. It was made clear that anyone who dared to show any form of opposition, or a mere hint of defiance, would be made an example for the others to witness. Just then, Danika witnessed the guards yank another young person from the men's line, take out a small caliber pistol and shoot him in cold blood, on the spot, in front of all the bystanders. There were no words of consolation for such horror. No time for pity or compassion. Danika's body began to tremble uncontrollably, while terror and new dangers lurked in all the shadows. Instinctively, she tugged her little son into her, pulling him tighter and closer, trying to believe this tiny gesture could protect him. At times like this it helped her to live in denial, to believe anything that might give her hope. Was she insane to think that pulling her son tighter, and that by camouflaging him into the side fabric of her woolen waistcoat would make them safer? It was curious, how a simple motherly tug could bring forth a moment of comfort for both of them.

Suddenly, Danika's attentions were diverted to the announcement from the loudspeaker by an SS officer pretending to welcome the incoming transports, spewing lies in an overall transmission to the entire Belzec camp. "Welcome to Belzec. My name is SS Christian Franzer, the first commander of this post," he announced. "Your stay here at Belzec will be temporary. You will move on to work camps wherever help is needed. There is work for everyone here. Even you housewives are needed to feed your families and keep the barracks clean. But first, I must have your cooperation so that we can get you on your way quickly." Immediately after the announcement, there was a ripple of applause from the officers and guards shouting, "Thank you, Heir Commandant!" He continued to speak. "We must have order and cleanliness. Before we feed you, you must all be deloused, and your clothes disinfected. First, it will be necessary for all women to have their hair cut off." The women gasped.

The commander continued his announcements. "I am issuing today's order. All men from Barracks #12 through 24 will be congregated together at the large registration hall. There, a selection will take place separating the able-bodied workers from the elderly, those in a weak state of health, or the infirm. After the selection, you will be assigned to special lines. Each line will be marched off in blocks, walking five abreast. When you arrive at the hall, all men will be directed to remove their shoes, tie them together with pieces of string that will be handed to you by assigned camp workers. There will be a strict supervision while the systematic removal of all belongings takes place. During the organization of property, you will hand over all clothing, personal property, and or any money you have with you. Move quickly and do not delay. It is imperative everyone follows the strict orders of the camp or you will face severe consequences." After the announcement, music was blasted on the loudspeaker, playing popular Polish melodies of the day, such as "*Drei Lillen*" and "*Highlander, Have You No Regrets*," a final insult to the incoming prisoners.

The women and children were ushered quickly into a cold and drafty room called the "*Sluice*", which was a place for de-lousing. They waited for what seemed to be at least an hour to have their hair chopped off in an indescribably brutal manner. Danika feared the worst, after seeing the ghastly sight of bodies, piled up to the side of the road, dead on arrival to the camp. Later, she learned that the sick, elderly, infirm, or the "troublesome" Jews were taken to the execution pit in Camp 11 and shot point blank. Fear was all encompassing. All she could hear was the blaring music and sorrowful cries all around her. The most wrenching, loudest cry was coming from deep within her own soul.

The hatred of other men destroys your own soul. -Sayings of the Fathers 2:15

Feeling Numb

After the traumatizing experience of being de-loused, Danika and Josef had to stand in an adjacent line among the other de-loused women and children. Despite the guard's warnings to remain silent, all the de-loused prisoners found it impossible to suppress the volume of mournful weeping, becoming seemingly louder each minute they had to stand and wait in line for the next humiliating ordeal of having their heads shaved. Frightened beyond imagination, Danika was thinking: How can they do this to us? I want to keep my precious hair! Will they shave Josef's head too? Sheer torture. Why are they so cruel? We have done nothing to deserve such treatment. To think that our crime is that we are Jewish and that's why they hate us! It's crazy!

Danika's panicky mind was spinning faster: We are trapped with no way out of here. Dear God, where is my husband, Samuel? Is he in hiding or held captive somewhere? Maybe he is not even still alive. If he is alive, is he looking for us? He would be worried sick. How could he find us? It would be impossible. Silently, in her mind, she began to recite the holiest prayer, '*Schema,*' desperately hoping and praying that Samuel was still alive and looking for them.

Suddenly without warning, a staunch-looking guard named Zosia headed straight towards them, making purposeful, heavy steps as she got closer. The fierce, determined look on her face was reminiscent of a hungry, salivating bear on a mission to capture its prey. She moved unsteadily with a prevalent limp, moving with the reckless hobble of a spasmatic ogre. Lurching forward, she positioned herself in front of the line where Danika and Josef were standing. In an exaggerated gesture, like a magician retrieving a surprise rabbit out of a hat, she pulled out a large pair

156

of oversized commercial shears from behind her back. In a threatening manner, she proceeded to hold the scissors in front of her large, buxom chest. Her eyes exhibited a crazed gleam with a hint of malice, reveling in the fact that she was making the prisoners suffer more fear and more humiliation.

Zosia lead Danika and Josef, who were first in line, along with the line of twenty other women and children into a large, windowless room with wooden walls and no air circulation, resembling the inside of an old factory mill. The foul-smelling room was previously prepared for the ritual hair-cutting ordeal, with an unavoidable stench similar to the odor of dirty feet mixed with sweat. It was similar to the smell of a men's athletic locker room soon after a ball game.

While Zosia stood in front of the rows of waiting women, she happened to lock eyes with Danika, resulting in a shocking jolt as she imagined how an angry cat might feel when a heavy foot mistakenly steps on its tail. All at once, Zosia held up her forefinger and emphatically pointed straight towards the first row of previously arranged stools. Focusing her gaze back to Danika, she ordered, "Sit down on this one, you stupid, pitiful Jew, and hold that little bastard of yours on your lap. But don't worry, my dear. You are about to have a new coif! This will be a hairdo like you've never had before, I can assure you!" She snickered, cackling like a witch making a poisonous brew.

Zosia shoved Danika roughly, her buttocks plopping down onto the base of the wobbly stool. Josef whimpered softly, afraid to cry out loud, as hot tears streamed down his face. "She's so mean, mama. We have to do what she says! She's a bad lady. I don't like her! Why can't we just go home?" Danika was at a loss for words. Instead of answering him, she said nothing. She couldn't seem to find the right words that would make any sense to him, nor did it make any sense to her.

157

Sitting on the stool, Danika was trying to ignore the waves of gripping panic. Afraid to look up at Zosia, she hoped to avoid triggering an angry reaction. She couldn't control the alarming questions that began to take over her mind: What happens if we fall off this stool? Will they shoot us, just to make an example? The meanness of these guards is overwhelming. Has someone like Zosia ever known kindness in her life? How does someone become so cruel? Does she hate herself so much that she takes it out on others? Danika decided she would think more about that at another time. She pulled Josef up onto her lap. As he nestled his head against the softness of her bosom, the rickety stool began to shiver and shake. Danika tried desperately to balance it, bracing her foot against the stool's unstable structure. At this point, Danika's remaining shreds of hope and trust were rapidly transforming into Arctic cold fear.

Just then, an unexpected omen appeared. A tiny sparrow flew into the room. Danika's heart started pounding against her chest as she remembered a folklore superstition. She heard the words in her mind: "When a sparrow flies into the room, it brings impending doom." The person who first sees the sparrow must catch and kill it, or loved ones will surely die. If the sparrow is not killed, then the person who first saw the sparrow will be the one to die. Danika decided that she mustn't put her faith in a superstition. It was absurd to think that a myth or an old wives' tale is able to determine one's fate. Instead, she chose to believe in God's protection, a spiritual promise of eternal life.

Suddenly empowered, Danika turned her head to face her son, Josef who was crying softly on her lap and holding fast to the sides of the wobbly stool. Wanting desperately to calm him, Danika whispered, "Please darling, don't worry. She is just cutting my hair. She isn't going to hurt me. Everything will be all right, you will see, my child." Danika wrapped her loving arms around Josef's tiny waist and held him tight.

On the stool next to them, there was a pretty, young mother with long blonde braids and a heart-shaped face. Out of the corner of her mouth she whispered, "You know they ship the hair out to processing firms in Germany. They use our hair to manufacture socks for submarine crews. They say the hair also makes felt stockings for railroad workers! Imagine if they knew their socks were made from Jewish hair? In school, we learned that human hair was used to make bomb ignition mechanisms, ropes and cords, even stuffing for mattresses! How would they feel if they knew they were sleeping on a mattress made from our Jewish hair? It would be like a Muslim finding out later that he ate the meat of a pig. How about an Indian finding out his own sacred cow was used to make his shoes!" she remarked.

Suddenly, the sound of Zosia's loud, raspy voice was nearing them. "Hey, you two, shut up! What do you think this place is, a beauty parlor?" Without warning, Zosia clutched a fistful of Danika's thick, dark, shoulder length hair. She pulled it roughly upwards and aimed the sharp shears dangerously close to her scalp, cruelly grazing it. Tiny droplets of blood appeared like polka dots on her camp blouse. Danika flinched and let out an involuntary loud yelp. Zosia worked with skillful efficiency, quickly clipping off Danika's luxurious cognac-colored tresses. As the precious locks of hair fell to the ground, Danika found comfort in her imagination. She fantasized that when each lock of hair hit the floor, it turned into a poisonous snake. The snakes gathered around Zosia's feet to viciously bite her, leaving her to writhe in unbearable pain from the venom before suffering a slow, agonizing death.

Danika was finding it more difficult to manage the anger that blurred her sense of right and wrong. She fought against an unstoppable flood of muddy waters clouding her logic and a barrage of vengeful thoughts bombarded her senses. Her weakened state of mind was caught in a tug of war between rational and irrational emotions, as she continued to contemplate: It is time to think about vengeance. If I had the opportunity to kill Zosia, would I be able to do it? Maybe I am just like her because I'm thinking about killing her. People can become evil. Maybe they can do bad things to others because evil had been done to them. The Nazi regime is based on fear. Zosia is a model Nazi. She has chosen to blame the Jews for all that is wrong in her life. Many people think is $\mathcal{J}$ easier to blame a victim for wrongdoings rather than for them to face their own shortcomings and imperfections. They don't realize that whenever the power of fear finds itself a comfortable place to rest, most of the time, it becomes buried deep within a person's soul.

In the midst of the greatest turmoil of her life, Danika held onto her strong will to survive, clinging like a small boat tied to a young tree during a storm. Was there anyone in the world who would be able to rescue them from this hell? Suddenly she had an epiphany; a comforting thought. She remembered that she still had three remaining gifts left in her life; the love of Josef and Samuel, and her faith in hope. No one could ever take that away from her.

When Zosia was finished lopping off most of Danika's hair, she put the shears in her back pocket. All that was left on Danika's head were patches of jagged brown hairs, like clumped blades of grass slowly dying in a sunburned pasture. Fortunately, there were no mirrors. There was no time for vanity. Stripped of her beautiful hair and of her dignity, Danika felt like there was nothing left but intense shame and humiliation. Danika took a deep breath and decided: The only thing that matters now is for us to find a way to survive. Like the wobbly stool trembling beneath us, somehow we will find a balance. At least Josef and I are together, though wobbling unsteadily on this stool, we are still in sync. There might be a new reality emerging for us. I pray for a miracle. Maybe Samuel will come and find us. I pray that he will find a way to save us from this place.

Something moved above her, which made Danika cast an upward glance. The same tiny sparrow flew around the room, looking for a safe place to perch. Danika met eyes with tiny sparrow and she began to think: Funny, that I feel a strange connection to that little bird. We are both looking for the same thing; a safe place to perch, to rise high above the evil that exists below us.

Justice for crimes against humanity must have no limitations.
-Vienna Documentation Center

Deplorable Conditions

The first night at Belzec, Danika was thankful she and Josef were assigned to the same barracks. It was nearly impossible to sleep amidst the anguish, the sounds of mournful sighs and heartfelt crying of everyone around them. All through the night, Danika feared the worst was yet to come, thinking: Could they be planning to kill us tomorrow? Considering the cruel treatment so far, it is suspicious, even somewhat strange that mothers and their children are allowed to remain together in the same barracks. I would think that by separating us, it would be more torturous. So why are they allowing us to stay together tonight? Does it mean something unthinkable will happen tomorrow? I can't let myself imagine something so terrible.

First thing in the morning, Danika was reluctant to feel her raw and ravaged scalp. She was strangely hoping the hair ordeal was merely a dream and instead her hair was still intact. She raised her arm to touch her hair, and her wishes were immediately crushed. Danika's shiny, chestnut tresses no longer existed. What remained on her head were only short clumps of hair, ugly protrusions on her scalp like the sporadic and rough skin of a pineapple. It was traumatic for her to wake up to the harsh reality of losing her hair in such an unconscionable way. It was as if her fingers had a mind of their own, as they continued to probe through the short stubs, the jagged coarseness of hair, wishing she could will away the horrible experience that left her with enflamed feelings of shame and humiliation.

At Belzec, aside from using the hair for war purposes, another reason for shaving their heads was to cut away personal feelings of femininity, to make the women look ragged and ugly, removing their last shreds of dignity. Danika was well aware that she had to accept her new existence, to live without vanity, to live without beauty, to live without color. Indescribable fear was becoming the normal state of being for Danika and for all of the other innocent women subject to such inhumane conditions.

In Danika's barracks, all the mothers and children were able to lie together on the primitive board and straw cots on the lower-level bunks. Single women were paired with another woman to lie upon the upper bunks. Although cramped and uncomfortable, they all tried to rest, maybe even sleep if they were lucky. Each woman was given a scratchy, woolen blanket; barely large enough to provide minimal warmth against the cold and drafty night air.

Through the darkening shadows of the barracks, Danika still managed to see through the blur of the impending darkness of the evening. Somehow, she began to sense the stare of a young, glassy-eyed woman appearing to be in her early twenties. In an instant, they both felt a curious connection, like an electric current, causing them to sit up abruptly. Danika was instantly stricken by the young woman's sad, compelling eyes, like the beam of a flashlight in the darkness. The young woman gestured a sign, offering a slight nod towards her. Just like Danika, her scalp was sparsely appointed with clumps of hair. A small, perky nose was centered between two finely chiseled Polish cheekbones in a heart-shaped face that was no longer framed by the former tresses of blond hair. Her natural beauty still came through. Danika admired her, thinking how resembled a lead actress she had once seen in a movie about a dancer who later became a famous legend. Unlike the actress in the movie, Danika's thought about how this young, beautiful woman's legend might end in a disastrous fate. Lying beside her, curled in a fetal position, was the small body of a little girl who was fast asleep.

163

Careful not to disturb Josef, who was still asleep, Danika decided to move towards the young woman's bunk, hoping that she had interpreted the previous nod as an invitation to come over. Danika moved closer and then took the liberty to sit down. She edged toward the far corner, trying not to appear too bold, careful not to disturb the little girl curled up next to her. The young woman responded with another nod, indicating it was okay for her to sit there. "My name is Katya," she whispered. "I am not a Jew. I am actually a devout Catholic. But I would like to have a friend in this hell hole. You look like a friend to me, would that be ok with you?"

Danika answered, "Of course! Friends are what get us through difficult times. We were meant to meet. My name is Danika and I am a Jew." Throughout many hours of the night, they shared their stories; talking through covered whispers, hoping not to be heard by curious ears of those still awake. They were two desperate people bonded by basic human needs: the desire to be free and the strong will to live.

Katya explained how she had been beaten, arrested, and taken prisoner before being sent to Belzec as punishment for committing a crime. She told how her own brother, a guard working at another camp, discovered that she had been harboring several Jews in the basement of an old, abandoned house. He immediately reported her to the authorities. His dedication to the Nazi cause was worth more than his devotion to his sister.

Katya's voice became shaky as she continued to whisper to Danika in the darkness. "Before I was arrested, my brother told me about what was happening, especially about the Belzec atrocities. He knew Belzec guards who worked at the gas chamber here. It is commonly known as the "Tube." My brother's friends who worked as guards knew about Belzec's secret operations. Male prisoners who are considered no longer able-bodied for work are weeded out from barracks.

They are made to strip naked and stand at the entrance to the "Tube." It is a well-rehearsed drill. Then the Ukrainian guards, armed with whips and bayonets prod and force the naked men into the gas chamber. After the doors are closed, they waited for a signal from the '*Scharfuhrer*' before gas was pumped into the chamber. Twenty minutes later, before turning off the engines, the guards check through the peep-hole in the chamber door, making sure the men inside were not moving, no longer alive. "This operation is practiced here at Belzec on a daily basis," Katya explained as she shook her head from side to side.

Danika leaned in closer, wiping away her angry tears, la-menting, "How can this be true? Aren't we here to work and then when our work is done, they will let us go? What you are saying cannot be true. No one can be that heartless, can they? No matter what religion, no one supports the doings of evil men. How can people turn a blind eye to such evil?"

Katya answered her wistfully, "People do what they need to do to stay alive. People never know how strong they are until they have to be. Sometimes they make deals that seem unthinkable to others. There are all kinds of arrangements. Some Jewish men can save themselves from their deaths by being lucky enough to be assigned to the job of a Sonderkommando. They are in charge of removing bodies from the gas chambers. After the gas is vented from the chamber and doors are opened, they shoot anyone who might still be moving. The Sonderkommandos have to throw the corpses out of the chamber, fasten straps to them and drag them to the waiting trolleys. From there, the bodies are taken to a mass burial ground, and they end up in mass graves somewhere. Any rings or gold teeth in their mouths are promptly removed before the corpses before being thrown into the pits."

Danika was speechless, trying to comprehend the reasons why any decent person would agree to do such things. She managed to say, "Now I can understand how sometimes people have to do anything, whatever is necessary, in order to survive. Before you told me, I never imagined a job so horrible as being a Sonderkommando. If a person chooses that job to in order to stay alive, I can understand why they do it. They want to live to see another day and for a chance to be with the ones they love. What is more important than that?"

Suddenly, the little girl began to stir, moving her head to the other side. Katya gently placed a calming hand on her back, lovingly encouraging her to stay asleep. Then Katya explained, "When I found her, this child was dirty, hungry and abandoned in the street. She is not my child. She told me she witnessed the Nazis shoot her parents right in front of her. She managed to run away and hide behind a garbage bin for several days. When I happened to notice her, I approached, she came towards me willingly and let me hug her. I told her I would protect her as best as I could. When I was arrested, the Nazis let her stay with me, thinking she was my daughter. She has been with me for several weeks. She has no one else but me."

Devastated by Katya's story and the terrifying news about the camp, Danika crawled back to her bunk and lay down next to her son. She lay in her cot and thought: I'm so glad the little girl was allowed to stay with Katya. At least they let Josef stay here with me. I couldn't bear it if we were separated, even for one night. I wouldn't be able to live without him. Life would have no meaning at all. No matter what happens, I have to manage to stay alive, not only for myself, but for the sake of my precious son.

For the dead and the living, we must bear witness. -Elie Wiesel

More Torture

Danika awoke listening to the sound of Josef's soft, rhythmic breathing. She watched him open his sleepy eyes and he managed a slow smile as he turned to look up at her. The vision of her son's youthful innocence touched Danika's aching heart. It felt like listening to the saddest song or recalling the memory of an unrequited love. In spite of the primitive surroundings, Josef was able to sleep through the night. "Mama, is it time for us to go home today? I don't want to stay here any longer. We have to go home and see daddy. Why didn't he come with us to this place?" Danika's heart broke and she searched for the right words to explain. Struggling not to reveal the fear in her voice, she smiled back at him, rubbing his small ear soothingly. With tears clouding her eyes she said, "Not right now, my child. Not this day. Maybe someday very soon, my darling boy," she responded gently. "Before they let us all go home, we have to do some work for them. We have to be very strong. Hopefully, they will send us home soon." Josef seemed satisfied, knowing his mother would never lie to him. He trusted that she would always protect him no matter the circumstances. Why would it be any different now? Josef rolled towards Danika and hugged her tightly. Their bodies felt safe, clinging together, as they sought loving comfort in each other's arms.

There was a sudden wake-up call coming from outside the barracks. Unmistakably, it was Zosia's shrill voice on the megaphone. Her razor-sharp words pierced through the quiet stillness of the morning air. Minutes later, the barracks door swung open in a fury. Zosia barged into the barracks, deliberately plowing ahead like a charging bull. She continued to shout in a pitch that could probably shatter glass. "Listen to me, you Jewish whores and little bastards, "Wake up! Get dressed, *und Mach Schnell*! Remember that

167

you are our prisoners and you are meaningless to us. We have your possessions and they belong to us now. You have nothing but the rags that you are wearing. You are poor, destitute for that matter. Now you all know how it feels. All your beautiful clothes, grand homes, all your riches and fancy friends- everything is gone! It'll serve you right to know how we regular folk have had to live. You Jews have robbed us of everything for a long time. Well, those days are over! Now it's our turn to be rich, to have all those luxuries. Even your hair is gone; imagine how horrid you must look! Lucky for you there are no mirrors because you look like monsters. Ha, it's for sure that no man would even look at you now! Just remember, you are nothing but workhorses. You work for us now. You are the servants; slaves for that matter, nothing else. If you can remember all that, you will have no trouble here."

As Zosia shouted, Danika saw how the image of hatred was etched into her face; the same facial expression as she had yesterday. During the hair-cutting ordeal she seemed to savor every moment, enjoying the tortured faces as she lopped off their hair. She paid no attention to the woman in front of her; it was as if she was cutting the hair of a lifeless mannequin. There was no doubt that she was infected by the disease of hatred, the same contagion running rampant throughout the Belzec Concentration Camp. The very same hatred was filling Poland, and sweeping rapidly throughout Europe.

For some strange reason, Zosia stopped shouting and pointed straight at Danika. "You, Jew girl with the boy, both of you get up and go to the front of the line. The rest of you will all follow behind." Zosia then turned to face the prisoners in the barracks. Before shouting the rest of the morning instructions, she puffed out her chest, took a deep breath and crossed her elbows in front of her low hanging, matronly chest. "Today, all babies and young children under ten years of age will be taken to another building," she commanded.

"Obviously, they are too small to work. All children aged ten and over will accompany their mothers and work alongside them. Work hard and there won't be any trouble. Calmly, you will hand over your babies and children to the guards already standing outside the barracks. There is no need to worry. We will make sure they are fed, cared for and brought back later," she snarled. "There is no time to cry or get upset. Now, move it, I say. Get up and get out quickly! I'll meet you outside. Get ready to work hard today. *Mach Schnell*, everyone!"

The women and children broke their silence. It was sheer pandemonium. The sounds of weeping and inconsolable screaming ensued. Danika and Josef covered their ears with their hands; trying to block out the shrill, screeching sounds coming from the terrified children. In the barracks that morning it sounded like the blaring sirens of a five-alarm fire. Waiting outside were three more guards assigned to take the babies and young children away from their mothers, who had no choice but to relinquish them into the arms of strangers. The defenseless mothers, standing in unhinged panic, were desperately weeping and screaming. They stood there, some falling to their knees, until they could no longer hear the drone of the babies' wailing and children's pathetic pleas moving farther away in the distance.

Zosia blew the ear-piercing whistle that hung on a string around her neck. "Mothers, shut up!" She shouted. There is no need to be so emotional. You will see them later tonight. You will learn here that work comes first. I hope you are not so foolish to think that you can have children with you during the work day. They will be back to you tonight, so get in line and move forward! We have plenty of work for you to do."

Danika was in the front of the line while the rest of the women followed. Most of them kept their bulging, blood-shot eyes to the ground, afraid to look at one another and be reminded of their own sadness. They didn't want see other

169

hairless women; mirrors to their own barren ugliness. To think it was only yesterday they were forced to surrender their last vestiges of dignity and femininity; robbed of the hair that was once their crowning glory. Marching forward in a single line, the sunlight seemed to brighten; drawing attention to their ravaged, mutilated scalps. Together they looked like a tribe of savages.

As she walked, Danika's tormented mind began to wander, searching for a guiding light of hope. Suddenly she remembered a friend telling her words of wisdom spoken by a Kabbalist, "You should live your life imagining that you are walking along a very narrow bridge, always trying to keep your balance so you won't fall off. The secret to keeping your balance is to keep on moving." Danika realized: That's it! That's what I'll do. I'll keep on moving and hold on to hope that everything will turn out all right. Where are you, my darling husband, my Samuel? You must be so worried about us, where ever you may be! I pray that you are alive and that you will find and rescue us. Just then, Danika heard Zosia turn around, displaying the same malicious smirk, before shouting the next order. "Okay, now we are here to work! Move inside the building in a straight line! Do as I say, dumb whores!"

Once inside the building, the women were made to shuffle through the floor's tangled debris from yesterday's newly shaved heads. Piles of hair clippings and tumbled tresses were left intentionally on the floor for the prisoners to sweep up, bag, and prepare for transport to surrounding factories. The floor looked like a hair mosaic of various colors, a creation made from the prisoners' lost tresses, intertwined with their last colorless shreds of dignity and self-respect.

Zosia grabbed a large broom from the corner of the room and began to yell contemptuously as a glob of white spittle collected in the corner of her mouth, "Halt! You are working too slow, lumbering along like fat cows!" She began to walk up and down the line, purposefully shaking the broom in front of their faces, further terrorizing them. Then she raised the broom high into the air and emphatically slammed it down to the floor. From the broom's pounding force, a thick shower of feathery hair ascended into the air and began to blow about like a gossamer splay of dandelion weeds in the early spring. "Clean it up, you whores! Grab a broom and a burlap bag from the stack on the side wall, then sweep the hair from the floor into the bag. Bundle each bag and pile it up on the right side of the wall. If there aren't enough brooms to go around, get on your knees and scoop the hair up with your hands!" Then she pointed to the left wall. "Those bulging sacks are already filled with hair and stacked. Stack your bags neatly on top of the piles. You have one hour to finish up, then we will go to work in the factory." The women and the few remaining adolescent children hurried as fast as they could to bundle and rope the hair-stuffed burlap sacks before lifting and stacking them up against the wall, ready to be taken away. After an hour of hard labor, the floor was cleared of hair.

While inspecting their completed task, Zosia paraded around the room, her beady eyes showing sparks of disdain. She seemed to enjoy shaking her head and making loud, dramatic tsk-ing sounds; pretending their work was not good enough. As Danika quickly worked, she thought: That woman is a despicable ogre. She is contaminated with the poison of red-hot human loathing, a disease for which there is no cure.

Finally, Zosia barked her last order. "Your work is done here. Not a great job, but I can't expect too much from Jews. Now line up in groups of five. You have two minutes to dig up holes in the ground to relieve yourself outside this building. Cover the holes with the dirt when you are done. When finished, get back into the line and prepare to follow me. You will get some food and drink before starting your afternoon work assignment."

The midday meal was a bowl of watery soup and a piece of bread, measured and doled out to each prisoner. They were forced to eat in silence during their fifteen-minute lunch before being taken to the factory. There they would be assigned various jobs in the German textile production to work on sewing, mending, knitting and other fabric-related projects. Throughout the work day, mothers were plagued with worry; hoping that their babies and little children had been fed and cared for with human decency. At last, the drudgery of the workday had finally ended. After eating their last sparse evening meal, they headed back to the barracks, desperately anxious to see their children as Zosia had promised.

As they neared the barracks, Danika was hoping to hear the sound of children's voices. Gripped with dread, she heard no noises, no sounds of anyone at all. The stillness was deafening. She was trying to remain calm and somewhat hopeful, but the prospect of being reunited with Josef was beginning to fade quickly. Once all the mothers lined up outside the barracks, Zosia gestured a curt nod to Danika, giving her the sign to take them all inside. Their fears were realized as soon as they entered the barracks. The children were not there as promised. Suddenly, there was an uproar of crying, groaning sighs, the sounds of mass hysteria starting to build among them. Zosia knew it was the perfect time for her to make a dramatic entrance, pretending not to notice the mothers' heartfelt tears and blatant disappointment after seeing that the children were not there to meet them. Oblivious to their despairing cries, she spoke in a voice sounding like a fog-horn, "Everyone, take to your bunks and prepare for the night. Tomorrow, you will await my new orders. By the way, there have been some complications. Two guards are sick and we cannot bring your children back yet. Don't fret, you will see them. They will be here in the morning."

172

There was an explosion of screaming, a cacophony of despair. "Where are our children? You promised us! We don't care about sick guards! Why can't someone else bring them back tonight? Why aren't you answering us?" Zosia dropped her chin, sported an expression of feigned empathy, and responded in a nonchalant manner. "Why would you ever trust a scorpion when it says that it would never sting you? So, you see, I've made my point. Plans change all the time. Get over it and go to sleep. You'll see them tomorrow." Zosia then raised her chin, seemingly satisfied with the outcome, and promptly stamped out of the barracks. She left behind a cloud of utter dismay. Mothers shook and cried, barely able to breathe. All you could hear was despairing sounds, like the haunting echoes of a funeral march.

Would someone ever believe us, we asked ourselves.
Would anyone be able to grasp it... -Simon Wiesenthal

A Mother's Devotion

It was late October, another dismal evening in the barracks. After a long day of physical labor, Danika lay on her bunk while endless tears streamed down both sides of her face. Feeling betrayed, she kept thinking about how Zosia had lied to them, how she broke her promise to return the children that night. The mothers worked hard all day, most of them obliging without protest. Why would Zosia need to punish them and deliberately be so mean and heartless? Danika's blood turned to ice as terror seeped through every pore in her body, shaking her into the harsh reality that she might never see Josef again. Numbness set in, as she berated herself just thinking how she could be so naïve to believe anything that a demonic creature like Zosia would say. Of course, she would never keep a promise.

Suddenly, coming from somewhere off in the distance, a series of shrill, random sounds broke the ominous silence of the evening. Danika froze and barely took a breath so she could listen carefully. Are those animal cries coming from the forest? I can't be sure. Is my imagination playing tricks? The strange commotion was growing louder and moving closer. As Danika lay wide-awake on her bunk, she felt certain it was the muffled sounds of children. She sat up and listened to the high-pitched sounds of youthful voices, the scampering of light, quick paced footsteps running over twigs snapping under their small feet and scurrying towards the barracks. Danika felt her heart burst with anticipation with the thought of having her precious Josef back. As soon as all the other women became aware of the tell-tale sounds of their children coming back, their faces lit up and they jumped out of bed, filled with excitement. They could barely contain their joy.

174

It was true! The children were really coming back! A miracle! All seven screaming children of varying ages, like piercing whistles, their shrill voices rang out. "We are back! Mommy, I'm coming! Mama, Mama! We're coming back! Mommy, mommy!" The loudest cries overpowered the muffled ones, as the eager children charged through the barracks door and stampeded in with reckless abandon, jumping into the waiting arms of their overjoyed mothers. Moments later, three more guards entered the barracks, each one carrying a baby. One guard was also holding the hand of an unhappy toddler who looked exhausted from a day of fear and misery. Seconds seemed like hours before the babies were placed safely into their mother's outstretched arms. It was a heartfelt display of tenderness, as the babies and children were smothered with love and kisses, their faces wet with frenzied tears.

Just then, Danika recognized Zosia's heavy tread resounding outside and stopping at the barracks' door. She entered in pompously, smirking as if she had a secret, barging in as if she expected a round of applause from an appreciative audience. Her demeanor was detached from the passionate scene between mothers and children, acting as if she didn't notice the jubilation, looking far off into oblivion. Picking up the megaphone, Zosia began to shout. "Well now, you must see that I am a woman of my word! You now have your children back. We are planning something special for you tonight. A celebration for such a happy reunion! It happens to be the end of the harvest season. We will be attending a Lozinski harvest festival to celebrate the autumn equinox and all the hard work of the Polish peasantry! As prisoners, you are all part of the peasants' alliance. The harvest moon marks the end of the reaping season. Surely it is a treat for you to see. Get dressed quickly, put on your coats, take your children, then form a single line outside the barracks and wait. You have exactly five minutes."

Zosia began her exit barreling down the five steps leading to the ground. Upon noticing a gathering mound of damp, rotting leaves lying at her feet, she swiveled on the heel of her boot and kicked it to the side, seemingly irritated that it dared obstruct her path. While taking her spot to wait alongside the two other assisting guards, Zosia stamped her heels together in a dramatic show of Nazi allegiance, keeping the distinct smirk on her face.

As they prepared to leave the barracks, the women began to worry as waves of unstoppable fear replaced the jubilation in their hearts. Their intuitions warned of impending danger. Danika tried to understand: Why are they making us take part in a Polish peasantry celebration? Why, as their prisoners, did it matter to them that we see the Harvest Moon? Certainly, Zosia doesn't care about our happiness. There was no reason for us at all to trust her. She is nothing but a hateful Nazi guard. Despite being grateful after being reunited with the children, their feelings of consolation and relief were promptly extinguished and replaced by clouds of fear and distress.

During the brisk October night, heading towards the Bronika Forest, they were forced to walk in single file for at least thirty minutes or more, greeted by the sounds of chirping crickets and groaning frogs. The wood pigeons cooed, while the glow of the bright orange moon illuminated the entire surroundings. They were ordered to stop along the side of a babbling brook at the bottom of a gorge. How strange it was that this was where they stopped. Danika wondered: Maybe we stopped here to drink water or to bathe our dirty feet in the brook. Was this the plan? What is their motive for taking us here? When is the celebration going to begin? Yet no one knew what to expect next, already surmising their lives were in grave danger.

As they stood waiting along with the quiet calm of the tranquil creek, there was a pungent aroma: a wild mixture of fallen pine cones combined with damp, mulched leaves. It was curious how the aromas seemed to emit a soothing combination of tangy smells, instantly becoming a temporary balm to the senses. The earth's natural scents could be so powerful, especially during an uncertain time filled with jittering nerves.

In the distance, Danika turned her head, spotting a large ravine several yards away, thinking: Thank goodness we stopped at the creek instead the ravine. I still can't imagine why it is so important for us to see the Harvest Moon. Who else is coming to the Dozynski festival? So far, there is no one else here. There is nothing to celebrate. How are we expected to enjoy gazing at the moon at a time when we are frightened to death? Maybe it's just another dirty trick, playing with our emotions. Dear God, are they going to kill us here?

The light of the coppery, orange moon continued to shine on the line of women, children and babies who had been ordered to wait while facing the creek; all of them forbidden to turn around. The moonlight was almost a melody, a sad, pathetic song in a minor key. Everyone was fearing the worst. Danika pulled Josef closer, holding him tighter, trying to hide her unrestrained panic; like a raging dam threatening to break loose. As hot, silent tears began streaming down her face, Danika whispered hoarsely, "Josef, look at the bird on the branch of that tree! Isn't he beautiful? Maybe he will sing us a song of freedom! Look up at the Harvest Moon and make a wish! Maybe the moon is sending us a sign that we will be going home soon! Always remember that God will always protect us, my beautiful baby boy." A slight, hopeful smile appeared on Josef's face as he replied, "I think so too, Mommy! Maybe we can even go home tonight after the Harvest Moon celebration! Maybe the guards will change their minds and be nicer, instead of always beings mean to us."

"Yes, my darling boy," Danika sadly replied. "Maybe so, 'Moije Kochana,' we shall see. We might go home. If not tonight, then maybe tomorrow."

Suddenly, Danika sensed a palpable omen, an intense fear and dread sinking into her bones. How long were they expected to stand there on the dense creek bed, their feet slowly sinking into the spongy mossy and still stare at the moon? Why couldn't they turn around? Was there really going to be a festival? Could it be that the cold-blooded haters were planning to shoot at their backs at any moment? Was this really the end of their lives? Everyone now feared the worst.

Shuttering with the familiar twinge of incredulity, Danika's throat went dry, trying to assess what was happening: These are cruel and despicable people who have trapped us here where there is no escape. All of us, afraid to breathe, are standing outside in the chill of night for only God knows how much longer. It is not about the Harvest Moon, it is just another maneuver to leave us to wait like ducks in a row, while they set up a firing squad. Oh my God, the babies, our children? They don't deserve to be the victims of this tragedy, snuffed out in the darkness, and never having the chance to live their lives. My dearest Samuel, if you are alive, or hiding somewhere, always know I love you! Josef loves you! May God keep you safe from harm.

By this time, the babies reacted to their mother's prickling tensions and began to wail even louder. Several stoic women remained eerily quiet, enveloped in their own tortured silence; seemingly able to bury their mental agony while the rest of horrified women tried desperately to quiet their restless children. All of them were constantly reminded to face the creek and wait while standing in the moon's spotlight. No one could possibly imagine the severity of the encroaching danger of this moment.

Suddenly, Katya, the young woman with a heart-shaped face whom Danika had befriended in the barracks, took the little orphaned girl's hand who always stood by her side. Katya turned around to face a large ravine in the near distance. She grabbed the little girl's hand, dared to step out of the line, and they both began to run away towards the ravine. One of the guards began shouting, "*Achtung*! Halt, I order you! Where do you think you are going? Return to the line immediately or I will shoot!" he warned.

But they didn't listen. They kept running and ignored the guard's warnings. In an instant, two deafening bullets were fired from the guard's pistol. Katya and the little girl fell to the ground as the two bullets tore through their young flesh, ripping away the last shreds of their innocent lives; murdered in cold blood. The killings were senseless. Ironically, Katya was a beautiful, young Catholic woman, punished for doing the right thing. She risked her own life for harboring Jews, and was deemed to be guilty for demonstrating kindness. How would killing her help the Nazi's plan to eliminate the Jews from the earth? She wasn't Jewish. But she didn't obey.

The traumatized tension thickened among the lineup of women and children after hearing the shots of the merciless killings, as they stood facing the creek, trembling and silenced in horror. Suddenly, there was an increasing rumble, a sound of distant engines, coming towards them from the direction of the camp. Seconds later, two military transport trucks were riding down the hill towards the stream.

Zosia turned around to see two Nazi trucks, armed with four SS uniformed men inside. She watched as both trucks stopped on the grassy knoll, strategically parking next to each other in front of a row of pine trees. The trucks kept a distance of several yards while having a clear view of the line-up standing at the creek. For some reason, the men didn't get out of the trucks right away. They sat there and waited. In each truck, two men were in the front seats and two in the back. They were there to carry out the mass executions.

After several minutes, Zosia was curious as to why the delay. She was eager to complete the planned execution. She dared move forward, careful to proceed with caution and not to show any disrespect to her superiors. She walked towards one parked truck, noticing the two SS-men sitting in the front with machine guns slung over their shoulders and engaged in light-hearted conversation. As soon as she tapped on the side windshield and interrupted the men, their banter stopped while their faces turned the color of gray, industrial steel. Zosia feared she may have stepped over the line as she gestured for the him to roll down the window. She witnessed the name, Otto Stuttgarter on his uniform. Forcing her words through tightly clenched teeth, she asked impatiently, "Sorry to interrupt. We have followed the orders explicitly. As you can see, they are lined up at the stream. When will you be ready? When should I start moving them closer in towards the ravine? We really can't be keeping them there too long. It might get too messy. We have already had to kill two of them. Please hurry up, as I am waiting for your signal to move them," Zosia implored as she hastily walked back down the hill towards the creek. Stuttgarter yelled out, "Move them to the ravine immediately!"

At that moment, SS Officer Otto Shuttgarter, Alek Chamatsky's contact at Belzec, sat patiently in the passenger seat. He was being bribed, paid by Alek's sister, Dr. Henrietta Charmatsky. Otto Shuttgarter was on the mission to remove Danika Rosenberg from the firing squad, before safely bringing her to another camp. In a flash, he yanked open the passenger door, quickly jumped out of the truck, and raced down the hill stopping in front of Zosia. He faced her head-on, exhibiting the same determined look of a prizefighter about to start the match with his opponent. In a swift motion, he reached into his back pocket and pulled out a paper. The official Nazi insignia in the left corner, as a beacon of early morning sunlight, illuminated the document.

Before Zosia responded, her thick-skinned eyes turned into slits, squinting against the glare of his document. She began to growl like an injured animal, forgetting her place as a guard speaking to a superior. "What is the meaning of this? What is this document? What do you want to do? Why are you blocking it? Move away from here. Go back to the truck. Set up the guns and let's get started." Otto responded confidently, "This is an official document that we are obliged to follow. One of the women in the line-up will be released to my custody. She will be taken to another camp."

Otto Shuttgarter whipped around to face the backs of the women, children and babies before walking briskly towards them. "Attention, Rosenberg!" he yelled. "Danika Rosenberg! Move quickly out of the line! Turn around and follow me!" Danika froze. She couldn't believe her ears. Yet, she took the risk. It was worth it. What did she have to lose? Her life? She'd probably be killed in the next minute anyway. Mustering up all strength and courage within her, expecting the bullets to hit at any second, she forced herself and Josef to step backwards out of the line. Still petrified to turn around, clutching desperately onto Josef's shoulders with both hands, she dared to take several steps backwards, still facing the stream. She and Josef waited, both glued in place, afraid to breathe, as the sounds of the SS-man shouts came closer.

"Danika Rosenberg! Come with me now! I need you for more work at the factory! As he leaned in closer to her ear, careful not to let his actions be noticed, and in a quick and lowest, possible whisper he could manage, said, "You are spared for today. Your husband is responsible for saving you. Ask no questions. Act like I am not talking to you. Look straight ahead. Now, turn around and send the boy back to the line, and quickly follow behind me."

Still holding tight to Josef's shoulders, she turned to face him and began to move behind him. He turned around to her, saying, "He can't come. Children must be killed, sentenced to die, without exception. Move along! We don't have all day!" Like someone just pressed an engine's off button, Danika stopped following him. She planted her feet on the ground, her heart no longer pumping, her life was bleeding out. Shocked, he turned around and warned, "Are you completely crazy? Have you lost your mind? I'm saving your life! What are you thinking? You either come now or go back to the line! You are a lunatic! Who wouldn't take such an offer?"

Suddenly, Danika made her decision. She felt saved, as if a cool, peaceful breeze of courage purposely blew by, enough to calm her fears. As thick, hot tears began to cover her cheeks, her voice barely audible, she managed to answer, "I will never go anywhere without my child! There is no life for me without him. I choose death. Please write a note to Samuel and tell him to always remember me and to remember Josef. I want him to know that we love him now and we will love him eternally. If he survives this hell, tell him to light a candle for us, because from wherever he may be, we will always feel his love." With Josef sobbing softly beneath the firm grasp of her loving hands on his tiny shoulders, she turned back. They headed towards the line, resigned to face their deaths.

Shuttgarter ran back to the truck, jumped in, and sat back in the passenger seat. The other seven SS-men were already stationed in a horizontal line, machine guns positioned in place, aimed directly at the line-up, ready and waiting to release the barrage of bullets. For some reason, Stuttgarter decided not to take part of the firing squad. Was it guilt? Did he actually have a conscience, or was he emotionally affected by the Danika's decision to choose death? Was he moved by her heartfelt words towards her husband? One thing for sure, he already knew that he would write the note to Samuel, at least to carry out Danika's request. It was the least he could do for the money and the vodka.

Shuttgarter remained in the truck covering his ears in an attempt to lessen the onslaught of the machine gun blasts he knew were coming. He looked down at the floor and heard the order, "Fire!" As the word "fire" echoed through the forest, a torrent of flying bullets bored holes, tearing the flesh of innocent women and children. Suddenly a thought he had heard during a church sermon came to mind. "We must all remember that the sun dries all garments without prejudice; no matter what religion, no matter whether people are rich or poor. It is the same for all of us. The most important right we have as human beings is the right to be free." His eyes misted over as he quickly brushed the moisture away with his sleeve, hoping that nobody noticed, especially his comrades.

As the tinny smell of fresh blood began seeping into the soil along the edges of the ravine, it marked its territory like the spill of red ink on parchment paper. The women and children's lives were snuffed out, like two wet fingers extinguishing a candle. Their lives ended ruthlessly, all because of their faith. Their only crime was that they were born Jewish. As a deafening silence blanketed the forest, there were no more sounds of babies crying, no more sobbing or screams. They were all silenced. All that remained that night was the putrid stench of evil.

God is closest to those with broken hearts. - Jewish Proverb

Guilt Ridden

Later that night, still in the throes of a drunken stupor, Commander Otto Stuttgarter lay in the dark unable to sleep. He and his Nazi comrades had been celebrating the accomplished massacre of the women and children at the ravine. It was predictable that his insomnia was the result of the night of heavy drinking. But it was his guilty conscience that bothered him more. Oddly enough, as far back as Stuttgarter could remember, this was the only time a guilty conscience affected him. This time it felt different, like being trapped by a heavy boulder lying on his chest. Last night he was just pretending to be celebrating with his buddies, but he'd never felt this way before; he had never felt remorse for doing bad things. As he lay there, he felt nauseous and disgusted by his role in inhumane tragedy that took place under the light of the moon at the ravine. Unfortunately, it was too late. There was no going back. He did what he did; even though only an accomplice to the killings, it didn't matter. The pain was unbearable. The torment of deafening shots, the sounds of the slain women and children falling to the cold ground would ring in his ears forever.

All at once, as if a heavy, dense fog lifted away from his obstructed vision of the world, Otto realized that he no longer wanted to be like his Nazi comrades. They were young men like him. They were friends. How could he have liked and respected them? They had pledged their loyalty to the Nazi cause, truly believing that Jews were responsible for all the ills of society. These were his friends who turned away from morality and who readily metamorphosized into cold-blooded psychopaths. They felt no remorse after the execution of such unspeakable acts of violence. How could he have been so blind? They worshipped their own bigotry and prejudice, misdirected men who kept justifying their despicable actions against the Jews. How was he not aware of how

184

they kept deluding themselves, thinking they would be absolved for any wrong-doings by merely attending church on Sunday, or going to confession with the priest? They believed it was their obligation to remain loyal to the Nazi party and to their country to get rid of the Jews once and for all.

Stuttgarter's self-reproach was creating a culpability in his mind; one he didn't recognize. He felt deflated, disappointed about his failed mission; not being able to save Danika nor her child. Overwhelming guilt was a powerful force in its wake. He was now on his own mission, to at least carry out Danika's last dying request. How could he think otherwise? Just before falling into a deep sleep, Otto muttered re-assurances to himself: It's not my fault entirely. The Nazi laws are very clear. No children could be left alive. Killing those women and children isn't my edict. I blame Hitler and the Nazi party! I am just following orders. So, according to plan, tomorrow at noon, I will meet Charmatsky at Barracks #1, at the back of the west guardhouse where I was supposed to bring Danika. I will keep my promise to her. I will write down Danika's last spoken words before she chose to sacrifice her own life, taking her son with her. I will give Charmatsky the note to give to her husband, Samuel. It's the least I can do. Maybe it will lessen this gnawing guilt that keeps squeezing my chest, making it hard for me to breath easily. I wonder if I even deserve to live anymore.

Early the next morning, Otto awoke to the annoying buzz of the alarm clock on the bedside table. The maddening noise worsened his blasting headache and he winced as he turned over to stop the alarm from blaring. When he tried to swallow, his dry tongue felt as if it was covered with particles of sand from a sun-parched desert. Despite the discomfort of a severe hangover, Otto managed to sit up and take a drink from the glass of tepid water balanced on the antique bedside table. As if drinking a few sips of the water might serve as a tincture to help clear his mind, Stuttgarter knew

185

he had to prove to himself that he was different from his comrades; that he was a man who still had a sense of human decency. He was a man who had a conscience, a heart that knew it was evil to kill anyone at all; no less to kill innocent people; even if they were Jews.

With the back of his hand, Otto swatted away the long, unruly strands of black hair parked in front of his eyes, wedging them behind his left ear. Then he stood up and leaped around the side chair that was buried under last night's uniform hanging over the back. He made his way towards the large mahogany desk against the wall. He carefully pulled open the heavy desk drawer, managed to find a sheet of paper, then rummaged further to find a pencil. He wanted to finish the promise he made to himself, to fulfill Danika's request. He would write the note and try his best to convey Danika's message to her husband, Samuel. First thing in the morning he would give it to Charmatsky.

Arriving promptly at 8:00 am, Charmatsky parked his jeep at the guard station at Barracks Camp #1. As he walked around to the back of the west guardhouse, he spotted Stuttgarter sitting on the bench without Danika and Josef. Immediately, he assumed there was a complication. While walking briskly towards Stuttgarter, he mumbled to himself. Without saying hello, Charmatsky began to question Stuttgarter gruffly. "Why are you late? What happened? Where are they? How could you screw this up? This is not acceptable! Have they been killed?"

Before Stuttgarter could reply, they were noticed by SS-officer Ludvig Sherman who came jogging over, stopping directly in front of them. Sherman sported a mischievous smirk and gestured a dramatic Heil Hitler salute. "Hey comrades, what's happening here?" he asked. "Officer Charmatsky, weren't you reassigned back to the Janowska camp? Why are you here today? Are you transferred back here permanently, or do you have some secret business going on?

Hmmm? Is there a problem we should all know about?" A long pregnant pause hung in the already tense air, making it hard for both Charmatsky and Stuttgarter to breathe. They were afraid of being caught in a lie; a deception of any kind. If so, there would be serious consequences to pay.

Charmatsky thought quickly, making sure to act non-plussed. He smiled casually, attempting to hide the truth behind his poker face. With the look of a professional card shark, he responded, "Yawol, comrade! I left my shaving kit here and am asking my comrade if he has seen it anywhere." Thinking on his feet, he put his hand to his face and added convincingly, "Why, look at my beard stubble! I haven't shaved for several days! I am beginning to look like a filthy beggar, or a dirty Jew for that matter!" With his fast-thinking and clever response, the tension among them lessoned and together they shared a contagious, hearty laugh.

"Okay then! If I see your shaving kit, I'll be happy to use it on the next dirty Jew I see who might need a clean shave! Especially the ones under those long black robes with the heavy, large fur-trimmed hats! If you know what I mean, that is!" he said jokingly. Just then, Sherman turned around and began to walk back to the front of the guardhouse. Turning his head to face them he shouted, "Hey! Hope you are telling me the truth about the shaving kit! Hope there is no funny business going on! You know, there is a rumor going around that some officers have been disloyal to the party. Some are even willing to take bribes! Would you believe such a thing? What fools they are to risk their own lives! We wouldn't want to find out that you would be among them, would we?" he remarked as he turned the corner, chuckling loud enough so that they could hear.

Swathed in a blanket of fear, they sat on the bench with wide eyes, staring at each other for several moments. Both Charmatsky and Stuttgarter stood up. With a sigh of relief Stuttgarter said, "Look Charmatsky, I have to go. There's no time to explain further. All I can say is that Danika Rosenberg wouldn't come with me. I tried to convince her. Of course, I couldn't take the boy. She wouldn't leave her son behind. Instead she chose to die along with him as well as all the others. But, I have something very important to give to you." Otto Stuttgarter reached into his back pocket and pulled out a small paper folded into the shape of a rectangle. He shoved it toward Charmantsky and said insistently, "Here, take this note. Danika told me what to write. Give it to her husband, Samuel Rosenberg. My mission is done here. Now give me the money you owe me. You can deliver the vodka to my barracks later."

Charmatsky was visibly shaken. He was shocked by Danika's decision to die along with her young son. There was no time to delay any further. Sherman's comments made him nervous. He had to hurry and leave the Belzec camp. In a swift motion, he took the note and shoved it inside the breast pocket of his uniform. The payment for the bribe was readily available, located conveniently in his wallet in his back pocket. He retrieved the money and handed it to Stuttgarter. Both men gestured a "Heil Hitler" salute and hurried back to their respective posts. Stuttgarter resumed his daily patrol of the de-lousing area at Belzec's Camp Barracks #1. Charmatsky was already in his jeep driving away, headed back to the Janowska labor camp to find Samuel.

Know that every human being must cross a very narrow bridge. What is most important is not to be overcome by fear. -Rebbe Nachman of Bratslav

A Failed Mission

When Charmatsky returned to the Janowska camp that afternoon, he felt a sense of urgency to complete his part of the bargain. He had to tell Samuel about the aborted mission at Belzec and the horrific news; the senseless tragedy of what happened to his beloved Danika and Josef. He planned how he would choose his words carefully and explain what happened in the most tactful manner. Then he would wait for him to calm a bit and watch to see how he handled the devastating news before giving him Stuttgarter's note, Danika's message to him.

Charmatsky felt tortured as he drove. How could he allow himself to make peace with such disaster? Things were getting out of control, going against the grain of humanity. Jews were being slaughtered like cattle and he kept thinking how utterly remarkable it was that ordinary citizens joined in on this catastrophic disaster against the Jews. He was embarrassed to be one of them and his heart was no longer drawn to the Nazi regime.

It was late afternoon when Charmatsky parked his truck and entered the carpentry factory, hoping to find Samuel. In these times, there was always the nagging doubt that Samuel might not only not be present at his work post, but might be gone permanently. Charmatsky knew that the situation in the Janowska labor camp was becoming more and more dangerous. There were frequent reports about prisoners who had started their day at work and then would suddenly disappear, never to be seen again. Nobody knew for sure what happened to them. Consequently, everyone suspected they must have been taken away to another camp, or eventually killed in a concentration camp.

Upon entering the factory, Charmatsky routinely gestured a Nazi salute to the two guards at the entrance door. He straightened his spine, taking on a corrective stance of his posture and assumed the authoritative air; the haughty look of a Nazi commandant pretending to be there on official business. Fervently, he began to scan the large room trying to spot Samuel; hoping he was not too late. Fortunately, within seconds, he noticed Samuel hunched over the work table, using a lathe to whittle and smooth out the rectangles of a large wood chunk in order to form a hammer handle.

Charmatsky bent down close to Samuel's ear and said in a low, discreet tone, "Rosenberg, just listen. I have news." Samuel looked up with a slight, hopeful smile. When he saw Charmatsky's grave expression, he knew something was wrong. "What is it? I'm afraid to hear…but tell me anyway," Samuel whispered in a hoarse voice, fingers trembling uncontrollably. He was cautiously fearful of the news. Gently, he released his hold on the lathe and turned it off before placing it down quietly onto the metal table.

Charmatsky took a deep breath, looked around to see who was watching, and continued. "Rosenberg, brace yourself for what I'm about to say. We found them. As we suspected, Danika and Josef were in fact prisoners at Belzec. When my contact, Otto Stuttgarter, got to them, both were already standing in a line-up of women, children and babies waiting to be shot by a firing squad. Just in time, he called for Danika to come away from the line and go with him. Sadly, he could not make that same offer for Josef. Saving children is prohibited. There are no exceptions. Unfortunately, Danika was adamant. She absolutely refused to leave without her son. I'm told she held onto him tightly the whole time she spoke. Before she went back to the line, she begged my contact to write down what she wanted you to know before they died. He wrote down exactly what she said. I have the note here in my hands. Read it only when you get back to the barracks tonight."

When he was finished speaking, Charmatsky stood up brusquely. He straightened his back upright, promptly readjusting the jacket of his Nazi uniform, pulling down each sleeve to level against his wrists. All the while his eyes darted back and forth, making sure to avoid suspicion. Then, making sure no one was watching, without missing a beat, he dropped the folded note on the floor, landing it strategically next to Samuel's left boot. With one swift, almost undetectable motion of an accomplished magician, Samuel picked it up and shoved the note deep into his boot. Without further comment, Charmatsky turned to walk away while searching the guards' faces; making sure that he had not raised any unwanted attention. As he left the factory, he thought about what he would say if any superior officer might question what he was doing. He decided he'd say that he was remarking on the progress of a prisoner's work. As he left the factory, Charmatsky bent down to wipe the sawdust off his own boot.

Slowly drowning in his own sea of despair, Samuel hung his head low; feeling grief pounding furiously at his heart. Careful to avoid attracting undue attention, he picked up the lathe and turned it on to resume his work, as if nothing had changed in his life. Nevertheless, Samuel was unable to stop the steady swell of giant tears clouding his eyes and streaming downward. Like the steady flow of a rain-shower, the unstoppable pitter-patter of droplets was falling onto the metal table, slowly creating tiny pools of sorrow. While his hands were able to brush away the watery droplets, there was no way he could brush away the misery of his shattered heart. He knew it could never heal. The folded note in his book was like the constant discomfort of a pebble in a shoe. It was an unwelcome messenger relentlessly rapping on the other side of the door, impatiently waiting to deliver the most devastating news.

Several days passed before Samuel could bring himself to read Danika's note. When he finally read it, the devastation was too much to bear. The folded piece of paper that held his loving wife's last words was his only remaining connection to her. He memorized every word and he pledged to keep her letter with him for as long as he lived. Every night in the barracks while crying himself to sleep, Sam never stopped asking God, "How is it that I am spared? How come you are allowing me to live without the rest of my family? Why am I left, made to live in this human torture? It should have been me instead of them. They were cheated, robbed of their young lives way too soon."

Samuel pleaded for a signal, an explanation. He waited and begged for God to send him a sign, some logical reason for him to grasp, to make sense of it all. No sign ever came. No resolution could ever quell his tortured soul, nor satisfy the unanswerable questions that only God could answer. Yet, Samuel was actually grateful for the numbness, the inability to feel anything. For self-preservation, the severe blow of losing his wife and child were buried away deep in his soul. Every day was monotonous, his motions robotic; he woke up, dressed, wolfed down the sparse amount of tasteless food just to stay alive, all before going to work long, grueling hours at the factory.

It was early morning in late November when flashes of light flickered on the horizon, heralding the unfolding of a new dawn. The sunrise sent rays of penetrating warmth to chase away the cold and darkness of the night air. Within minutes there was a gradual illumination of the dismal campgrounds. It was soon blanketed with a yellowish-gray transparent haze, a film-like quality similar to the pallor of an abandoned graveyard. Feathery beams of sunlight began reaching inward, penetrating through the cracked crevices within the barrack's walls. As if intent on awakening the sleeping men, a beam of sunlight like a long, thin finger lightly tapped Samuel, and he opened his eyes.

Most of the trees were already barren, yet some were left with a few surviving leaves that were left to die on the branch. Other leaves were left waiting, slowly withering from a lack of water until it was their turn to fall. For so many prisoners, life seemed to be waning with each passing day. Heart-broken to the core, Samuel lay very still on his bunk, listening to the outside rustling of leaves on the trees. The remaining leaves clung and swayed back and forth, fighting to maintain their place on the home branch. While the morning wind tried to dislodge each leaf, the fallen leaves were waiting to decompose back into the earth as if they never before existed. Samuel thought, "We are all like autumn leaves, fighting to hang on to our lives. Aren't we just like the last of the leaves, desperately left to hang onto a branch on the tree of life? Perhaps we are worse off than the leaves because many of our branches have been cut away; our loved ones, our families lost. We have nothing left to hold on to anymore, we can only hold on to ourselves."

Suddenly, Samuel's thoughts shifted, as a new positivity began to push aside his sadness. "We do have something more powerful than the stability of the trees. We have our human spirit; a constant source of strength we can tap into, and it can serve us. It can be our stronghold, something to hold on to! Our faith and hope can become powerful branches on which we can rest our souls." Energized by his positive thoughts, Samuel sat up while rubbing the sleep from his eyes. He thought: Maybe if I can change the way I see a problem, I can find a way to change my perceived reality. It was Hillel who said, "We do not see the world as it is, for the world is as we see it."

If the mountain was smooth, you wouldn't be able to climb it. –Anonymous

A Talented Singer

It was early December 1942. Louisa continued to spend the afternoon hours at the sewing factory, keeping her mind occupied by her favorite pastime, singing songs. Throughout her life, everyone she knew she was a talented singer. Since she was a mere child, she was a singer; always entertaining her family and friends with an exceptional voice. Louisa's parents were proud of her, urging her to entertain family and friends whenever an opportunity arose. Every Sabbath, she visited her grandparents and delighted them by singing their favorite songs.

During the afternoon shift at the sewing factory, Louisa would sing songs while working on her machine. She sang a variety of her favorite current day and old folk Polish, Russian, German, French, and Yiddish songs. She sang songs from when she was a free woman, when the world seemed normal and familiar. Her coworkers in the sewing factory always made requests. It was their only entertainment of the day. Music was the common language among them, their human senses deeply entangled with memories of the past, bringing about a gentleness and thoughts of a better time.

Louisa was exceptionally talented. Whenever she heard a melody and lyrics of a song, she could sing it again acapella without a glitch. Her voice was so captivating, even the stern-faced guards enjoyed the entertainment. They never once cautioned her to stop singing. In fact, they often encouraged her to sing, as they loved to listen to the voice that melted their hateful expressions, making them sway to the music that filled the sewing room. It didn't take long before word spread around the camp about Louisa's natural aptitude for entertainment. There was no need for a radio when she was there. Many of the officers and guards heard how

194

she was always singing at the factory during the day, and for her bunk mates in the barracks at night.

One afternoon something happened, a turning point in her life of captivity. While walking towards the sewing factory ready to begin her work day, Louisa's arm was yanked gruffly, pulling her away from the rest of the queue. A guard named Matylda Kassenhoff, a tall, young woman with long, silky blonde hair and square shoulders, turned Louisa around and stopped her abruptly. Taken aback, Louisa stood in shock while her heart clamored in her chest. She was feared that she was being punished for something she might have done. Was it her habitual singing? She couldn't imagine what she did to draw unwarranted attention to herself. Was it because she was meeting Samuel every evening outside of her barracks? Did someone report them? When Samuel and Louisa would meet in the early evening at the back of her bunk, she always sang a romantic song to him before kissing goodnight. She chose songs that stirred emotions of past memories and offered a glimmer of hope for the future.

As the rest of the line of prisoners entered the sewing factory to begin their work, Louisa and guard Kassenhoff remained outside the entrance, still facing each other, like in a standoff before a fight. Kassenhoff leaned down close to Louisa's ear and whispered loudly, "Pay attention to my instructions. I have been contacted by a Nazi officer who has heard of your singing talents and he wants you to sing at his engagement party celebration. After tonight's evening meal, I will come to your barracks and bring you to the Nazi official's house for a few hours, then I will bring you back. The guard in your barracks has already been informed. When your bunk mates notice that you are gone, they will ask you tomorrow about what happened to you. Tell them you were chosen to sing for an engagement celebration. Tonight, you will sing famous torch songs and then you will take requests from the audience. You will be accompanied by a pianist; a

Jew from another camp who was a well-known concert musician before he was taken prisoner. Do you understand my orders? In preparation for tonight, practice your voice and review the melodies and lyrics for as many songs as you can remember. Be ready when I come for you." Satisfied with her instructions, Kassenhoff stood up and didn't wait for Louisa's answer before nudging her side rib, indicating that she go inside and return to her post at the sewing machine. As soon as Louisa was inside, she quickly turned around to see that Kassenhoff was already gone.

As Louisa sat at her sewing machine that afternoon, her mind raced; thinking about Kassenhoff's instructions. She wasn't sure what to think. Should she be happy about her dream to perform for an audience, or should she be very concerned for her safety? How could she trust any Nazi guard? Was this some kind of set up, a plan to take her away from the camp? Maybe she was going to be assigned to be a sex slave to service the Nazi thugs, a common occurrence these days. Maybe they would make her sing first and then dispose of her altogether? Louisa was absolutely terrified.

Suddenly, one of the factory guards yelled, "Hey songbird, sing us an Edith Piaf song, the one you sang us yesterday!" Louisa turned around to spot the short and stocky, unsmiling German guard who made the request. Louisa responded, "Of course, she's one of my favorites!" Without delay, Louisa began to sing La Julie Jolie passionately, tapping into her best voice. Although her mind was seriously doubting the safety of that evening's plan, she was able to sing the poignant, heartbreak song with great feeling. While she sang, she imagined that her own life might be like the short life of a once beautiful, withering rose; close to wilting away before ever fully blossoming.

That evening at Louisa's barracks, Kassenhoff waited impatiently. As she paced back and forth she took long, deep inhales of her unfiltered cigarette, releasing slow smoke rings into the air. As soon as she noticed the queue of prisoners being ushered back after a long work day, she flipped the cigarette to the ground and stomped on it furiously, as if to put out a serious flame. Making herself known to the guard leading the line, in a resonantly confident voice, she yelled, "Louisa Drimmer, it's time to go. Move out of the line. Come over here and walk with me!" The sound of the guard's voice prickled her skin and as she stepped out of line her throat went dry. She was terrified and took a deep breath in attempt to calm her frantic heartbeat. Louisa stood alongside Kassenhoff, and together they began their walk towards the camp entrance.

As Louisa nervously walked, she tried to prevent her boots from being sucked into the muddy ground. Her thoughts drifted to Samuel, and she was upset that there was no way to contact him to explain why she wouldn't be meeting him that night. She knew he would be fraught with worry. As soon as they passed through the gates, Kassenhoff signaled a "Heil Hitler" salute to the two front guards and smiled smugly. Both guards nodded, returning a knowing look. It seemed they were aware of the evening plan.

When they arrived at the gates, a young man wearing a beret was leaned up against a jeep while smoking a cigarette and staring up at the moon. When he saw the guard escorting Louisa, he gestured for them to get into the vehicle. As they drove away from the camp, no one in the jeep uttered a sound. The young driver and Kassenhoff sat in the front seats while Louisa sat in the back. Twenty minutes later, they pulled up to park in front of a decorative eight-foot iron fence with a gate. Behind the fence was an ivy-covered, three-story wood and stucco chalet. The home was appointed with a medieval-style, high-arched front door. The property was surrounded with well-manicured trees and bushes leading up to a stone walkway. Louisa sat looking out of the window, glancing upwards to see six octagon-shaped windows on the left side of the chalet before noticing

197

the silhouette of a tall, slim man peering down at the jeep through one of the upstairs windows.

"Stay put, everyone," ordered Kassenhoff. "Someone will come to escort us into the house through the back door. Inside, there are clothes for you to change into for your torch song performance," she chuckled sarcastically. Within moments, the same elegantly dressed tall, young man Louisa had noticed in the upstairs window appeared. He was wearing a black tuxedo with a red bowtie and a meticulously pressed white shirt. After coming out of the massive entrance door, he walked down the steps and made his way over to the stone walkway to greet them. As soon as Louisa saw his face, she was shocked. Her face paled. Was it really him? She blinked several times, trying to make sure it wasn't her imagination. She couldn't believe her eyes. Was this happenstance, a strange coincidence? These days, she doubted everything, but how could she be mistaken? Her breathing became shallow and her heart pounded relentlessly against her ribcage.

Demonstrating the class of a refined gentleman, he opened the jeep's back door and while smiling broadly, offered his gloved hand to Louisa as if he were handling precious crystal. The kindness of his gesture suggested that he might have been expecting her. As soon as their eyes met, he winked appreciatively through a half-smile. Now she knew for certain; it was him. How could she ever forget the familiar wink? It was his trademark; the language they shared without words. A hopeful realization came over her that maybe he would be able to save her life once more.

No. No... that isn't true. Don't let them have that victory...
Don't you dare! -Vesper Stamper

What a Surprise

Louisa felt as if she was under a spell as she watched Wladek Manheim's loving face. She was unable to break the connection between them. It was the same handsome young man who left her alone in the bedroom on the night of the Aktion in her hometown. She would never forget that nightmare, forever etched in her mind; the dreadful night that her family was marched down the stairs and taken away. After that, they were never heard from nor seen again. For some strange reason, this same young man always seemed to show up for her at the last moment, like a brave fireman facing danger at the scene of a blazing fire. She was perplexed, thinking: But why is he here, at this house? Is he somehow related to the guard, Matylda Kassenhoff? Could it be that he is an invited guest to the engagement celebration? It is the strangest coincidence. Does he know I am here to sing this particular evening? If so, why would he be greeting us here at the jeep? Could he have something to do with why I am singing here tonight?

Manheim released Louisa's hand quickly, hoping his chivalrous behavior was appropriate, as he sought to disguise his true feelings towards her. While his blue eyes released cupid arrows into the vast greenness of her eyes, he admonished, "We must all run along now. They are all waiting in the main parlor. They will most definitely wonder to where I have disappeared. Follow me inside. Be careful as you walk, the stone walkway is somewhat uneven. Oh, and... I must say, as they say in show business, Louisa, 'break a leg' tonight!"

The driver remained in the parked jeep while the three of them entered the impressive looking home. The massive entry foyer had cathedral ceilings with long walls appointed with

199

illuminated oil painting portraits showcased in gilded frames. As they made their way into a larger room, Louisa could hear the merriment of many voices coming from the next room. There must have been at least thirty people in the parlor when the three of them entered. While standing in the door-way, Louisa scanned the room with her eyes. The parlor was decorated with colorful tapestries, mahogany furniture with tufted velvet upholstery, and several antique tables. The ta-bles were topped with crystal vases filled with fresh lilies, permeating the evening air with their captivating scent. The room maintained the exquisite motif expressly designed for a wealthy home. With a fleeting glance, Louisa noticed the black Steinway piano diagonally situated in the corner by an octagon-shaped window. Already seated at the piano bench was a stern-faced young man dressed in full Nazi regalia. He seemed preoccupied while sipping a cognac-colored drink and he barely noticed them enter the room.

Kassenhoff gestured a customary "Heil Hitler" after nod-ding cordially in the direction of the piano player. She in-formed him of their plan. "The singer will begin as soon as she has changed into an appropriate gown, perfectly suited for this performance. I will bring her back in a few minutes." Then she pointed towards an adjacent room and said to Louisa, "Follow me, now. It will be like magic. For a few minutes you will be transformed; outfitted into an authentic torch song performer."

The female guard led Louisa into a bedroom to stand in front of a large canopy bed draped with a hand-knitted, cream-colored afghan. On the bench in front of the bed was an open trunk filled with theatrical accessories: blonde wigs, colorful boas, pairs of long white gloves, jeweled evening bags, faux jewelry pieces, and various other luxurious items. Kassenhoff went over to the side wall flanked with an arched wooden credenza. She pulled open the double doors to re-veal several glamorous gowns hanging inside. Placed neatly on the floor, side by side, were the same number of high heeled satin shoes dyed to match the colors of each hanging gown.

Kassenhoff ordered, "First, you will select a gown of your choosing and a pair of matching shoes. Then you will sit down at the vanity table and I will put on your makeup and a long blond-haired wig. Now, take off your clothes and sit down here on the vanity chair." Skillfully, she applied the eyeshadow and cream mascara like a professional makeup artist. She pulled the wig to fit over Louisa's head and re-adjusted the sides to hang naturally. The long, silky blonde hair framed her face beautifully and rested alluringly on her creamy white shoulders. As Louisa glanced in the framed oval mirror on the vanity table, she was stunned by her re-flection. For a moment, she almost didn't recognize the woman in the mirror. She looked so elegant and her eyes glowed like sparkly green pools twinkling in the sunlight.

"Now hurry and step into the gown. Be very careful," Kas-senhoff warned as she helped Louisa to slink into a back-less, emerald green, tight-fitting taffeta gown. Louisa then slid her feet into a pair of high-heeled emerald green strappy satin sandals. As a finishing touch, Kassenhoff reached into the trunk and pulled out a long, black feathered boa and wrapped it around Louisa; balancing onto her bare shoul-ders. She stood back and examined Louisa's presence ap-praisingly and then she said, "Looks like we are ready, *frau-lein*. You look like a wealthy and fancy German young lady!" Kassenhoff snickered to herself, seemingly satisfied with her ability to change Louisa from prisoner rags to a woman of prominence, at least for a few hours.

Kassenhoff led Louisa back to the engagement party in the parlor, which was already bustling with guests eagerly waiting for the promised entertainment to begin. Louisa no-ticed waitresses dressed in short skirts, costumed with pris-tine white aprons tied in the back with large, perfect bows. Each waitress held a tray that contained a wide assortment

201

of delicacies. The waitresses mingled among guests who chatted amicably while balancing their cocktails in one hand and tasting food with the other. When Kassenhoff and Louisa entered the parlor, guests were engaged in light banter; some were laughing while others were standing around comfortably enjoying the festivities.

Louisa was led to take her place and stood next to the piano. The pianist was still seated on the bench, shuffling around the sheet music and getting ready to accompany her performance. Louisa felt like caged butterflies were flitting around inside her stomach, trying to get out. As she stood there, it occurred to her that she, too was in the same situation; trapped as the imaginary butterflies, wishing for a way out. Suddenly, a man's voice broke through the noisy frivolities. He clinked his wine glass with a spoon and with a serious face, requested the crowd's attention. He scouted the room with his eyes, making sure everyone had stopped talking and was ready to hear his announcement. He then declared, "Here, here, everyone! I want to make a toast to the newly engaged couple! Everyone, raise your glass to these two fine people. It's a beautiful thing to see young people fall in love, care for each other, and promise to always be faithful and true. I may add, we send good wishes to our brave, strong sons and sweet, beautiful daughters. May your sons grow up to be loyal to our Nazi cause! On behalf of our Fuhrer and the Third Reich, may your sons become devoted German soldiers! May we fight to end the war and become the supreme ruler of the world! Heil Hitler!" The room rose their glasses and cheered in unison. The man continued to speak. "The time has come for us all to congratulate my niece, Irena Kassenhoff, who is now officially engaged to SS officer Wladek Manheim! Let us say, 'Heil Hitler' and praise be for the Third Reich!" All at once, the previously silent room erupted into enthusiastic stamping of feet and boisterous applause as the engaged couple made their way to stand in front of the piano.

Louisa, already positioned to the right of the piano, was standing next to Waldheim. She was still in shock over seeing him again, and her head was swirling. She could smell the masculine fragrance of his tobacco and his vanilla-scented cologne. Louisa's throat constricted and she found it difficult to breath as she stood in front of the crowd. Frightful thoughts filtered through her mind as she silently worried: Why was I chosen to be here? How did Wladek know I was in the Janowska camp? Did he have anything to do with my being chosen to sing here tonight, no less at his engagement party? Are they planning to dispose of me afterwards, maybe send me away to another camp, possibly a death camp, when I am finished singing? Why am I feeling conflicted that Wladek is celebrating his engagement? What is wrong with me? He means nothing to me. Louisa took a deep breath and pulled herself together so she could focus. All that really mattered was her love for Samuel, and she vowed to let his love strengthen her. Louisa was going to sing from the bottom of her heart at the top of her lungs.

Just then, the male pianist turned to face Louisa and asked pleasantly, "What song are we starting with, *fraulein* Louisa?" She cleared her throat and asked, "Can someone please give me a glass of water?" Just then, the kind pianist waved his hand in the air, flinging his wrist, motioning to Kassenhoff to bring Louisa a glass of water. After drinking the entire contents in the glass of water, Louisa, prompted herself to remain composed so she could appear confident. "I'll start with *'La Julie Jolie* by Edith Piaf," she smiled. The pianist nodded, and then began playing the introduction. His hands moved expertly up and down the keyboard, the chords bittersweet and enticing. Suddenly, Louisa felt a surge of adrenalin and the lyrical quality of her voice enhanced. As she sang, she captivated the crowd; sending chills up and down their spines. Louisa had a way of reaching deep within and warming even the coldest hearts.

The evening passed with Louisa singing guest requests, many of which were popular Edith Piaf songs, such as: Je N'en Connais, Les Momes de la Cloche, La Java de Cezique, Mon Apero, La Danser, De L'autre Cote de La Rue, and Les Hiboux. At the end of her performance, Louisa was surprised and delighted by the enthusiastic and thundering applause. Some audience members were even screaming, "Brava! Brava! You must come back! What a fine voice! 'Wunderbar'!"

Immediately after the performance, Kassenhoff must have gotten her cue from someone who was watching. She whisked Louisa away from the piano and brought her back to the bedroom, urging her to change quickly. She pulled off her gown, removed the wig, kicked off her high-heeled sandals and left the fur boa on the bed. Moments later, Louisa wore her original camp garb in which she had arrived. Together, Kassenhoff and Louisa snaked their way down the back circular staircase, the party crowd growing louder and more boisterous by the minute. They passed through the servant's door and followed along the narrow stone path leading towards the front of the mansion to where the jeep was waiting. All the while Louisa felt a strange sense of relief, extremely grateful that the ordeal was over. The crowd obviously loved Louisa's singing, and she couldn't dispel the gnawing fear that they would demand more performances from her. She worried: What else will be required of me when and if there is a next time? Am I now beholden to the Nazis, to be used at their every whim? There is always a price to pay. Louisa could almost smell the primal scent of advancing danger in the cold Nazi air.

Kassenhoff took the passenger seat of the jeep and Louisa sat in the back. As soon as the driver was about to pull away from the curb, Louisa heard a familiar man's voice coming towards them from a near distance. She detected an urgency in his tone demanding their attention as he shouted emphatically. "Wait! Wait! Stop right now! Halt, I say! Do not pull away!" The driver obliged and stopped the vehicle. No one spoke. As the voice grew nearer, the three of them sat in wonderment while they waited. Louisa felt a chill, an icy tremor tearing up and down her spine as she began sorting out her thoughts: I knew it. This was exactly my fear. My days are numbered. The Nazis cannot be trusted. Kassenhoff knew about this plan all along! How could I let myself think she had anything but bad intentions? Most likely, I am going to be taken away immediately to some death camp. But what about my new love, Samuel? How can he survive another loss? Please God, save me from these wicked people!

Suddenly, the rear door where Louisa sat was yanked wide open. Wladek stood outside the car door breathing heavily, as if he had just finished running a 5-mile race. He drew a deep breath and managed to shout a firm command, "Oh no, you don't. Not so fast! You all will leave when I tell you to leave. Now, get out of the car, quickly! Your work is not finished here. Don't delay! Get out before I wrench you out of your seat. I have something more for you to do."

Louisa froze, wondering if she was hallucinating. Was Wladek really standing there? What did he want with them? Why wasn't he with his fiancé? Kassenhoff whipped her head around and spoke sternly. "Well, what are you waiting for, stupid girl? You heard him. Get out!" As Louisa quickly stepped out of the jeep, Wladek stepped closer and stopped to shut the door. Trembling with trepidation, Louisa couldn't imagine what was happening, and why did Wladek need to pull her from the jeep? Why was he acting like this? Were they all part of a set up? Did Kassenholf know this was going to happen? What about Wladek's fiancé? Was she aware of what he was doing? Didn't she wonder where he was going? The tension was thick in the air, making it difficult to breathe.

Wladek glanced over to see that Kassenhoff and the driver were facing forward. Quickly, he brushed his face across Louisa's cheek, stopping close to her ear. In an almost undetectable whisper he said discreetly, "Don't worry. From the very beginning, you must have known my unquenchable feelings for you. From the minute I laid eyes on you, you stole my heart. I have never once stopped thinking about you; your face, your eyes, the spell you have cast over me. All through the war, I've kept track of your camp assignments. Please believe me; I'm not like the others. You must trust me. I'm not a true Nazi. Be patient. I have a plan. I am going to help you."

Wladek opened the jeep door, sweeping his hand inward, cueing Louisa to get back into the jeep. Louisa's heart was flipped over, barely able to sustain the chaos she felt; the stirring of new, runaway emotions. Confused and bewildered, she obliged and got back into the jeep. As she sat there, she felt a light-headedness; a sense of floating, as if her body seemed to be separating from her mind. For the sole purpose of deceiving the others, Wladek deliberately shouted, "Okay. You heard the orders. You had better prepare yourself to sing your best, for you will be back here soon. Be aware that your life may depend on it!" Then, Wladek moved towards the passenger window. He knocked on the window hurriedly, anxious to get Kassenhoff's immediate attention. She quickly rolled down the window to hear him. "Kassenhoff, it is imperative that you listen carefully, he said sternly. Be mindful of my future plan. I just told the girl my explicit orders. Special singing talents cannot be wasted. She will return to sing here in two weeks. She will be the singer at my wedding. You are to bring her here, exactly as you have done this evening. My contact will inform you as to the date and time she needs to be here. Make sure she is ready. There will be no possible changes. You will abide by my orders. I'm sure my instructions are clear. Now, hurry up and get yourselves back to the camp." Without waiting for a response, he turned towards the stone walkway, casually strolling back towards to the house, whistling the "*The Blue*

Danube Waltz." His face showed a certain look of content-
ment, a prideful display, as if he had just accomplished a
most challenging task.

As the jeep pulled away from the curb and headed back
to the camp, they rode in uninterrupted quiet for at least
twenty minutes. Kassenhoff broke the silence when she
turned around to face Louisa and commented sarcastically,
"Well, Jew girl, looks like you've got yourself an official job
working for the Reich! Bet you always wanted to entertain
the Nazis. Maybe they'll make an exception for you, let you
stay alive as long as your voice holds out! Don't worry, my
unlucky *'fraulein'*, they'll eventually dispose of you like a
piece of trash, just like they do to all the other Jews when
they are done with them. Don't get too comfortable, girl. It's
all temporary. Not one person before you has been lucky
enough to survive. I wouldn't feel too confident if I were you."

Louisa tried desperately to make sense of Wladek's will-
ingness to help her. Was he really in love or just infatuated
with her? Was she so vulnerable as to believe the kindness
of his words? Isn't it said that kindness is a language that the
blind can see and the deaf can hear? She decided to believe
him. Despite the gravity of the situation, she couldn't help but
feel a strange sense of elation.

reatest mistake of all is to do nothing because you can only do little. -Sydney Smith

Where is Louisa?

The evening of the performance was the fourth night that Samuel and Louisa planned to meet secretly outside the barracks shortly after dinner. Samuel waited impatiently, kicking the same pebble around the barracks' back door, worrying: "Where is she? Why hasn't she shown up? It's been at least ten minutes. Did she change her mind about meeting me? I miss her radiant presence, the brightness of my life. The time I spend with her is the only joy left for me in this miserable existence. The moments we share are so beautiful; so precious, because we cannot keep them forever. Everything we have is only here for a brief moment. After losing my Josef and Danika, I know that for certain. Samuel picked up a handful of pebbles and started throwing them, one by one, into the neighboring field. He stood there throwing pebbles for a long time, watching each one disappear into the distance. He was trying desperately to expel his frustrations and control the angry ache of his yearning. As he watched the pebbles disappear into the darkening night, they were suddenly gone like the vast sands on a rocky beach, overpowered by one powerful wave.

Samuel's hopes faded with each moment and his mind swayed with more fears: Maybe Louisa is a tease, a frivolous type who is just biding her time with me, trying to fill a gaping hole in her life. After all, I really don't know her. But what am I thinking, what if she is in danger? Did one of the guards do something to her? I won't let myself think the worst. Maybe she's just not feeling well." His mind was running rampant in all directions.

Just as Samuel was about to give up and leave to return to his barracks, he heard someone call his name. He spotted a young woman's head poking half-way out past the back door of the barracks, holding it tightly against her chest; just in case she was forced to close the door quickly. She whispered loudly, "Samuel, wait! It is Monika, Louisa's friend. Listen carefully. Plans have changed. Louisa isn't here right now. She was assigned to sing tonight for some Nazi couple's engagement party. Don't worry. You'll probably see her tomorrow morning before work. Now, hurry back or else someone might see you here. We don't need any trouble!" A cold finger of fear and suspicion tore at his heart as he watched her move back inside; slowly and quietly closing the door behind her.

As Samuel lay on his cot, sleep eluded him that night. He stared through the arresting darkness and saw nothing but the emptiness of his existence. All he could think about was how his life changed so quickly. After hearing about Louisa being requested to sing for Nazis and not knowing where she was, his head pounded with worry: Where did they take her? Was the request to sing just a cover for something more devious? Will she be coming back? I pray she is safe! Immediately, Samuel realized it was a foolish idea to think that any of them would ever be safe while in the hands of the Nazis. He kept wondering why they picked her. Did one of the guards or officers take a special liking to her? Did they have impure motives to take advantage of her in some ugly, unthinkable way? Not only did Louisa have a beautiful voice, she was young and exceptionally pretty. Samuel couldn't stop the choking, obsessive thoughts. He was trapped in the tarnished prison of his own making, and he prayed that his fears were unwarranted. While intense anxiety kept him awake, he could not wait to see Louisa back safely at her post. Daylight couldn't come fast enough.

The next morning, Samuel awoke to the color of smothering grayness. Throughout the night, icy air blasted cold into the barracks and seeped into his aching bones. Chilling thoughts about Louisa kept flooding his mind. He couldn't wait to see her and make sure she was alright. Though tired and emotionally spent, Samuel felt thankful that it was almost time to get up and begin the next miserable day. He lay there for a few more minutes, listening to sounds of the morning shuffle; with bare feet scuffling across the wooden floor. Prisoners made their way towards the exit door, stopping at the excrement pail for the first pee of the workday.

As usual after roll call, Samuel and the other carpentry workers were led into the reception area to pick up their equipment before starting the workday. Samuel craned his neck upwards to look ahead of the queue, anxiously hoping to catch a first glimpse of Louisa. Finally, as the queue moved forward, Samuel felt an internal hot flash when he spotted the back of her dark hair. He noticing how her slim, seductive body was leaning forward to help someone remove a hammer from the toolbox. His heartbeat quickened with gratitude. Louisa was back, absconded and returned. She was safe! Louisa was also eager to spot Samuel. She happened to turn around to scan the queue and their eyes met. Thousands of silent words passed between them and it felt as if time stood still. Their emotional connection was strong, continuously building the truest realization of how much they both needed each other in order to survive.

When Samuel finally stood directly in front of Louisa, his soulful eyes brimmed with tears. "Thank God you are here! I'm so happy to see you, my sweet Louisa!" he whispered passionately. "You gave me such a scare when you didn't come out to meet me. All I care about is that you are back here safely. Tell me nobody has hurt you in any way. I wouldn't be able to stand it if you were disrespected in any way." Louisa turned her face to smile back at Samuel demurely, her loving eyes shining with kindness and understanding. She answered reassuringly, "Everything is alright, Samuel. I'm fine. Meet me tonight and I will tell you where I was and about the strangest thing that happened." Samuel couldn't stop staring at her and admiring her fresh vitality. He was captivated as he stood watching her speak, listening to

210

the encouraging tone, the penetrating sound of her voice, feeling the soothing softness and warmth of her words. He thought to himself: She could have read me a recipe and I would have felt the same way. Later on that evening, Louisa told Samuel all about her experience being a singer at the Nazi engagement party.

The next two weeks seemed to pass by quickly. During that time, Louisa was constantly singing while at the sewing machine and performing her songs every night for her bunk mates. Feeling jittery and extremely nervous, the day finally-arrived for Louisa to sing at Wladek's wedding. This time, Kassenhoff brought the dressing costume and incidentals in a suitcase with her to the barracks, along with eye makeup, red lipstick, and an array of accessories. This way, Louisa could be elegantly dressed when she arrived at the wedding ceremony. The dress was a bare shouldered, long and fitted red silk gown with a plunging neckline. She wore an over-sized black-sequined shawl trimmed with white fur, long matching gloves, and a tiara with twinkling multi-colored crystals. On her feet she wore matching red satin high-heeled shoes. Louisa looked more like a guest at the elegant wedding rather than a young woman who owned nothing but a marvelous singing talent; a gift far more valuable than dia-monds and jewels. Ironically, no one would ever know she was forced to live a life as a prisoner of the state in gut-wrenching conditions, never knowing if she would be al-lowed to live for one more day. After being fully attired in all the beautiful pieces of her costume, Louisa stood the middle of the dirty barracks floor. She began spinning around to im-agined music, like a toy ballerina pirouetting on a jewelry box. Louisa's bunk mates gasped in astonishment when they saw her. Their eyes sparkled and their mouths hung open at the vision of loveliness that stood before them; a welcome light amidst a backdrop of dust and gloom that cir-cled the air with every graceful, twirling movement.

It was one hour before the wedding reception that was scheduled to begin at 8:00 pm. The driver pulled up to a partially hidden side of the large ivy-covered, fifteenth-century white stone mansion. The long cobble-stoned pathway was flanked with elaborately sculpted shrubbery, framed with rows of fragrant eucalyptus trees. The long path sparkled with many small glass lanterns; each one appointed with a flickering candle. They stood elegantly, lighting the way down the path of the estate leading to the mansion.

The driver remained in the jeep while Kassenhoff proceeded to jump out quickly. She slammed the passenger door shut as a reminder to Louisa that she was solely in charge. In a gravelly voice she bellowed, "Raus! Hurry and get out of the jeep, prisoner! No one would believe you are the same person that you were several hours ago. Now look at you, don't forget that you are nothing but a Jewish whore with a measly singing talent. Don't get any bright ideas. Your only purpose here is to be a servant at this wedding. After you have performed, you will return to the barracks, back to your place; a worthless Jew prisoner of the state!" Kassenhoff put her face close to Louisa's face and continued to spew her ugly words. "Tonight you better sing like a nightingale. If you disappoint them, there will be hell for you to pay tomorrow! Actually, I'll see to it myself if I have to, you stupid Jew." Louisa wiped the guard's angry spit from her cheek, careful not to mess up her makeup.

Following Wladek's explicit instructions, Kassenhoff led Louisa down an adjacent path, paving their way between dense bushes. When they reached the servants' entrance in the back of the mansion, Kassenhoff pounded on the back door. A young housemaid of a similar age to Louisa answered the door. She wore a classic white uniform and a matching cap that topped her long, crimson locks of hair. She greeted them with a cordial nod, and as she smiled she revealed crooked, overlapping front teeth. The housemaid quickly ushered them up the majestic stairs of a gilded stair-case. As they continued up the stairs, Louisa dared to touch the sparkling gold of the hand-cast banister with her gloved fingers. As they walked through the entrance hall on route to the grand music room, Louisa was mesmerized by the high gothic arches framed with curved moldings ornately etched in Baroque décor. Palace-worthy chandeliers hung above them, shining brightly. Louisa stopped short for a second to admire the intricately carved oak paneled walls that climbed up to the ceiling. She eyed picturesque windows dressed in floor-length red velvet, collections of artifacts, and a show-case gallery of rich tapestries and famously large oil paint-ings.

Noticing Louisa's fascination, Kassenhoff sneered, "Hey 'dummkopf,' don't be gawking at the riches. That is some-thing you will never have and never know about. For sure you will be dead before that could ever happen. Don't forget that tonight you will be merely entertainment; nothing but a servant to the Third Reich! Keep on walking behind me and remember your place. Don't dally. We are almost there."

The grand music room's high-ceilinged walls were richly patterned in deep-set red wallpaper and offset with furnish-ings of dark mahogany with inlaid bronze detailing. Situated around the large room were three round side tables, each appointed with Baccarat crystal vases set on white lace doi-lies, abundantly filled with wedding bouquets of white tuber-oses, baby's breath, and stargazer lilies. The intoxicating scents perfumed the air. While captivated by the resplendent luxury of elegance and the regal feel of the grand music room, Louisa's eyes became transfixed on the luminescence of a silver candelabra resting splendidly on a grand Steinway piano, where twenty-five long tapered candles burned bril-liantly.

The second Louisa spotted the piano, she started to become undone. Gripped with a sudden tightness in her chest, she found herself at war with her nerves. All at once, she became distracted by the distant sounds of cheery voices and occasional laughter coming from the direction of the mansion's main staircase. The wedding guests were on their way to the grand music room. Louisa realized that there was no way out, and she was petrified. The soon-to-be festive scene was now about to become a reality. She was expected to perform like a professional singer; to sing for her life. Suddenly, she recalled something she read years ago in a children's fairy tale. "After all, every castle needs a princess." Louisa thought: Just for this evening, I'll pretend that I am that princess. This may be the most important night of my life. May the hand of fate wave its fairy wand and cast a spell, enshrouding me with just the right amount of luck to survive.

Life is not the way it's supposed to be. It's the way it is.
The way you cope with life makes all the difference.
–Anonymous

Praises for Louisa

Wladek was the son of a prominent businessman, Walter Waldheim; a loyal member of the Nazi party. He was a well-known man who wielded a great deal of influence in Third Reich affairs. Since the beginning of the war, Wladek had slowly risen to a position of command. As a teenager, he joined the Nazi youth and participated in multiple 'Aktions' taking place in and around Louisa's neighborhood in Borislow. Meeting Louisa during such a dire circumstance was a twisted finger of fate; one that would change his life, as well as hers.

The war marked its distinctions among the affluent, the working class, and the persecuted. Since luxuries were at a premium for most, the rich didn't seem to be affected by the food shortages in the slightest bit. By the looks of tonight's audience, dressed in their impeccable attire, the guests had little else to worry about but to luxuriate in the glorious wealth of the mansion. The well-healed socialites in attendance that evening seemed to be oblivious to the maelstrom evil happenings. They lived in extravagance while prisoners were trapped like animals, suffering terribly and living in inhumane conditions. All of that seemed so far away from the overflowing decadence of the evening.

Louisa sang even better than she had performed on the first night at the mansion. She captivated her audience with soulful songs that pulled at their heartstrings, meaningful lyrics that triggered personal memories of unrequited love and broken dreams of romance. People were filled with nostalgic feelings of days long gone. For several fleeting hours, Louisa was able to forget she was a slave, a Jewish prisoner of the state. Instead, she felt she was an equal, a free person like

215

all the other admiring guests in the grand music room. Throughout the duration of her performance, at least for one night, she felt like the mistress of the manor.

At the end of Louisa's captivating performance, she remained standing next to the piano. Relieved that it was over, she looked up at the group of more than one hundred invited guests, all standing next to their high-back chairs, clapping enthusiastically. Careful not to look directly at their faces, Louisa lowered her gaze to admire the luxuriant Persian rug beneath her red, sandaled shoes. As the applause began to wane, she took several modest but graceful bows. Satisfied with her performance, Louisa felt pleased with the choice of songs, especially with her decision to end with a German song of pride and hope. She couldn't help but think how ironic it was, that a Jewish prisoner like herself had transformed into an inspiring entertainer for an enemy that was capable of killing her at any moment.

The audience clapped, cheered and roared. "Brava, brava! Encore, encore!" shouted the Nazi dignitaries, wives and mistresses, family and friends of the wedding party. The guests were among prominent circles of affluent European society. Their presence was not only to celebrate the wedding, but an opportunity for them to gather together, cheering on the future successes of the Third Reich. While the guests settled back down in the comfort of their seats, Louisa remained next to the stand-up microphone adjacent to the piano. Feeling curious and afraid, she couldn't stop trembling. She was fearful as to what would happen to her now that the performance was over.

From the back of the room, Louisa heard a familiar voice. It was Wladek, swiftly approaching, making his path between the aisles and horizontal rows of seats. Handsomely clad in a splendid black tuxedo, he was moving forward in a long and purposeful stride, most assuredly, as if nothing could stop him. He finally stopped and stood next to Louisa. Almost immediately, while shooting her a half-smile, his eyes shining brightly, Wladek applauded her performance. "Wunderbar, wunderbar, fraulein! Your singing talent has captivated our hearts. You sing like the sweetest songbird! 'Danka, dankashein, fraulein.'"

Wladek reached across Louisa's shoulders, bringing the microphone closer to his mouth. "Ladies and gentlemen, I'm sure you have enjoyed this concert as much as I have. The choice of music and this fine performance was a fitting tribute to our special wedding celebration tonight." Looking squarely at Louisa he added, "Fraulein, we thank you for your fine talents. You have added greatly to the joyousness of this special evening. No doubt you will return to sing for us again in the near future!"

With Wladek standing next to her while expressing his appreciation for her performance, Louisa felt uncomfortably self-conscious, out of place. Keeping a keen focus on the intricate designs of the sepia-and rose-colored carpet, she made sure not to meet eyes with him or with anyone in the audience. After hearing Wladek's kind words, Louisa dared to look upwards at him, knowing she had no choice but to face him. The magnetizing lure of his sky-blue eyes drew her to him, like walking into a cool pond on a hot summer's day. Louisa responded in a barely audible whisper, "'Danke,' it was my pleasure to perform for this happy occasion." Wladek peered into her eyes and they were held together in a mesmerized connection. They shared a soulful embrace, without touching; momentarily unaware that anyone else was in the room. Suddenly she noticed the familiar gesture; Wladek's quick, conspiratorial wink she came to know so well.

As the guests were being ushered from the music room to the grand ballroom for a night of dancing and more celebration, Kassenhoff quickly appeared and began pulling on Louisa's elbow. Wladek said, "Guard, wait for her back at the jeep. I need to tell her about a few more future singing engagements in the next few weeks. Hurry up, get back to the jeep and wait. I'll have my butler bring her back down through the servants' quarters in five minutes." Kassenhoff remained silent and nodded quickly. Without a moment's hesitation, she then turned away and proceeded to scurry down the back steps leading to the side exit of the mansion, following Wladek's order to wait for Louisa back at the jeep.

When they were finally alone, Wladek moved his face close to Louisa's ear, whispering every so softly so only she could hear. "We have only a minute. Listen carefully, I am talking to you with the voice of my breaking heart. This marriage is arranged by my family for many reasons. It is an important union for their benefit only; a political move. She, my wife Katerina, really means very little to me. I am not in love with her. I can only say that sometimes we are forced to do things for the greater good of others rather than to follow one's heart in matters of love.

The anguish the Wladek felt was becoming more apparent as he tried to explain. His face was a picture of worriment as he slowly released strained words. "Louisa, you must know that ever since I first laid eyes on you, breathed in the same air, felt your heavenly presence, I fell in love with you; it was truly love at first sight. Every morning, the image of you; your beautiful face visits me, leaving me breathless. Every day I yearn for you. You are my unquenchable thirst, my fairy-tale princess. I will always love you. Maybe, at another time, at another place, or in another life, we could be together. But now, it is impossible. As sad as it is, we have no choice but to leave it to destiny.

I want to tell you about my plan that I have already set in motion. I have arranged for a potato farmer to get you out of the camp. He will keep you safely hidden at his farm until all of this is over. Tonight is Saturday. In three days, at Tuesday's evening meal, you will feign a painful cramping from a

218

case of dysentery. You will beg to spend the night in the infirmary. At the crack of dawn, after the potato farmer finishes his daily delivery to the cafeteria, he will hide you as a stowaway underneath the emptied burlap bags. My sister's friend, Magda Schenck, is the nurse who regularly works the night shift. In the early morning hour, she will smuggle you out of the infirmary to meet him at the wagon. The farmer is well known to the guards. It is my hope that the guards will not check the truck on his way out."

Louisa was stunned, unable to speak; her expression downcast while brushing away the unstoppable tears streaming down her face. Finally, when able to find her voice, she responded, "Wladek, I don't know what to say. You have saved my life before and I believe you will again. For that I am forever indebted to you, moved by your words, grateful for everything. The powerful feelings that exist between us are surely present, in fact, heartbreaking. On Tuesday night I will act sick, in the hopes the guard will send me to the infirmary. You are my messenger from God, my savior. May almighty God send his blessings to both of us."

Wladek's eyes were moist from tears that he tried to contain, and his voice shook as he spoke. "My darling Louisa, I only hope and pray that someday, when this hell is over, I will see you again. Only then will I be at peace and happy knowing that you made it through; that you survived, my love. Always remember that no matter where you are, my love is always present. Let it be an everlasting protection. Go now, 'moije kohana' and stay safe." Trying to control the raging tempest of emotions inside, Wladek turned away sharply. He then snapped his fingers and nodded to the butler, indicating it was time to escort Louisa back down to the jeep.

219

Determination, patience, and courage are the only things needed to improve a situation. If you want a situation changed badly enough, you will find these three things.
–Anonymous

Dangerous Liasons

The next morning as glints of daylight crept into the barracks, early April snowflakes swirled around the camp; leaving only a few moist snowdrops sticking to the ground. Louisa awakened from a restless sleep, contemplating Wladek's plan: Did last night really happen or was it a wistful dream, a figment of my imagination? I don't doubt the feelings that Wladek has for me. But how is it possible that he is willing to jeopardize his whole life for me? If the plan goes awry, it will bring dishonor upon his family and death to him. I can't help but be suspicious and question his motives. Yet, he was the one who saved my life before. He must mean what he says. I really do believe he has true feelings for me. Why else would he take such a gamble and jeopardize his existence? Still, I am terrified. This is such a great risk; something definitely might and could go wrong.

Lost in the haze of conflicting thoughts, Louisa's heartbeat quickened; just thinking about the possibility that the plan might not work. She hoped to be lucky enough to escape from the hellish inferno and finally rid herself of the daily hostile conditions, dank smells, menacing guards, and all the other tortures of living in captivity. Louisa willed herself to get up and face the routine of the new day. There was little to be gained by wasting more time letting gnawing fears rule her life.

That evening, struggling against the bite of an icy wind, Louisa and Samuel met at the usual spot in the back of her barracks. She told him about Wladek's plan to have her hidden by a local farmer at his nearby farmhouse. Samuel listened in rapt attention, his glistening eyes tense with anxiety, unleashing an army of tears that spilled down over his cheeks. The putrid stench of danger was hitting them both like a runaway locomotive.

When Louisa finished relating the plan, Samuel took her in his arms and held her tightly in a warm embrace. Time seemed to stand still for the next few minutes. They remained in companionable silence, holding each other like two terrified mountain climbers afraid of losing their footing on a mountain well beyond their level of competence. They shared a life-or-death secret; a desperate attempt for Louisa to be free from bondage.

Samuel was the first to break away from their embrace. While resting his hands on Louisa's shoulders, he held her at arms' length and spoke to her from his heart. "There are no fitting words to describe how I feel, Louisa. Of course, I don't want to lose you. You are the only light of my days. To me there is no sun, only you. When I lay my eyes on you or even think of you, please know you are the only spark of joy left in my existence. But one thing I do know for sure is that you must do this. This plan is a miracle sent by God. The 'Almighty' has blessed you with this opportunity and you must take it. Who knows, maybe this is the necessary risk that you must take for both of us. Maybe it is our one chance for survival. We both know that our days are numbered and the longer we stay here, the less time we have." Samuel pulled Louisa towards him and kissed her as if he was sending her away, a farewell journey into the heavy air of doom.

Tuesday evening couldn't come soon enough. In the mess hall at dinner, Louisa battled against worry and anxiety as she finished her watery soup and stale bread. In front of an audience, she was always able to put on a great show. The time had come for her to test the power of her acting skills and put on an award-winning performance. Louisa had to execute Wladek's plan perfectly, feigning serious stomach cramps. She needed to appear to be in a tremendous

221

amount of pain so the guards would send her to the infirmary.

All at once, Louisa's soup bowl fell off the table and rolled across the mess hall floor. She let out a great scream and cried loudly. Doubled over and bracing her stomach with both arms she screamed, "Oooooh… my God! The pains are so bad! I cannot tolerate it! Someone please help me, I think I may have the dysentery again!"

Kassenhoff rushed over to Louisa and placed her rough, calloused hand on Louisa's forehead. "You don't seem to have a fever yet, are you sure you have dysentery? When did it start?" she inquired with no hint of empathy. Louisa screwed up her face in misery and continuing to grasp her belly like she was wounded by a bullet. She fell to the floor in a heap and began to sob loudly, hoping that Kassenhoff wouldn't notice that her crying was not accompanied by tears in her eyes. While feigning intense pain, Louisa managed to answer in a shaky voice, powerless as a slowly deflating balloon. "It started right after work when I returned to the barracks. The pains had stopped for a few minutes, but they are back and much worse now. My body is exploding. Please help me, I beg of you!" Louisa's expression was that of terror.

Kassenhoff continued to stand with hands on her hips, her eyes narrowing as if trying to focus on something through a tiny hole. She responded quickly, apparently believing Louisa's winning performance. "Get up, you worthless piece of garbage! Listen to me and stop all of that screaming. You are causing a disturbance here! I don't have all day to deal with such trivial inconveniences." There was a noted change of timbre in the mess hall and a thick silence of fear blanketed the room. The prisoners became still, suddenly quiet while witnessing Louisa's performance. Kassenhoff noticed the women staring and she quickly re-directed her fury towards them. "What are you all looking at? Mind your own business, you ugly sluts. Turn around and finish your food! I am taking this worthless pain in the ass to the infirmary. If she does have dysentery, you better kiss my feet because I have saved all you from getting it from her!"

Roughly pulling Louisa to her feet, Kassenhoff did not hide her aggravation. She huffed and complained that she did not have time for such childish behavior. Fortunately, the infirmary was situated next to the mess hall, so it was a just a short distance away. As they walked, Louisa kept the charade going. The volume of her weeping echoed into the woods and she took short strides as if she was barely able to walk; paralyzed with gripping pain.

Kassenhoff dragged Louisa by her arm into the infirmary, all the while trying to hold her breath so she would not get sick. Showing no consideration for the ailing patients in the infirmary she yelled, "Can someone help us over here? We may have a serious problem with this prisoner and we need a bed immediately. If she has dysentery, we may all be in danger. Imagine getting sick from a stupid Jew whore!"

Just then, a young, petite blond nurse named Margarite looked up while tending to another patient's needs. Peering through round, wire-rimmed glasses that rested on her nose, she stood up and faced them. "I can help, Kassenhoff. We fear there are others in here that may have dysentery too. We are doing the best we can. There has been a new outbreak. Has she been here before?"

Kassenhoff, impatient and seemingly annoyed, responded condescendingly. "No, she hasn't been here before. Listen here, 'fraulein' in charge, I'm much too busy to attend to this irrelevant wretch now. My work is far too important to be dealing with sick Jews. To me, none of these Jews are worth one 'zloty'! The only reason I brought her here is so that she doesn't spread her disease to everyone else, including us!"

223

Margarite remained indifferent and unaffected by Kassenhoff's sarcasm and spiteful words. Pointing to the empty high-backed wooden chair beside the small mahogany desk by the entrance door she calmly said, "Please sit her down there. I will get to her when I am finished with my rounds." Kassenhoff stormed out of the infirmary door leaving Louisa sitting on the chair, moaning melodramatically. When Kassenhoff was gone, nurse Margarite approached Louisa and whispered, "Do not talk or answer. Just sit tight. I know who you are and why you are here. I will be taking care of you." She took hold of Louisa's upper arm, pulled her up off the chair, and led her to a secluded bed near the back exit. "You will remain here throughout the night. I will awaken you when it is time for us to go. No questions at all. Just lie down and wait until morning." Margarite then walked away with a purposeful stride.

Throughout the long and never-ending night, Louisa hardly slept. All she could do was stare at the cracked ceiling and watch the foreboding darkness slowly turn into daylight. She kept rationalizing, trying to prepare herself for any possible outcome. She prayed that the plan would work; it was very dangerous, but she had to try. If discovered under the burlap sacks in the truck, she and the farmer would be killed instantly. Suddenly, Louisa was shaken awake. Nurse Margarite began to whisper, her hot breath close to Louisa's ear, "'Raus, muetzen auf,' It's time to go."

There is no hope un-mingled with fear, and no fear un-mingled with hope. -Baruch Spinoza

The Courage to Trust

Leopold the farmer stared straight ahead nervously as he drove, trying desperately to stop his heart from beating like a drum. The tension of the moment ignited an almost intolerable heat that radiated from his body. He reached his hand to his head, removed his sweaty 'kepi' and quickly tossed it onto the passenger seat of his truck. He wanted to avoid trouble at any cost.

For the past two years, after having made regular early morning deliveries, Leopold was a familiar and trusted entity to the Janowska camp guards. However, what the guards didn't know is that he was the potato farmer who was secretly hired by Officer Wladek Waldheim to take Louisa from the labor camp and hide her on his farm until the war was over. If discovered, not only would Louisa be severely punished, but Leopold and his whole family could be immediately shot on the spot.

Leopold pulled his truck up close behind the first truck in the exit queue and waited to be cleared by the camp's two guards stationed at their posts. As he inched towards the exit, the truck's engine was revving like a windmill. Leopold peered ahead through the dirt- cracked windshield, carefully watching two familiar guards. One of them spit on the ground while the other leaned casually against the wall of the guard house, smoking a cigarette.

Louisa tried to remain motionless in the back of the truck, crouching down beneath a high pile of smothering burlap bags. A nauseating mix of gasoline, burnt rubber and petroleum, combined with the odors of potatoes and onions made her stomach turn. She trembled like an injured baby bird on the uncomfortable hard truck floor, resting in a strained fetal position. Inch by inch, she tried to extend her legs; hoping to relieve the discomfort while her spine tingled with icy-cold fear. While Louisa's ears keenly awaited hearing the verbal exchange between Leopold and the guards, she prayed he was more than just a trusted friend to Wladek. She hoped he was a credible actor as well. Her mind wrestled with trepidation while her pulse raced on like a run-away horse.

Leopold's truck crept forward towards the gate where he greeted the guards, immediately gesturing to them with the Nazi salute. Trying desperately to maintain a bored expression on his face, he hoped to mask his intense anxiety. "Good morning, Leopold!" shouted one tall, ramrod straight guard who threw his cigarette to the side and grinded it into the ground with the heel of his boot. He walked over to the truck, motioning for Leopold to roll down his window. As Leopold sat with his window down, he was careful to keep a bored facial expression; appearing disenchanted with the mundane monotony of his life. The guard smiled in a friendly way, leaned in closely, and rested his elbows on the bottom of the open window.

"Yawohl, Leopold!" the guard said cheerfully as he looked up at the sky. "Looks like we might be getting more snow. It'll be a real Polish winter that just won't quit! Wish we had this weather when it was Christmas, it would have been good for us all to celebrate the holiday in a winter wonderland; cozying up by the fire with our families. How is everything with you? Has your wife recovered from her illness? I know a good German doctor; they are the best, you know. Just let me know if you need him and please wish her well from me." The guard stopped talking and stared at Leopold, waiting expectantly for his response.

Leopold turned his head to face the guard, searching for any trace of suspicion. Throughout the casual exchange, Leopold was unable to stop the freshly released rivulets of sweat seeping into his armpits and beginning to roll down his

226

back. In contrast to his own body heat, he couldn't help but notice how the guard's breath readily formed a cold, icy mist in the cool April air. Leopold attempted to keep his voice calm as he replied. "Yes, everything is the same. Day by day, my wife is getting stronger. Thanks for asking. All I can do is hope the cold weather will end soon. That's the life of a farmer, always worrying about what mother nature has in store."

Just then, Louisa could hear heavy footsteps of a second guard approaching the truck. She was unable to see him pausing to throw his arm over the first guard's shoulder. The guards stood, locked together as Nazi comrades, while one guard nodded a wordless gesture; indicating that they begin the routine surveillance. As they began circling the truck, Louisa held her breath. There was nothing left for her to do but wait in abject terror and hope for a long shot, praying for a miracle that she would not be discovered.

Leopold's insides were shaking and he tried to calm himself by taking slow, deep breaths. He stared straight ahead, pretending to be self-absorbed in his own thoughts, careful not to show curiosity as to what the guards were doing. The guards were getting close to where Louisa hid, and Leopold had to do something fast to redirect their attention. He needed to think of a distraction, a way to get them refocused on something else. Secretly observing the guards circling around the truck through the side rear view mirror, Leopold made a quick decision. He decided to use an old trick, a possible detour during the security check. He shouted out the window to the guards. "Hey guys, I just remembered something very important! Do either of you happen to know anyone who might want to buy some vodka, really cheap? I have quite a few extra bottles back at the farm. I could bring them here during my next delivery tomorrow morning! Let me know if either one of you is interested."

It was as if Leopold had given them a secret code, a password to unlock a safe. The distraction worked like a charm. In an instant, both guards looked up, serious and wide-eyed, and came back around from the back of the truck to face Leopold. Apparently delighted with thoughts of vodka coming their way, one of the guards remarked, "Of course, we are interested! We will be happy to take the vodka off your hands! Bring the bottles here on your next delivery tomorrow morning. We will put them to good use!" The guards laughed as they waved the truck on through the gate. Within moments, Leopold shifted into first gear, stepped on the gas and moved forward through the gate; leading them away from the Janowska camp. As she felt the truck accelerate, Louisa breathed a deep sigh of relief and prayed in gratitude. She was elated and cautiously hopeful that her life as a prisoner would soon be over. Leopold whispered cautiously, "Hey you, back there. We got lucky! Don't move. We are not completely safe yet. There could be random road checks ahead. It might be a while so be patient and stay very still. I'll let you know when you can sit up. You never know what could happen from here. Hang in there, Louisa!"

On the road towards Leopold's country farm, the truck rode over frozen tumbleweeds, gnarly hills and bumpy roads. Louisa lay listening to the crunch of the gravel along the way. Even though she quivered under the damp and heavy burlap bags, a wave of relief washed over her. Shifting her body slightly to rest on her right thigh, she began to think how strange it was she was no longer minded the physical discomfort; it was a small price to pay for her freedom.

Hope is the one thing that can get us through the darkest of times. -Anonymous

The Kindness of Strangers

Within an hour, the truck pulled into a long, winding drive-way that led to a stately stone structure built in the 1800's. Leopold turned around and finally spoke to Louisa. "We are here at my farm." Louisa and Leopold shared silent feelings of relief as the truck moved across the field that led to the red barn behind Leopold's farmhouse. Before pulling into his parking spot, Leopold proceeded to remove the Walther pistol from under his seat and put it in his back pocket. "This shitty war has made me a nervous wreck," he said. "I live in constant fear of arrest and imprisonment and I sleep with a pistol under my pillow every night."

Leopold parked the truck, stopping in front of a securely bolted, arch-shaped door. The door was framed by wooden logs and encased between heavy stone. Behind the door and down the stairs was the root cellar where Louisa would be hiding. After Leopold wiped the sweat off his brow with the back of his hand, he pried apart the wrought iron lock and pushed against the large wooden door and swung it open. Then he turned back around, offered his outstretched hand to help Louisa get out from under the burlap bags, help-ing her to disembark from the back of the truck.

Leopold promptly spun around to face Louisa. "With the help of almighty God, we made it. We are honest, God-loving Christians who value the lives of all human beings. We don't know how long this unconscionable war will last, but for now this is where you will stay, 'mloda kobieta' Louisa. In the root cellar, you will not be alone. There are a few other Jews like yourself hidden there too. Later, my wife Krystyna will bring you what you need to be more comfortable. We are risking our lives to do what is right. We are here now, hiding in a somewhat protected bubble, like a band-aid covering a

229

wound. Every night we pray that we won't be discovered by the Nazis. They are insipid enemies of humanity and we just can't stand back and watch it happen; we feel compelled to do something to help. Go inside, beyond the door. The stone steps are very uneven, so go very slow. Please be careful not to trip or fall down. After all of this, we want you to stay safe."

Moved by Leopold's kindness and sincerity, Louisa's eyes filled with grateful tears. "There are no words for me to express how I feel, she said. "All I know is that you are an earth angel. No, you are more like a saint. After losing my family, after almost losing my own life and facing the danger of each day, I am deeply grateful. I thank God that there are still righteous Christians like you, risking their own lives to help us. If I am able to survive, I will always remember the compassionate people like you, the ones that no matter what happens in this cruel world will always treat other people with respect and decency; regardless of their religious beliefs."

Not waiting for a response, Louisa turned around quickly before beginning the slow and careful descent to the root cellar, trudging her way downward through the narrow, darkening stairway. As she neared the last step, her ears perked up like a guard dog hearing the shrill sounds of a whistle in the distance. She froze in place for a moment, thinking that they had been discovered. Louisa stood on a crooked stone stair for a few minutes, hardly breathing, then she continued her careful descent. When she reached the bottom, she thought she heard undertones of muted whispers and hints of movement coming from the dense air in the cool basement.

The root cellar was damp and dark, smelling like loamy dirt after the rain. It was the perfect setting for vegetables and food storage. Amidst the darkness, Louisa could see two small windows on the walls perpendicular to each other, the only source of daylight. In one corner were two half-melted white candles, secured in thickly formed wax, planted on two small, chipped plates; used nightly to light the cellar for its inhabitants.

Louisa's roaming eyes continued to peer through the hazy darkness of the small root cellar. Instantly, she spotted the hidden people, seated with their legs crossed on the dirt floor, supporting their backs against one of the multi-shelved walls covered with glass bell jars of preserved food. There were three adults, appearing to be in their forties, one elderly woman probably in her eighties, and two small children aged between five and eight. As Louisa carefully walked down the dark stairs, they stared at her with silent dread. Their fears were palpable and Louisa thought she could hear their hearts beating loudly. They were all frozen in place, staring at her as if they had just seen a ghost who had come to take them away. These poor souls all lived in a constant state of fear, distrust and insecurity. Louisa understood the feeling all too well.

Louisa whispered calmly, hoping to lessen their fear. "Please don't be afraid of me, I'm a Jew just like you. I'm here to hide from the Nazis and the kind farmer has brought me here." Louisa sat down against the wall, situating herself next to the youngest child; a little girl with long, brown braids and a heart-shaped face. As Louisa sat, she looked around at the place she would now call home. She thought how ironic it was that the cellar now had another clandestine purpose, to also exist for the purpose of preserving innocent human lives.

The little girl with the heart-shaped face had big, expressive eyes that were the shade of sky blue. Her eyes looked a bit too large for her adorable face. Just looking at her melted Louisa's heart and she thought, "I hope I live long enough to have a little girl of my own, just like her." No one spoke for several minutes until the little girl broke the silence. Turning to look at Louisa, she spoke softly in a diminutive

231

voice. "Will you help us?" she asked shyly. "Of course!" Louisa kindly said. I will do whatever I can." The little girl said, will you play with me? I don't like it here. We are usually cold and bored most of the time down here. There is nothing to do. It's no fun at all. I want to run outside and play. Will you be able to take us home?" The girl's young mother had a thin, pallid face that showed signs of stress and premature aging. She finally spoke in response to her child's request. "'Sha, zoll zien schtell, Ruchelle, mein kindt.' This lady can't do anything to help us leave here, but I have good news for you; she can still be our friend! How do you like that? Maybe a new person to play with sometimes?"

The little girl looked up at Louisa and her face lit up like the sun. With a big smile she said, "I am Ruchelle Kupferber. My brother's name is Josef Kupferberg. That's my 'zeide' over there. Her name is Hannah. My mother and father's names are Paulina and Pietr. We are a family. We used to live in our own house. I used to have a dog named Boris and a cat named Stella. They aren't with us. But maybe they are also hiding somewhere safe. What's your name?" Louisa smiled back warmly and said, "My name is Louisa. So nice to meet you, beautiful girl. I'm sure your pets have found safe places to live for now. And yes, I'd love to play with you sometimes."

Just then, their attentions were redirected by the sounds of the outside latch being opened, the scraping of descending footsteps, and a sudden gush of cold air began to chill the room. All eyes were fixed on the bottom of the stairs. It was Krystyna, Leopold's young wife. She was a kind-looking, pretty Polish woman who wore a long country skirt and she was wrapped in an oversized, hand-knitted shawl. A handkerchief was neatly tied around her long, blond hair. Krystyna was holding the braided handle of a large straw basket covered with a red-checked cloth. She set it down on top of an empty box that was used as a makeshift table.

With a sweet voice she said, "I made some hot oatmeal for you. Brown sugar is scarce these days, but there is a jar of maple syrup and fresh milk from our dairy cow. There are also wooden spoons in the basket for you to use. Welcome to our new guest, Louisa. We are glad to have you with us, and we will keep you safe here as long as we can. I'll be back later with the dinner meal, and then I will light the candles for you at dusk. I will not lock the door latch, just In case you need to relieve yourselves outside during the night. In the meantime, try to pass the time in prayer and gratitude for the new day."

That night, each person lay sleeping on a bale of hay, covered with old woolen blankets that Krystyna had brought them. Louisa awoke, feeling cold and uncomfortable in the primitive surroundings. Moving ever so slowly as to not disturb her new friends, she dared venture up the steep stairs to explore her surroundings. Pushing open the creaking door, she was able to step into the night air. Standing outside in front of the door, she watched her breath condense into mist. It drifted against the peaceful backdrop of a pitch-black sky dotted with sparkling stars. Deeply inhaling the fresh air, for a fleeting moment, she was able to feel free again.

Suddenly, Louisa felt something fluffy tickling her as it ran across her feet. Looking down to see what it was, she saw the small kitten stop and turn around, then it looked up at her as if to say, "Welcome to my home." Louisa thought: Thank you, my God. Now I am sure I will be free again one day. You sent me that cat, a sign to remind me not to give up. I will keep hoping for the day that Samuel and I can survive together. I believe that one day we will be able to live in freedom and no longer in fear for our lives. For now, we need to live one day at a time. Louisa took one more look at the starry sky, took a deep breath and turned around to return to the cellar. After closing the cumbersome, wooden door behind her, Louisa carefully made her way down the steps, anxious

233

to get back to her sleeping companions; an adopted family of survivors.

When one dog barks, he easily finds others to bark with it.
-Exodus Rabah

The Power of Song

It was towards the end of the month of April 1945. Like burrowed animals finding safety in an underground shelter, Louisa and the Kupferberg family had been hiding in the root cellar for six weeks. During that time, Leopold's wife Krystyna was an excellent caretaker; treating them with humane dignity and respect, helping them feel more at ease with their primitive surroundings. She brought them daily nourishment, limited supplies, and clean clothes. She did her best to accommodate them with as much as she could spare, especially in war times where everything was scarce and hard to get. Considering that food and clothing supplies were so limited, she was able to provide decent living conditions for them to stay healthy and comfortable while they all prayed for the war to end.

One evening when it was time for supper, Krystyna carried down a large pitcher of water and a steaming hot tray of kapusta, polenta, and kielbasa. She was careful to balance the tray of food as she navigated her way down the uneven stone stairs. She always made sure to announce her presence in a lyrical tone with a sing-song voice. "Please don't be frightened. It is only me, Krystyna! I'm bringing down your dinner." When she reached the bottom of the stairs she was eagerly greeted by her thankful stowaways. "I have some promising news!" Krystyna announced as she stood there holding the dinner tray. "Tonight may be a special night for us all!" she said with a hopeful gleam in her eyes.

Krystyna set the heavy tray down carefully on the makeshift cardboard box table before striking a match to light each one of the eight candles strategically placed around the root cellar. The candles were their only source of illumination. Louisa and the others sat down on the floor to gather around the hot, aromatic meal that Krystyna had lovingly prepared. "Please take your spoons from the basket and eat the food I've prepared for you. This is a meal of anticipatory celebration, and I will explain as you eat. So now, just close your eyes and eat slowly. Savor each spoonful and imagine that maybe you will be tasting flavors of freedom that might be coming your way."

"Freedom?!" they gasped, and all eyes were on Krystyna. "Tell us more!" The little girl implored with big eyes. "Well, Leopold and I listen to the news radio broadcasts every day and night," Krystyna said. "Like all of you, we are very anxious for this terrible war to end. We listen to stay informed of the latest political developments, always hoping for any turn of events so that the time will come that you will be able to leave here without fear. More than anything, we want you to have your freedom back so you can restart your lives once again. What I am about to tell you is most promising because it seems that the end of this hell is near, that the war will end soon. The smiling faces in the cellar lit up the darkness, and they all beamed with hope. Louisa's heart soared, thinking about the moment she could reunite with her beloved Samuel.

Krystyna continued to explain. "This morning's broadcast informed us that the Battles of Nuremberg and Hamburg have ended with American and British occupation. The Western Allies have captured many thousands of German troops. Many troops have surrendered on the Western and the Eastern fronts. The Battle of Berlin has ended with the Soviets surrounding the city, leaving no escape routes for the Nazis. Mussolini was executed in Italy. Oh, and I have saved the best official news for last. The rumor is that Hitler, along with his long-time partner, Eva Braun, have committed suicide. It is the final fall of the Nazis and the third Reich!"

Stunned by Krystyna's pronouncement, no one dared to move a muscle. They just sat in disbelief, frozen in stone

236

silence. Astonished by the news, it seemed they were all afraid to react for fear that the good news would disappear, and what Krystyna just told them was nothing more than a fleeting dream.

Ruchelle, the youngest girl, broke the silence and stood up with her hands on her hips. "Mama, what does Krystyna mean? I don't know those people she is talking about. Will we be able to go home now?" She scooted over to sit in between her mother's crossed legs. She began hugging both arms tightly around her mother's neck and started crying soulfully, as if she had lost her favorite doll. Suddenly, there was a release; like a dam giving way to a water surge. They all began sobbing tears of relief, trying to free themselves of pain and indescribable losses, letting go of the fretful tears from the past and present, and overwhelmed with their unknown futures.

As blurring tears were running down Krystyna's face, her voice cracked with emotion. "Please hush. Dry your tears, everyone. Please try to calm yourselves. We must remain vigilant and not let our guard down just yet. Stay quiet and take no chances, for no one should hear you. Freedom may be days or weeks away. Remember that living in captivity has changed all of you. It won't be easy to start your lives over again, but you will. I promise you that. Although the next step for you will bring great challenges, don't think about that right now. You must be brave and optimistic. You will need your strong willfulness now more than ever. But for now, we must hang on a little bit longer. Please try to be patient that it will all work out for everyone.

Smoothing down her apron and wiping the tears from her eyes, Krystyna wished them all good night, then she swiveled around to begin her climb back up the rugged flight of stairs. When she closed the door to the root cellar behind her, she looked up into the Prussian blue and starlit sky. With a hopeful sigh, she reflected on everything they had all been through. Krystyna and her husband lived in constant fear of being discovered. To the Nazis, the harboring of Jews was forbidden and considered to be the greatest crime. If anyone from the Nazi authorities ever found out, there would be no further questions. Krystyna and Leopold would be either tortured or immediately murdered in cold blood. Their lives were in constant jeopardy but despite the risk, they believed in their hearts that what they were doing was right. The fear and constant stress had taken its toll, but being Christians, Leopold and Krystyna believed in helping others. They were strongly committed to their choice to save human lives.

When everyone else was asleep, Louisa wrapped herself in a blanket and began her habitual climb up the steep stairs to get a few moments of freedom. She sat in the darkness on her usual stoop next to the entrance to the root cellar. As she sat there, Louisa's passionate heart was clamped with fervor and nostalgic emotion; recalling past memories and profound sadness for the loss of her family, friends and loved ones, yet simultaneously inspired, thinking about her love for Samuel. She was careful not to allow herself to think about any future beyond this night, knowing that at any moment her life could change again. Hoping she would be lucky enough to greet the next day, she began staring up at the gleaming stars sprinkled amidst the inky sky. With her softest and most heartfelt voice, Louisa sang 'My Yiddishe Momma.' Before Louisa finished singing, her faithful feline companion appeared and began snuggling against her thighs. Leopold's cat, with his clearest green eyes like a river in a mountain valley, stared straight into her soul and offered her hope.

Choose to be the tail of lions rather than the head of foxes.
-Hebrew Proverb

Love Prevails

It had been several weeks since Samuel was first questioned by the Nazi authorities. The time seemed to fly by quickly. He was wrapped up in his own grief, burdened by waves of melancholy. Every day, he worried about Louisa; wondering about her well-being, fearing that he may never see her again and petrified of what would happen to him.

Fortunately, the routine of work at the carpentry factory served as a welcome distraction. While working, Samuel spent his time contemplating, wondering if Waldheim meant what he said and if he could trust him. Like all the other victims of the war, living in such torturous times created distrust and suspicion. It left him unsure if anyone told the truth anymore.

One evening, when Samuel returned to the barracks, he felt sad and discouraged. He was physically exhausted from the tediously long workday and he was looking forward to some rest. Suddenly, a guard approached him and said, "Hey you, come with me. You are ordered to report to the administration office immediately. Leave your boots on and take your coat. We are walking there now. Hurry up, Jew!"

Now familiar with the Nazi interrogation process, Samuel was ushered into the administration office and told to sit down on a wooden chair positioned in front of a large mahogany desk. The guard left Samuel alone in the room and as he closed the door behind him, high-pitched sounds of squeaky hinges disturbed the oppressive stillness. As Samuel sat waiting for someone to enter, his heart was galloping in his chest. He felt the foreboding chill of the sterile room and he tried to avoid the watchful eyes of the Hitler portrait hanging on the wall above the desk. Suddenly gripped with the urge to run, his throat constricted and he was desperate to catch his breath. As threatening waves of apprehension rolled over him, finally someone opened the door.

SS Officer Wladek Waldheim stood at the door looking stone-faced and serious. He came in quickly, taking his seat behind the massive office desk. Samuel was surprised to see that he neglected to gesture the customary 'Heil Hitler' salute to the painting. Waldheim positioned himself on the desk chair, moving it closer. He clasped his hands in front of him on the desk and leaned in towards Samuel. Looking Samuel straight in the eye, he began to speak. "By now, I imagine that know who I am. After all that has happened, you must believe that I am a man of my word. The war is coming to an end and the Third Reich will be defeated. The Jews will soon be set free. My family and I are in great danger, and we will be leaving the country as soon as possible. He looked nervous as he sat there ringing his hands."

Wladek looked up at the clock on the wall, and then back to Samuel. "There is no time to waste," he said as he began to speak more quickly. You will probably never see me again and that is likely of no importance to you, but the most important thing is our mutual concern for Louisa. You must already sense my feelings for her. She is my priority and I know she is yours as well. It seems we both love the same woman. So, you must listen closely and heed my warning or else we will all be killed.

He looked back to assure that the door was closed and he leaned in closer, speaking in a hushed tone. "The information I am about to convey to you is only between us and must be kept in strict confidence. It is crucial that you will tell no one about the plan or of anything you are about to hear. Otherwise, you could endanger Louisa's safely as well as the people involved in hiding her. You could jeopardize your safety too. The war has changed everyone. People that were kind and good have become monsters, ogres; men with no

240

conscience. Many have become murderers. There is no justification for the evil that surrounds us, as well as for my participation in the cause. There is no excuse for the burning rage, the hatred towards the Jews. But you must know, you must always remember that there are some of us who are different; people who still care about each other. I had no choice but to keep my feelings, my thoughts and opinions silent. But it's much too late for me to explain further. I have been entangled in this Nazi web, like a lightning bug held captive in a glass jar with no way out. When the war is over, I will seek a way to escape. It's too late for me to try to disentangle myself from my association with the Nazi regime. Even though I was obligated to act in support of the Nazi party, still it is no excuse. But what's done is done. So you see, I have no other choice but to escape like a coward and run like a thief in the night."

"It is critical that you listen carefully," Wladek continued with a look of extreme intent. "Louisa has been hidden on a potato farmer's farm. The farmer's name is Leopold Krasnovosky. He is well-known to the guards at the camp's service gate where he makes his daily deliveries. I had prompted Louisa to feign an illness; a bad stomachache, so she would be sent to the infirmary. The plan was carried out successfully. Early the next morning, the potato farmer managed to smuggle Louisa out of the camp in his delivery truck, hidden underneath the emptied burlap vegetable sacks. Since Leopold was well-known to the guards, he was able to get through the security check with no problem. He took her to hide in a root cellar at his farm. I am told that Leopold's wife has been very supportive. Louisa is being hidden along with several others in the cellar. His wife is cooking them meals and keeping them comfortable. I have been compensating Leopold for his efforts, as well as for the rest of the Jews being hidden in the food cellar."

"I must explain the current political situation. Right now, the Allies are gaining ground; closing in on the German-held

241

territories. It is evident that the war will be over soon and will be won by the Allied forces. When it's official, this camp will be disbanded, and you will be free to go. It is my great hope that you go and find Louisa at the Krasnovosky's farm. If you are too late to find her at the farm, all camp prisoners; including Louisa and other hidden survivors will be congregating at the city hall on Yanivska Street. Louisa will, no doubt, be there with them. I hear that American soldiers are setting up displaced person camps; formerly established US army barracks from World War 1, to provide temporary housing for the remaining survivors."

"If and when you do find Louisa, please take care of her. She is my one true love. Tell her that she will always be the woman who stole my heart and the memory of her will always be tucked safely away in my dreams. Tell her to remember me; the dangerous risks I took for her. Tell her that if there is such a thing as love at first sight, then I am living proof of that theory. Tell her that every night when I close my eyes, I will dream of the vision of her loveliness. I will feel her heart close to mine."

Trying to inhale deeply, Waldheim could take only jagged breaths. He was trying desperately to stop the bittersweet tears, choking on overpowering emotion. Still, he managed to say, "I will always love Louisa. Maybe someday our paths will cross again in this lifetime. If not, then maybe another lifetime. For eternity, my heart will always belong to her." For the next minute, he lost his composure and cupped his face in his hands and began to sob, releasing his pain and shameful frustration. Samuel could do nothing else but remain a witness to Waldheim's distress and underlying guilt.

Finally, after what seemed to be an eternity, Waldheim tried to wipe away his embarrassment with the back of his sleeve. He was unable to control the stream of relentless tears. It was a catharsis for him, the final release of the pent-up years of frustration. While sniffling and sucking in the awkward air, he began to speak. "Pardon my outburst. I can't help it. You see, there is no way out for me from all of this disaster. For as long as I am able to escape, to stay alive, my irreparable heart remains broken. All I ask of you is that you please take good care of my truest love, Louisa. You are a good man, Samuel. No one deserves to go through such indescribable trauma and then try to heal from such a ruptured life. From the bottom of my heart, I am sorry for the hatred, the despair, and the lack of human decency you had to endure. God speed to you and to Louisa."

Suddenly, Waldheim stood up and quickly pushed the screeching office chair away from the desk. He called to the guard waiting outside the office. "Comrade, come and open the door! Remove this prisoner at once and return him to the barracks." In the flash of a second, before quickly disappearing through the side door, Waldheim turned to face Samuel, and like a stamped signature, he shot him a tired wink.

That night, when Samuel lay awake and unable to sleep, he kept trying to concentrate on everything Waldheim told him. He lay there in worry: Maybe it's all just rumors. It's too soon to bank on the war ending shortly. The winds of change could turn against us. Nothing is certain yet. Anything could happen. All I know is that if I am set free, I will find Louisa. Even though my deprived life has been shattered with unspeakable losses and loneliness, I must move forward and create a new life. Maybe when the storms of war truly end, there will be a rainbow. Like the Irish say, "There is a pot of gold at the end of a rainbow," and Louisa will be my pot of gold.

For the first time since the war began, Samuel was able to be comforted by pleasant thoughts and glimmers of hope. He was starting to believe that it might be possible to find Louisa and start a new life together. Samuel smiled in the darkness, sighed deeply, then he fell into a deep and peaceful slumber.

One week later, in the early morning, Samuel woke to loud sounds above. Allied planes were flying overhead, disturbing the eerie silence that hovered over his barracks. A blast of frigid air filled the room from the open back door; abandoned by the guards. Prisoners began to slowly awaken and begin their morning rituals while a few men stood carefully peering out the open door. Samuel could hear the far-off sounds of people shouting. Could those voices be the glorious cries of victory? So many unanswered questions began spinning around in his head; like a school of neon-colored fish swarming around a coral reef.

Just then, Sergi jumped up off his cot looking bewildered, scratching his thick mop of black hair, scanning the barracks with a perplexed look on his face. Making his way over to Samuel's cot, he was barely able to grasp the shocking turn of events. While speaking in shallow breaths he looked around and exclaimed, "What's happening here? Could we really be finally free? The guards are gone. Did they just run away like scared rabbits? Can it be that the war is over?" Samuel just looked at him, shaking his head in disbelief, gazing at the gaping open door. "Your guess is as good as mine, but it looks like we might be experiencing a miracle at last!" Samuel responded hopefully, listening to the welcomed roar of Allied planes flying overhead.

Filled with joy and relief, Samuel and Sergi embraced; both sobbing uncontrollably. Sergi was first one to break away. With his face still wet with tears, he suddenly looked lost. "Samuel, what should we do now? Where do we go? Where will we live? How will we find our way in a world that has hated us for so long?"

Samuel swiped his forearm across his tear-filled eyes so he could see more clearly. He cleared his throat, stood up taller, and with renewed faith he held his hand on his heart. Samuel then looked up into heavens and spoke with a strong, clear voice. "By the grace of our Almighty God, we

244

have been spared so far. We must believe in his powers now, more than ever. We must have faith in His will and trust that he will continue to protect us and bring us to safety!"

Sergi sat down on Samuel's cot, resting his face in his hands. With firm conviction he said, "The Almighty God has come back. He has not forsaken us. Let us pray, my brother." It was the first time in years that they began to chant the familiar, ancient Hebrew prayers they knew so well.

Do not fear to hope…each time we smell the autumn's dying scent, we know that primrose time will come again. -Samuel Taylor Coleridge

Victory at Last

On the morning of May 8, 1945, the wood-fired oven was blazing and the aroma of freshly baked bread filled the house. Krystyna and Leopold were listening to the radio and drinking coffee when suddenly there was a broadcast announcement claiming, "Victory in Europe!" Their eyes grew as large as the saucers under their coffee cups. In rapt attention they listened to the radio broadcast, informing the world that the war had finally ended. Krystyna and Leopold jumped to their feet and embraced. "Finally, my love!" Leopold cheered in exuberant celebration. "We did it! By the grace of God above, we are alive and free!"

Stunned, Krystyna stood staring through the streaked glass of her kitchen window. As she looked out beyond the trees, the resounding words of victory replayed in her mind. Cautiously optimistic, she tried to grasp the reality of what had just happened. These days her heart was beating stronger. There was a new vitality of spirit and hope in the air, something she hadn't felt for years. Inhaling deeply, she allowed herself to relish a few euphoric moments of lightness, a sense of utter relief. Then she started to worry. It had been seven years since the start of the war. What should they do about the hidden guests in the root cellar? What could they do to help them? Where will they go now?

While gazing out at the pinkish-white, cone-shaped buds of the large chestnut trees, she wondered what would happen to all of them now after the war was finally over. She worried what would happen if people found out that they harbored Jews during the war. Would she and Leopold be harshly judged, even punished by the remaining supporters of the Nazis? Would they ever be free from the fear of being misjudged for their good deeds; their Christian values? Surely the prejudice, bigotry and hatred of others doesn't just disappear; evaporate into the air, just because the war ended. Krystyna shook her head in bewilderment, wondering: If anyone ever found out what we did, would we be punished for breaking the law? Hiding Jews was a great risk, yet we were not alone. There were many other Poles like us who hid them and so far have lived through it. Who knows, maybe we would be praised for defying the Nazi's inhumane campaigns to wipe out the existence of the Jewish people. Although some might protect us if they knew the truth, others may accuse us. There are stories of farmers who lost their lives by the betrayal of other Poles they believed they could trust with their secret. When found out, they were shot and killed on the spot. How can I still believe in the goodness of other people?

Faced with the impossible dilemma of whom to trust, Krystyna made the decision to tell nobody what they had done. God has seen our kindness, and that is all that matters, she thought as she wiped her hands on her apron. Krystyna turned around to stir the large pot of savory cabbage soup that was simmering over a low flame on one of the four iron burners on the stove. She leaned over the pot and inhaled the delicious scent, then closed her eyes and allowed her face to absorb the soothing warmth. For the first time in years, a hopeful feeling began to wash over her.

Suddenly, Krystyna's thoughts were interrupted by the sounds of horns beeping vigorously outside, seemingly intent on waking up all the farm residents. She turned back to peer through the kitchen window and saw a procession of slowly moving vehicles passing in front of the farmhouse. The heads of soldiers were leaning outside the open windows of at least eight army jeeps and trucks. The soldiers were cheering loudly and waving American flags in a joyous victory parade.

247

Leopold was hauling a rusty wheelbarrow loaded with bushels of potatoes towards the root cellar when he heard the commotion. Instantly dropping the wooden handles to the ground, he ran towards the front of the farmhouse. He cautiously chose to hide behind the piled bales of hay while watching the army trucks and jeeps pass by on the dusty dirt road. Suddenly, Leopold heard the sound of their front door bang open abruptly, slamming hard against the house. Shouting at the top of her lungs, Krystyna hurried down the uneven, weather-beaten steps and began to run down the path leading to the road. Frantically waving her hands high in the air, she yelled in her native Polish tongue, "Stop! Please! American soldiers! I beg of you! Stop, stop!"

Leopold was stunned as he watched his wife run across the front yard towards the trucks and jeeps. With his heart gripped fear he thought: How could Krystyna be so bold and take such a daring risk? How could she take such a chance and possibly have us all killed? Who knows if this is some kind of set up by the Germans? Maybe it's a dirty trick to catch those of us who were harboring Jews, thinking it is now safe to let them go! Leopold's eyes were red and swollen with dread as he watched from behind the bales of hay.

Just then, he noticed that Krystyna's frenetic display of wild behavior must have caught the attention of the driver of the last truck. The truck made an immediate stop and pulled over to the side of the road while the rest of the procession continued onward. Leopold continued to wait for several more minutes, observing that Krystyna was leaning forward at the open window of the vehicle, talking to the driver. He could only assume that Krystyna must have found a way to communicate with at least one soldier in the truck. He figured that maybe someone spoke Polish, or maybe it was a combination of sign language, common sounding words, and more importantly, the urgent desperation to be understood.

Unexpectedly, Leopold saw the driver reaching his hand out the window to give Krystyna something small, like a piece of paper. Promptly folding it and putting it into her apron pocket, she watched the truck pull away from the side of the road. Its wheels stirred up a large cloud of dust, turning it into an apparition and disappearing from sight. Suddenly Krystyna looked feverish, her face pale and gaunt, as if afraid to make her next move, standing stoically in place. Her exchange with the American soldiers made it clear as to what she had to do in order to protect herself and Leopold. The only thing left to do was to evacuate the hidden Jews from the root cellar and bring them to a safer place. Without a moment's hesitation, and with the determination of a mother set out to rescue her toddler from a potentially dangerous situation, she lifted up her long skirt and began to run back to the farm house.

Leopold raced towards the farmhouse, pushed through the unlocked back door, almost tripping over the black cat lazing sleepily on the braided oval rug. He yelled loudly, "Krystyna, where are you? In the kitchen? Are you all right? Talk to me, 'moija kochana!' I am very worried about what I just saw. Who was that who you were talking to? You were so courageous and daring running out to the road! Who knows what could have happened to you!"

As if nothing had just transpired outside, Krystyna was acting strangely calm as she stood by the stove, stirring the fragrant soup in a tantalizingly slow motion. When she turned around to face Leopold, he noticed that her pale cheeks had warmed into a faint-colored rose; like the blush of a newborn's tender skin. With a voice that was completely composed and at ease, she responded. "Yes, Leopold, I am right here. I must tell you something. Everything is going to be all right, you know. It has become clear to me now exactly what to do. We have to accomplish our last mission, to bring the people in our food cellar to safety." Leopold moved toward Krystyna, taking her in his arms. With happy tears in their eyes, they held each other in a warm embrace as their fears began to slowly ebb away. The dangerous choices they were forced to make amidst the wildness of the times were turning out to be the right ones. It was all starting to make sense. Basking in the distant glimmer of fleeting moments of future happiness, they remained standing; locked together as one. Together they silently reveled in gratitude that they had decided to choose courage over fear. They knew they did the right thing to help others who were in desperate need of safety.

Krystyna pulled slowly away from their embrace and while grasping onto Leopold's shoulders, her face looking earnest as she spoke. "Throughout this war, death was all around us. It was in the present, the past, and it felt like there was no future. But that seems to have changed; the tides have turned. Maybe now there is new hope for us, for them. Now, turn around and prepare the largest truck we have, as if to make a delivery. The address to where we are going is written on a piece of paper in my apron. It is a place only several kilometers away. For extra safety precaution, make sure you load the truck with plenty of empty potato sacks."

Kindness which is bestowed on the good is never lost.
-Plato

A Sad Farewell

Krystyna had to move quickly. There was little time to complete her final task. It would be her last act of kindness towards the Jews in her root cellar whom she had grown to love like her own family. The risks were still not over. She knew that after her precious friends left the farm, they would continue to lack any sense of security. Even though they were considered liberated, they would not yet live in freedom.

Krystyna began to think about the new problems they were about to face. Countless times when she and Leopold were in town, they heard disparaging comments among townspeople about the Jews and even witnessed blatant acts of anti-Semitism right in front of their eyes. Krystyna worried about the liberated Jews who went back to their neighborhoods. When they did, were they going to be treated with hostility or would they be subjected to more violent incidents? What would happen when the liberated Jews tried to return to their homes and retrieve their property? There was a strong likelihood of strangers already living in their houses and claiming legal ownership. There was no doubt that what lay ahead for the surviving Jews were only more dangerous challenges; among them was trying to fit into an unsympathetic society that refused to accept them back.

Nevertheless, despite the emotional chaos she and Leopold had to endure, her conscience was clear, brimming with a strong sense of responsibility towards saving as many Jews for as long as possible. She began to smile slightly, praising herself to think how it took a great deal of courage and generosity of human spirit to do what she and Leopold did; a worthwhile risk they would remember for the rest of their lives. She thought: At least, no matter what the outcome, we will always know that we did the right thing for others.

Suddenly, Krystyna remembered the note that was still in her apron pocket. The Allied officer had written the address of a temporary refugee reception camp set up in a nearby town center. He told her that, upon arrival, the displaced persons (DP's) would be organized into groups for processing, then sent either to a DP camp or be repatriated to their country of origin. He told her that DP camps were set up by Allied military commands and the United States Relief and Rehabilitation Administrations in Germany and in Austria.

Krystyna could still hear the voice of the Allied officer at the road that morning. Before pulling away, he shouted emphatically in her native Polish tongue, "Hey lady, don't wait a second. Get them out of here! You know the dangers of being found out. Take them to the reception center now. It's their only chance to start a new life. If they are lucky, living in a DP camp will be their first taste of freedom."

Krystyna had grown accustomed to serving and nurturing her hidden guests, and being concerned for their well-being and comfort. Although inspired by the Allied soldier's encouraging information, she couldn't help but feel sad that they were leaving the farm, knowing she was going to miss them. Taking care of them gave her a worthwhile purpose, a way to demonstrate caring about others. She enjoyed preparing delicious soup for her guests and seasoning it with heartfelt compassion, kindness and gratitude. She knew how much a meal made with love can nourish not only the body, but the human spirit. She decided to cook a farewell meal, a small celebration of hope.

After counting out enough spoons and dropping them in her apron pocket, she grabbed two freshly baked loaves of bread and placed each one to fit snuggly under both arms.

252

Lifting up the pot of fresh hot soup, carefully balancing and bracing it securely against her chest, she made her way through the slushy, wet cobblestone pathway towards the entrance door of the root cellar. Krystyna set the pot of soup down, anchoring it in place on the dewy ground, nestled among the early spring's sprouting grass. While endeavoring to open the heavy wooden entrance door to the root cellar, she was struck by stone silence. It was as if there was no sign of life living there. Down below, the harbored Jews were always listening for the creaking sounds of the wooden entrance door being pulled open. To them it was like a blaring alarm; a warning of a dooming destiny, the possibility of haven fallen into the grasp of enemy hands.

Scampering down the steep and uneven stone steps, Krystyna felt elated; exploding to tell the awaiting Jews what had transpired, that they were to be liberated! They had made it through seven hellish years. She couldn't wait to hug each one of them, assure them that from now on things would be better and better. As she reached the bottom of the stairs, the little six-year-old girl named Anya broke the profound silence, saying, "Whew! I'm so glad it's only you, Mrs. Krystyna! We were so scared that when we heard the door open, we started to pray. But it was only you and not the bad Nazis. Mommy always says you are the kindest person in the whole world! She ran over to Krystyna, instantly wrapping her short arms around her aproned waist and squeezed her tightly, showing the warmth and love of an innocent child.

Krystyna's heart was so full that she felt she could explode with joy. Barely able to contain her own excitement, she spoke almost too rapidly for them to comprehend its meaning. "Well, everyone, today is a day for celebration! The war has officially ended. The liberation of the Jews is approved by the state. You are free people! Please take any belongings you may value and make your way up the stairs to the outside. You will never see this root cellar again. Praise be to God! Today, you will be eating your soup and bread outside, in the freshness of early spring, taking in your first breaths of freedom. After you have finished your lunch, Leopold has prepared the truck to take you to a refugee center in the town. While you are there, you will be registered as displaced persons and assigned to an Allied-controlled military barracks camp for displaced persons. You will be sent by train destined for a DP camp in either Germany or in Austria."

While the others remained frozen in disbelief, Anya released her tight grip on Krystyna's waist. She pulled away quickly and scuttled back to her mother, sobbing uncontrollably with a stream of tears spilling down her pudgy cheeks. She cried out defiantly, "No! I will not go away on some dirty, noisy train! I want to go back to my house! I want to sleep in my comfortable bed. I miss my friends and my teacher! I don't want to go to any camp. I've waited long enough. I'm not going there. I only want to go home!"

By now, Louisa and the Kupferberg family were crying tears of joy, yet their hearts hammered with warning pangs of fear and trepidation. They were afraid to let themselves feel the happiness they deserved. After spending so much time in captivity, they were unable to grasp the concept of freedom. The miracle for which they were praying and hoping for had come to save them. But, why weren't they able to feel joy and happiness now that they were free? Still troubling them was the gnawing fact, that from this day forward, as free Jewish people, their new existence in this world was stained with a dark smudge, covered with an irreversible film of distrust, and locked away in an unreachable place of their memory.

For Louisa, the only happiness and joy she wanted was to find was Samuel. From the second Louisa heard Krystyna's long-awaited words, all she could think about was how was she going to find him. Incessantly agonizing over the doubting thoughts and troubling fears, she worried inconsolably: What if I never find him? What if he's no longer alive? I don't want to live without him. He is all I have left. Where will I begin my search? I don't even know where I am going. It will be almost impossible. It might be easier finding a lost diamond at the bottom of a deep, vast ocean. Only God can help us.

After the Kupferberg family had boarded Leopold's truck with everyone camouflaged under burlap bags, Louisa was the last one to board. Taking hold of Leopold's hand to assist her and pull her up onto the remaining space on the truck's flat platform, Louisa looked at him, her eyes expressing the excruciating pain of a desperate woman. She said quietly, "Please help me find my love. His name is Samuel Rosenberg. He was at my camp at Janowska. Maybe he is still there. Please go back there and look for him. Tell him that I am going to a DP camp. It's worth the try. I beg you to do this last favor for me, my dear man. May God bless you both."

Before Leopold threw the large canvas over Louisa's head, he responded. His voice revealed a firm conviction, like a Judge who had just imposed the final sentencing. "Listen to your intuition, young lady. Let it be your guide. Think about what you want and then really believe you can create it. Believe in your own magic. Speak kindly to yourself, make your world into being whatever you want it to become. If you think you'll find him, you will. May the stars be in your favor. Who knows, while you are searching for him, maybe your true love will come and find you first!"

As they boarded the truck and prepared to leave, Krystyna stood nearby. When the truck pulled away, her feet were planted on the side of the dirt road. She was unable to move away from the backlash of dirt kicking up from the tires; biting at her face like tiny needles. She felt a mixture of joy and sadness as she stood there alone, missing them already. What if I never see them again? She thought. She stood stoically, wanting to be happy for them, but at the same time wincing from the pain of her shattered heart. For so long, those people were her world, her hope, her purpose. Krystyna's withering spirit began to crumble and fall like a shattered building hit by the last war bomb to strike Poland.

All flesh is grass, and all the goodliness thereof is as the flower of the field. -Old Testament, Isaiah

Does Love Still Exist?

For the survivors living at the Janowska camp, the first morning of freedom felt unrealistic and surreal. Some of them were happy, yet many seemed confused and bewildered; wandering out of the camp like zombies. No longer belonging anywhere, most of them had no idea where to go. Bittersweet feelings of joy, fear and loneliness toyed mercilessly with their hearts and tortured their minds. For the survivors, the only constant thing in the world they could rely on was to manage their own feelings of faith and hope. They needed to push away the anger, humiliation and pain in order to move on to the next chapter of their lives.

The first morning of freedom was in early April, and the wonder of nature brought forth its dewy spring freshness. Birds sang their hopeful promise of new beginnings. It was as though nature had been missing for a while, opting not to engage in the calamities of war; ignoring the human degradation, filth, and destruction of the times. The world could always count on nature to change the seasons, but during the war it seemed as if Mother nature closed her eyes; quickly turning the pages in a book that had become too difficult to absorb and too painful to read.

Prisoners left Camp Janowska in droves that morning. The German guards and officers had run off to hide, afraid of what the Allies might will do to them if they were caught. Everyone at the camp had fled to places unknown, except Samuel and Sergi. They were running through the camp, hoping it wasn't too late to find someone who might know the location of the farm where Leopold the vegetable farmer lived. As Samuel and Sergi neared the entrance of the food hall, the door was left wide open. Dashing in, the silence seemed to indicate that there was no one around. Samuel yelled, "Hello, is anyone here? We need to talk to someone. Hello?" They waited for a few seconds and no one answered. Samuel and Sergi hurried into the kitchen just to make sure. As they turned the corner, they spotted a man. He was dressed in faded overalls that were pulled up over an old ragged shirt marked with round perspiration stains under his arms. His clothes indicated that he was a farmer. He was squatting in front of an open food cabinet, taking out vegetables that were left behind. He quickly filled his burlap bag with potatoes, beets, carrots, leeks, and heads of cabbage. Samuel and Sergi reacted with a simultaneous response, both yelling, "Hey there! What's going on? What are you doing here?"

The startled farmer stood straight up, popping up like a jack-in-the-box. Now facing them directly, he was quick to remove the soft, large-brimmed hat from his head, holding it like a shield to rest against his chest. His facial expression was that of a thief caught off guard in the middle of a planned heist. Slowly opening his mouth to speak, he began fumbling his words. It was apparent the was very nervous and he tried to explain what he was doing there, but his words stumbled clumsily into each other. "Please don't judge me harshly for helping myself to these supplies," the farmer said. "They will go to waste anyway. As a good Christian, I can justify what I am doing since I'm really not stealing from anyone now. I'm taking these supplies so my family can have food to eat and be able to move forward and build a new life."

"We are not here to cause you any harm," Samuel said. "We don't care at all about what you are taking. Stealing from the Germans only means taking back what was ours in the first place, so go right ahead. Feed yourself and your family! All we want is some important information." Instantly, the man relaxed and breathed a sigh of relief. "You must be prisoners," he said. "I can't imagine what you have been through, and I am so sorry. I am a local farmer. You must understand how difficult the food situation has been for farmers here in Poland. It has been oppressive, cruel and unpredictable. The Germans have had total control of everything we do. We have been permitted to have only one sustenance garden, one milk cow, and only one horse. But if any German officer, even of the lowest rank, ever chose to confiscate any of our possessions, the Germans always approved of it. Most of our livestock had to be turned over to the Reich. If they ever found out about an unauthorized slaughter of any farm animal, we might be killed. Many farmers lost their lives for this. As you can see, Polish farmers have become desperate. Even our chicken egg production was controlled and scheduled by the Germans. If our chickens had a bad week, we were forced to buy eggs on the black market. As for our families, we were permitted to eat a diet of staples: only bread, potatoes, cabbage, carrots and beets. If Germans found out about any other desirable foods we kept in our home, we had to turn them over immediately to the Germans. Today we celebrate no longer being ruled by the Reich. For your sake and mine, praise be to God, the Reich no longer exists!"

Samuel dared to walk over to the young farmer. As a gesture of understanding, he took the liberty to plant his hand on his shoulder before saying tenderly, "We understand. After what we all have suffered, we will never judge you nor anyone else for that matter. I will speak for both of us. We wish you and your family a life filled with promise and the best of good luck!" The young farmer's eyes filled with tears of hope and encouragement. He answered with a kind tone. "Thank you, my friends. I wish for you the same. May God bless us all."

Since the time seemed right for Samuel to ask him the important question, he began. "I am hoping you are able to help us. We are trying to locate the farm and the farmer who delivered vegetables to this camp every morning. Please, if you know anything, tell us." As soon as Samuel finished his request, the young man seemed overly anxious to blurt out his response, saying: "Of course I do! That's Leopold! He and his wife Krystyna live on the first farm on the right side of the main road about seven kilometers away. He happens to be a good friend of mine! We farmers always stick together. Considering the troubling times, the struggles we have endured throughout the war, we learned the importance of having each other's backs. Hey, if you want, I'll take you there! Wait for me in the back. You'll see my horse attached to the cart. I just have a few more bags to fill before loading them and I'll be there in a few minutes."

Samuel shot Sergi a quick glance, searching for a sign of mutual agreement. Sergi cheerfully said to the farmer, "Yes! How kind of you to offer. What a twist of fate for us to find you!" "God works in such mysterious ways," the farmer replied as he tossed the remaining vegetables into a bag. The young farmer smiled as he used his calloused hand to rub the short stubble on his unshaven face. "My name is Henryk. What are your names?" he asked. "My name is Samuel and this is Sergi. We are so thankful to meet you!"

"Have you fellows eaten anything yet?" Henryk asked. "Everyone who worked here has run away like scared rabbits." Not waiting for an answer, Henryk began pulling sugar beets out from one of the overstuffed vegetable bags, immediately offering them to Samuel and Sergi. Suddenly aware of their growling stomachs, they took them without hesitation, biting down hungrily. They closed their eyes and relished the explosion of sweetness on their tongues. It was a taste sensation neither one had felt for years. While devouring the beets, they hopped up into the back of Henryk's horse-drawn cart. They sat on bales of hay and leaned their backs against open crates filled with bags of rye, oats, barley, and wheat; supplies that Henryk had already confiscated from the camp's remaining food supply.

After several minutes, Henryk pushed his way out through the back kitchen door, lumbering along with three more heavy sacks of vegetables. Samuel and Sergi jumped out of the cart to help and together they lifted each heavy sack, tossing them one at a time into the cart. Rubbing his rough hands together and salivating like a king about to begin a scrumptious meal, he chuckled, "I hope there is enough room in there for you and the potatoes!" Before Henryk untied and mounted his horse, he grabbed a branch of low-hanging peaches on a nearby tree, picked some fresh peaches and tossed them into the cart. "Enjoy your dessert, fellows!" Henryk smiled. "I bet you haven't had a dessert or eaten anything sweet for many years. I sure hope the tides have turned for you; for all of us. Today, we are all freedom winners. It is truly a day of celebration!"

Old men shall dream dreams, while young men shall see visions. -Old Testament Joel 11-26

Reconnecting

While heading towards Leopold's farm, Samuel and Sergi sat in Henryk's horse-drawn ramshackle cart, leaning on lumpy overstuffed bags of vegetables and trying to balance on lopsided bales of hay. Samuel and Sergi were so happy to be free that they didn't even notice their discomfort. The rickety cart twisted from side to side along the flinty, dirt road; trudging over bumps and occasional rocks. As they rode through the countryside, they passed ravaged farmlands with toppled barns and rusting debris left as wartime souvenirs.

It was Samuel's first day as a free man. He tilted his head back, gazed up at the cloudless, blue sky and said a prayer of gratitude. He envisioned his dream of freedom, a hope for peace and serenity. He began breathing deeply, inhaling the fresh spring air. While breathing he hoped to erase the imagined blackness, the discoloration that had been gathering inside his tainted lungs. As they moved along the road, he started thinking about his childhood on the family's farm in early May. He remembered the morning bird calls, the small animals flitting around the large oak trees, the pleasure of the intoxicating fragrances of lilac trees, lilies of the valley, wild lavender, moist green mosses, and especially how the grass smelled after the rain.

Looking out over the vast farmlands on both sides of the road, Samuel started thinking: I've survived so many years of darkness and the most despairing losses. How will I ever be able to replenish my soul and awaken from the dreadful past? Is it possible for me to overcome my pain and recreate a new life? My heart breaks more and more every day with the thought of having lost most of my family and then Danika and Josef. I know I'll never feel whole again. My sweet Danika, my first and only love, I can never forget the stabbing pain of losing her. I don't know if I can ever forget, my everything; my life. They are gone forever and they are never coming back.

Samuel quickly realized that recalling the pain and misery of the past was depleting his energy, pulling him downwards into even lower depths of despair. He stopped himself by taking another deep, cleansing breath; managing to gain control of runaway emotions. He sat up and consciously chose to think loving thoughts instead. He needed al of his energy to find Louisa. His heart began to flutter at the image of reuniting with her and he thought: The only thing I need to complete me is to have Louisa by my side. She is like springtime to me, like the first sprouting bud on a barren branch after the winter frost. Since the first moment I saw her, my eyes continued to bask on the kindness of a face laced with understanding and compassion. It was a welcome gust of comfort. Louisa was sent to me from the heavens above. Her presence caressed me like a breeze to cool the disappointment; the grief and the fury I was feeling. Her very presence soothed my tarnished spirit. I must find her.

Swarming dust particles swept up from the road, as Henryk's horse proceeded to stop. Henryk shouted to his horse, "Whoa, Whoa! We are stopping right here! Whoa! Yes, that's a good boy! Hey men, brace yourselves for an abrupt stop in the cart. We are here at Leopold's farm." The horse stopped on the side of the road in front of some tall shade trees. Beyond the trees was a run-down, crumbling brick farmhouse set back from the main road.

Henryk hopped off the wagon, tied the horse to the iron post, and walked around to face Samuel and Sergi who were still holding tightly to the wooden slats of the dilapidated cart. "Okay, we are here! Come on out," he said. "I will take you up to the front porch. Krystyna and Leopold are longtime friends and I would be happy to stay with you while you talk to them. If things go well, maybe your girlfriend is here!"

After knocking on the farmhouse door, they stood waiting on a decaying wood porch that was weather-beaten from the lasting effects of another harsh Polish winter. Samuel's heart was skipping beats while Henryk thumped three more times on the door. Suddenly, Samuel felt a swift movement around his feet, noticing a lazy black cat looking up with an unrelenting stare. There was a gleam in his golden eyes, burning brightly against the shade of the covered porch. Henryk exclaimed, "Wow, that's so strange how this cat just appeared out of nowhere! Maybe it's a good luck omen that we will find your young lady friend here."

Samuel spotted the image of someone peeking through the side window. A woman pulled the curtain back, checking to see who it was and if was safe to open the door. Recognizing that it was Henryk, Krystyna slowly opened the door. She was dressed in a long, white peasant dress, a blue apron, and a flowered headscarf. "Hello," she smiled shyly as she brushed back several unruly tendrils of hair that blew in the breeze.

Before Henryk began to speak, Samuel couldn't help but admire the pretty, young woman who stood before them. Her luminous face projected sheer kindness and hope. Krystyna was holding the door partially open, grasping onto the frame's edge so she could shut it quickly, if warranted. "It's nice to see you, Henryk!" She said with a gentle smile. "It's been a long while, hasn't it? With this awful war and all, there hasn't been enough time for friendly gatherings like we used to have. Remember the polka dances? We used to have fun, didn't we?" she recalled with a gleam in her eye. "We sure did have fun," Henryk responded with a smile. Pausing to examine Samuel and Sergi, Krystyna felt guarded and slightly concerned. "How can I help you gentlemen? I am sorry but if you are looking for food or supplies, we are depleted of everything."

In the next moment, Leopold appeared from the door, having just returned from taking Louisa and the others and dropping them off at the town center. Still feeling uneasy and suspicious of everyone, he stood protectively behind Krystyna like an iron shield of armor, ready to slam the door shut if necessary. Leopold was a whole head taller in height than Krystyna, the width of his massive shoulders was several centimeters wider than her slim and narrow-boned body. He looked at the men and began scratching his forehead, giving himself more time to search for the right words. Finally he said, "Henryk, I'm glad to see you. But I don't know who the others are and why they are here with you. We don't want any trouble, nor any involvement in anything that puts us in danger."

Henryk was quick to answer. "Oh yes, Leopold, I understand your concern. We are only interested in any information you may have about a young woman named Louisa who escaped from Camp Janowska. Pointing to Samuel, Henryk said, "Louisa is the girlfriend of this man and he is trying to find her. They met at the camp and he hasn't seen her since she left months ago. He was told that she was kept here at your farm. Is she still here?"

Before Leopold could open his mouth to answer, Krystyna took over. "I am sorry. You are quite mistaken. No one named Louisa was ever here. We would never harbor any Jews here and put our very own lives in jeopardy. But I must tell you that since the war has ended, there is talk amongst the townspeople. Any survivors from the camp are being organized in groups at the Lwow town center before being transported to Allied-sponsored displaced persons camps in Germany and Austria."

Before she could finish her last sentence, the three men turned around quickly and started to run down the porch steps towards the wagon. As they ran, they swerved around the friendly black cat laying in a sunny patch of grass. "Thank you for this information! We are on our way! And may the almighty God bless you, Krystyna and Leopold!" Henryk yelled.

Suddenly, Leopold had a change of heart. "Wait! He shouted as he ran down the front porch steps after them, I have a better idea. I'll drive you back to town in my truck and get you there much faster than your cart can travel on these dirt roads!" Picking up his glossy haired cat, whom he called Czarny, and nuzzling him to his neck ever so lovingly, "I'm taking this cat with us. Just look at his intuitive eyes. They seem to shine with the wisdom of a soothsayer. No doubt, Czarny always seems to bring with him a stroke of luck whenever he comes around."

Suddenly taking on a look of contemplation, like he was deciding whether or not to divulge a secret Leopold's face lit up, "Okay, I admit it. I took Louisa and the others to the town center and dropped them off two hours ago. Maybe we won't be too late! But I must say, that when they were all in my truck, and when we were pulling away from the farm, I noticed that Louisa blew a kiss to this cat. I asked her if she loved cats. She told me that every night, when she dared venture out of the root cellar to breathe the fresh air, he appeared as her loyal companion. She told me how she looked forward to this cat coming to greet her in the middle of the night and snuggle up in her lap. She said his presence served as a hopeful reminder that maybe tomorrow would be a better day.

I don't have to tell you how her words inspired me. We've all risked our lives to save other lives. For this reason alone, we are taking him with us. Maybe Louisa can keep him with her. She might want to take him with her wherever she

266

goes." Leopold pointed to his truck parked to the left of the faded red barn in the mud-spattered and trampled grass. Showing the fortitude of a commanding officer, he implored, "Now, follow me and get in the truck! Remember, time is of the essence! I'll bring you to the place I dropped them off. We are going to find you that young woman named Louisa if it's the last risky thing we do!"

Out of suffering have emerged the strongest souls; the most massive characters are seared with scars.
-Kalhil Gibran

The Charm of a Feline

Riding in Leopold's truck on the way to the town center of Lwow, they passed by faded-colored barns and weathered silos that were peppered along the country road. Sheltered behind large shade trees were century-old farm houses with large front porches. The houses seemed to peek through tree branches, hunkering down to the deepest roots, as if trying to prevent the sadness; the immeasurable sorrow and the melancholy of the times from further seeping into their homes. Throughout the half-hour ride, no one in the truck uttered a word, everyone seemed lost in their own thoughts. Czarny the cat jumped from lap to lap, craving for attention.

Bursting with hopeful anticipation, Samuel could barely contain his wishful longing to find Louisa. He tried desperately to ignore the daunting prospect that he might not be that lucky, knowing it would be a challenge to find her amongst the mobs of displaced people in the town center. He worried he might be too late. If he did miss her, how would he find her? Where else could he go to find her? Panic began to stir the sourness lingering in the pit of his stomach.

Finally arriving in town at the old market square, Leopold stopped short and parked at the edge of '*Staryl Rynok*'. Hundreds of displaced persons had already gathered in front, crowding around where the Tempel Synagogue once stood. With a look of desperation etched deep into his face, Samuel was first to jump out; eager to push his way into the throngs of people. Sergi followed close behind while Henryk hesitated, stood back and yelled, "Wait! I'm going to take the cat with us. I'm not leaving him here alone in the truck. What if someone takes him away? We can't take the risk of anyone stealing Czarny, our good luck charm." Carefully, Henryk lifted the cat to his breast, handling it like a newborn baby. With the cat secure in his arms, he followed closely behind Samuel, Sergi and Leopold. Together they weaved their way through the dense hordes of people.

While pushing his way into the thickening crowd, Samuel felt a prickling of self-consciousness, suddenly acutely aware of his unkempt appearance and unwashed body; still dressed in tattered prisoner's garb. After living in the primitive conditions of the labor camp, appearance was the last concern. Samuel's goal was just to stay alive, remain invisible to the guards, and to avoid danger. Despite all his rationalization, having a scruffy appearance only exacerbated the dizzying worries that kept swirling in his head: If I get lucky and find Louisa, will she be happy to see me? After all, she is eighteen years younger. Maybe it was just a temporary friendship. I may have read too much into it, assumed too much. Now that we are free to be together, she might think I'm too old for her and may prefer to start a life with someone younger; closer to her age. No, I cannot let myself become discouraged, worrying about what can or will not happen; it is simply a waste of time. I'm just hoping I get the chance to find out.

Suddenly, a commotion started. A young man in the crowd began to climb up, posturing himself to stand high on the top of the temple's demolished building wall. Filled with firm conviction, his loud voice bellowed out above the crowd. "Look at this place, it's another emblem of Nazi degradation. Another despicable gesture of disgrace towards our people. Look at the large chunks of rubble on which I am standing. These are the synagogue's collapsed walls, laying in shameful defeat. It looks like the Nazis must have used dynamite to blow up this synagogue and left the ruins for all to see the evidence of their hatred. Just like the synagogue, they dynamited our lives too, gutted our souls, leaving us to rot in our own despair! They destroy everything in their path. They succeeded in destroying this once beautiful and esteemed synagogue, and they succeeded in destroying our lives." He pointed and said, "Look over there! The one thing those self-serving bastards didn't ruin are the wooden benches lined up along the park! They probably needed a place to sit down, drink their ale, smoke their cigarettes. They needed a place to sit and gloat about all the tortures and killings, and think about what they could destroy next."

Suddenly, a young man of about twenty years clambered up the crumbling wall to stand next to him in solidarity. His right cheek was marred with an ugly scar, as if his skin was sliced with a dull, jagged knife. He chimed in, shouting, "Yes, leave it to the Nazis. They're experts in destruction, like desecrating Jewish lives along with their sacred places of worship. But, luckily for us, we are all here today to show that they didn't succeed! We must recover from the horrendous past. Life must go on. Who could ever imagine this day would come? A liberation has come, freedom abounds, and there is renewed hope for us! Let's breathe in the fresh, new air. We have a chance, a choice to pick up the pieces of what is left from our broken existence; an opportunity to recharge our waning spirits, to become resilient again, and rebuild our lives. Let us survive the horrors of our past and become strong again. We will rebuild this temple! We will make it an even more exalted sanctuary of worship, more magnificent that ever before!!"

The crowd began to cheer and hail the enthusiastic speakers. Raising clenched fists in unison, many of them began shouting praises of approval. Yet amongst the excited crowd there were many who remained down-trodden, blinded by the darkness of their own despair, unwilling and unable to see the light of a new day. They wandered among the others in confused silence while the throngs began to swell and intensify with an array of mixed emotions. The variety of emotions in the crowd was like a multi-colored tapestry of optimism, pessimism, and apathy. It became an intermingling of the desperately lost, weaved in with those whom

270

were ready and willing to embrace the concept of reconstructing their lives.

Hundreds of additional survivors were pouring into the area, all heading together towards the Lviv Municipal center. Amongst the noise and chaos Leopold shouted, "Samuel, why don't you hop up on this crumbling wall and start calling Louisa's name? It's worth a try! Take Czarny. Maybe Louisa will notice him, even if she doesn't hear you!" Samuel moved fast, grabbed the cat from Henryk's grasp and said, "Hand him to me. I will hold him up in the air and shout out for Louisa. Maybe he will attract more attention! People are always interested in watching crazy people." In an instant, Samuel clambered up the collapsed wall to stand at the top. Towering over the crowds, he held the squirming cat high above his head, adrenaline coursing through his veins, and began to shout Louisa's name. "Everyone, please listen to me. I'm looking for a young, beautiful woman named Louisa! Louisa, darling! Please look up and see us! It's me, Samuel! You remember us. This cat was your loyal friend! Louisa! Please, look up here! Please see us, Louisa!" Samuel's idea worked. He succeeded in creating a disturbance, a hubbub to stir the crowd's curiosity and people began looking up to see what was happening.

It was early afternoon when Samuel's fate decided to offer a glimmer of hope. He spotted a young woman, the bright sun illuminating the warm, dark brown hair framing her face. He recognized the outline of Louisa's profile, the shape of her body moving underneath the thin bare dress, as she was pushing towards the wall where Samuel stood. Amidst the drone of the crowd, Samuel could see her moving, weaving through the swarms and pushing people aside with indisputable determination. Her expression was radiant as the glow of sunlight that shone upon her face. She looked up at Samuel with passionate eyes, filled with her truest love and loyal devotion. It was a vision that would be etched forever in his

271

mind. It was then that Samuel was sure he knew everything he wanted and needed to know.

Upon hearing Louisa's desperate pleas to let her pass, people in close proximity began to create a clear path for her to advance towards Samuel. All the while, she continued to scream, "Yes! I'm here. Yes, it's me, Louisa! You found me! I found you, my Samuel! Wait for me! I'm coming there, stay where you are!"

Louisa struggled, stumbled along, making her way towards the broken wall. Looking upwards at Samuel, she began climbing, holding tight to any protruding edges offering to lend support, before finally reaching him. Samuel dropped his arms at once, promptly releasing the cat to run down and into the mob. Louisa fell breathlessly into his outstretched arms. The moment they touched, they felt as if they were living their last fleeting moments together on earth. Louisa and Samuel remained locked in a fervent embrace, no longer aware of their surroundings.

Sergi, Leopold, and Henryk stood staring up at them from the bottom of the crumbled synagogue wall; their eyes wet with tears. There was a hush in the crowd as people looked up in awe. It was the kind of event that people needed to witness in order to rekindle their hope. After a while Leopold yelled, "Hey you two! That's enough! There will be plenty of time to show such affection! Meet us back at the truck. You cannot leave us without saying goodbye."

Samuel looked flushed, tingling with the reddish tinge of love, as he and the others walked amongst the homeless survivors. He couldn't help but observe the mixed assortment of faces. Some were tainted black, marred with the soot of doom and despair. Others were drowning in grayish fear, shadowed by their dismal pasts. Most of them looked colorless, blanched to a ghastly white. How similar they were to lost ships having drifted off the original course, gone astray with no place to drop anchor. He looked at Louisa walking beside him, her delicate hand in his. She was his anchor, his home, and he felt extremely blessed. He looked up into the sky and silently thanked God for his amazing good fortune. It didn't matter that they were left with nothing because together, Samuel and Louisa had everything.

Out of the corner of her eye, Louisa noticed a wheelbarrow several millimeters away, filled with a profusion of colorful Mayflowers. It had been a long time since she had seen flowers. Impulsively, she gave in to the reminiscent longing to feel and breathe in the intoxicating air of springtime. Bending down over the wheelbarrow, she hovered over it to inhale the sweet floral scents. She examined the vibrant colors and caressed the soft petals. As she inhaled, her nostrils filled with the promise of spring.

As Louisa stood up she noticed an overturned pail lying on its side, resting in a pool of spilled milk. A black cat, marked with a white-tipped tail was lapping hungrily at its newfound treasure. Louisa blinked, and not believing her eyes, she shook her head in disbelief. What a strange coincidence! How could it be that the same cat that Samuel held high in the air standing on top of the rubble was able to find them? She recognized the cat by the unique splash of white at the tip of his tail. Could it be her beloved Czarny? The cat looked at her with penetrating, golden eyes and she knew for certain it was her favorite cat from the farm. The same loyal cat that found her outside on those lonesome nights, sitting on the frozen ground surrounded by the chill of hopelessness. Czarny was her rescuer, keeping her warm when she was cold. He was her reminder to stay positive and believe her life would change for the better again.

Suddenly, Louisa remembered a cherished childhood memory. She recalled the affectionate pet name her beloved father used to call her when she jumped up to sit on his lap. She remembered how she loved the familiar scent of his pipe, his tobacco-stained fingernails stroking lovingly on her back. He used to say, "My ketzeleh." It was a Yiddish term for little kitten, but to Louisa it was the same as if he said, "My precious darling." Her heartbeat quickened, moved by the nostalgic, bittersweet memory of the past. She crouched down to pet the Czarny, gently rubbing her loving fingers through his soft, thick fur. She said softly, "You are my ketzeleh." Czarny responded knowingly to her touch. He weaved himself around her ankles with his tail in the air and then looked up at her with his golden eyes. Louisa bent down to pick him up and scooped him into her arms. She held him close and he melted into her arms. Czarny purred as she walked with him held tightly to her chest. Samuel reached his hand over to pet Czarny's head and said, "What a beautiful cat."

Samuel and Sergi chatted about future plans as they all walked together, and Louisa walked beside them in blissful silence with Czarny safe in her arms. She was overcome with emotion as she whispered into the cat's soft ear. "I knew you would find me, my precious 'ketzeleh'. You always have. You were my comfort, my loyal companion, my hero. In the middle of all the lonely winter nights, as soon as I came up the stairs of the root cellar and stepped outside the door, you always found me. When I was so cold and frightened and when the world abandoned me, you were my Godsend. Your goodness warmed my heart. Don't think I don't know why you are here, my kismet. You are my reminder to always to believe in faith, to never to let doubts rule my thoughts."

When they finally reached the truck Leopold said, "you found Czarny! I searched for him the whole way as we walked back to the truck. He is yours now, he belongs with you!" Tears of joy and gratitude streamed down Louisa's face. Samuel and Sergi expressed their appreciation for the risks and sacrifices that Leopold made, and for Henryk's incredible kindness and generosity. "We are all together because of you, and we hope to one day repay your kindness,"

Louisa said. All five of them cried heartfelt farewe
waved as the truck drove away.

Sitting on a park bench next to Samuel at the town center,
Louisa sat thinking: I have learned important lessons from
this horrendous war. I will not let myself drown in waves of
despair. The Nazis have proved to me that nobody can rob
us of our own hopes and dreams. Those our ours to keep
forever. Even though I have lost everything; my family, my
friends, my freedom and my youth, what still remains is most
important; the most valuable gift of all. What is left for me is
the hope that tomorrow will be a better day.

To everything there is a season and a time for every purpose under heaven. – Ecclesiastes

The Expected Arrival

Three years passed since Louisa and Samuel had been living at the Allied-sponsored displaced persons' camp in Bamberg, Germany. The medieval city was set along the Regnitz River in Bavaria, the northern region of Germany. Originally, Bamberg was an important fort on a hill and its view enabled soldiers to watch for and guard against potential enemy attacks. As far back as 1891, the Warner Barracks was built as an infantry barrack. After World War 2, the headquarters of the U.S. Constabulary was located there, created to occupy Germany and responsible for patrolling the American occupied quarter. Many survivors, including Louisa and Samuel, were housed in the Uhlan Barracks at this location.

Samuel and Louisa awoke each morning feeling extremely blessed. They often spoke of the relief they felt and how far they had come. It took a long time for them to decompress and unravel from being wound up so tight during their captivity. Many tears were shed. Former prisoners at the camp gathered in support groups to help each other process their trauma. They shared stories and sorrows, and found solace in each other. Deep bonds were formed and as they slowly healed, they basked in an ever-present lightness; grateful for having survived the war together. In front of a gathering of their dear friends, Louisa and Samuel were married; united in love under the bright blue sky.

Slowly, Louisa and Samuel settled into the routine of camp life and started to build a new life together. Samuel worked as an actor, putting on shows about the Holocaust for people at the camp. Louisa blissfully kept house, with Czarny the cat laying in sunny windows. Life was happy and they felt truly blessed, making plans for the future.

It was towards the end of September when a heat spell surrounded them, making the afternoon temperatures uncomfortably hot while the dense air felt thick as molasses. The windows of their small apartment were always left open in the hopes of capturing an occasional breeze. Even a small gust of hot air from the portable fan was a momentary welcome for them. Every afternoon after lunch, they would sit on the former military raggedly worn couch, perspiring through their clothes. They sat listening to the hum of the fan, eagerly awaiting the next rotation of air to come their way.

This particular morning, overlooking the city, the sunrise started to appear from behind the hill. Louisa woke up in a sweat, nine months pregnant, seized by intense pain. Clutching her belly, she began praying for it to subside. She'd had false alarms this week, but the doctor at the Bamberg Hospital told her it was only Braxton Hicks contractions. Louisa was not sure what to do this time, but she had a feeling that she was in real labor.

Deciding not to awaken Samuel, she rolled to the side of the bed, stood up, and began rubbing circles around both sides of her swollen belly trying to ease the pain. She didn't bother to change from her nightgown into day clothes thinking she might not have enough time to get herself to the hospital. Instead, she grabbed the oversized, hand-knitted shawl strewn over the top of the chair. For a split second, she thought how, coincidentally, she had just finished knitting it yesterday. Quickly, she wrapped it around her cumbersome body. Seconds before leaving the flat, she slipped on her shoes, softly closed the door behind her, marking her path by leaving a watery, bloodied trail on the linoleum floor. Making her way towards the hospital, she was headed in the direction of the Bamberg city center. To no avail, she was trying to quicken her pace but her body took charge; forcing her to move slowly. She ambled along *Von Norden Street*, past the Karmeliten Platz 1 and across the upper bridge

(Obere Brucke). She rested for a moment under the famous archway leading into the city square and then made her way beyond the center to an area called Bad Kreuzach. At this pace and stopping for contractions, it took another ten-minute trek up the hill until she reached the Kaserne hospital. Adjacent to the hospital was the Karmeliten Cloister, a place that housed nuns and monks of the Franciscan order, many of whom worked at this hospital as nurses, clerical staff, or medical technicians.

Finally, in the near distance, Louisa spotted the street leading up to the hospital which was perched on a hill, nestled back from the street. The stone front façade was covered with a dense latticework of ivy, sheltered by several weeping willow trees. Louisa had been forewarned that it was a Catholic-based hospital run by nuns who worked as nurses. Suddenly, panicky thoughts shot through her veins like ice water: What if the nuns won't help me because I am Jewish? Surely bigotry and hatred of Jews didn't just disappear with the liberation. What if they ignore me? Even worse, what if they harm me or the baby? How can I trust anyone anymore? At this point, after all Louisa had been through, all she could do was hope that somebody might show some compassion.

Louisa trudged her heavy body up the stone steps leading to the ornately carved arch above the entrance way. She began to look upward, her eyes becoming fixated on the massive doors. Subconsciously, she braced her arms around her protruding abdomen, trying to ignore the drizzle of the amniotic fluid trickling down her legs. Suddenly, she was flooded by a deluge of panicky thoughts: When I knock on the door, will the nuns have mercy on me? Will they even agree to help me, knowing I am a pregnant Jewish woman from the displaced person's camp?

A fast-moving distraction caught Louisa's attention. A beady-eyed crow landed onto the top of the stone stairs, poised like a statuesque ornament with magnetic eyes. Its piercing eyes shined unnaturally bright. It held a steady gaze while seeming to peer directly into her soul. Louisa's heartbeat quickened, wondering if its presence was some sort of bad omen. She promptly looked away but then, out of the corner of her eye, dared cast a second glance. She looked straight into its eyes and her heart warmed. She immediately felt protected as if the crow was a token of good luck, a shielding amulet sent by someone in the heavens above; someone who once loved her and who would always protect her.

Just then, another gnawing pain returned with a vengeance. Waiting for the pain to subside, she recalled how someone recently told her about the nature of labor pains, saying, "They take over the body like clockwork. They begin rolling in like waves at high tide, washing over everything in their path, then they slowly recoil and subside before they return again." She began to console herself: Be brave, there is no time to worry. I must do whatever I can to get this baby out safely! Please God, let it be an easy birth and bring forth a healthy baby into my arms. I have survived so many traumas. For the rest of my life, I promise you that every day I will pray, express my gratitude and honor for your ever-presence. So far you have spared me, saved me from the grips of evil; helped me to survive. Please, I beg of you, more than ever before, you must help me now!

Soon, another more intense contraction caused Louisa to double over and lean against the massive entrance door. Balling up her fists, she began pounding fiercely, the intensity of her contraction fueling her insistence to make her presence known. There was a sense of urgency in her voice as she shouted, "Please, somebody help me!" Finally, the massive doors began to strain forcibly, making creaking noises as they widened open. All at once, Louisa's nostrils were overtaken with the sickly air laced with antiseptic smells coming from the hospital's reception foyer. She froze. She began to breathe deeply, trying to inhale small doses of courage, praying that she would meet with the face of a kind person with an empathetic soul.

Towering over Louisa, an exceptionally tall nun stood at the doorway. Her stocky body was clad in a crisply ironed bleached-white habit, trimmed with blue facings. A regulation headdress framed her pallid countenance, revealing no distinguishable expression at all. Louisa watched as the nun slowly lifted her chin, peering down through the frameless spectacles that were resting atop a pug nose, shielding her faintly colored gray eyes. Her string-like lips separated as she began to speak in German, the guttural sounding language of Louisa's nightmares. "Are you a Jewess from the Uhlan Displaced Person's Camp?" the nun asked with an air of disgust.

Nodding her head in quick succession, Louisa answered the nun in basic German conversation, "Yes, please, I need help! I am in enormous pain and nine months pregnant. Water is dripping from my body. I think my baby is coming and I am very frightened. Please help me. I am alone and I don't know what else to do." The dispassionate nun offered a silent nod. She stepped closer to Louisa's side and held onto the back of her waist before guiding her through the entrance way into the receiving area of the hospital. She sat Louisa down in a wheelchair and pushed her down a long, green corridor, past thick plaster walls and onto a ramp leading to the upper hall of the maternity ward.

Louisa heard the sounds of torturous moans and screams of other young women in labor and delivery. While stationed in a room that smelled like a combination of alcohol, disinfectant and the faint scent of cloves, the nun helped her lie down on a cot and told her to wait. By this time, she was in a state of delirium. The harsh contractions were coming faster, becoming intolerable, causing Louisa's body to thrash around the narrow receiving cot. Soon, another stoic-looking nun appeared; staring at her wordlessly. Dressed in the same regulatory uniform, she seemed to ignore Louisa's pain and suffering. Without delay, she began to follow the well-practiced routine, stripping away Louisa's outer garments, pulling the nightgown off over her head, and wrenching the amniotic-drenched under-panties down to her knees. She shoved two penetrating fingers into Louisa's vagina, reaching up to feel the opening of the cervix to determine how many centimeters she was dilated.

When the contraction subsided, Louisa became conscious of her new surroundings. The hospital room was quite barren. A single-bulb lamp shed a vague, dimming light on the weathered window shades. A bleached white hue reflected ample light onto ice-cold walls, allowing her eyes to adjust to the partially lit room. Adjacent to the bed was an open window, infusing the room with earthy scents of the early morning dew. Centered on a white doily on a side oak table was a large pitcher placed next to a glass half-filled with water. Permeating throughout the antiseptic-smelling room was the subtle odor of freshly scrubbed and scoured bare floors. The hospital room became a new type of captivity, a place where she had no choice but to survive the unchartered territory of childbirth. She would have to succumb to the nuns' apathetic treatment, make her way through the blinding fog of their emotionless neglect.

Feeling crazed, Louisa lay terrified, just waiting for the next relentless contraction to seize her defenseless body. Alone in a strange hospital and at the mercy of the nuns, she was left with no support; plagued with the worst physical pain of her life and having no knowledge of what to expect or what was about to happen to her body. Her mind was spinning: Oh my God, who is this person who is trying to help me? Is she a righteous nun? Does she mean well? I feel so violated by her gruffness, powerless against her superiority. I hate being so vulnerable, unable to get up and walk away from it all. Does she treat everyone the same way? Is it because I am a Jew? This is the way one would handle a doll, an inanimate object. Is this a routine exam? Is she a witch or an angel? Louisa assured herself: I can do this. I am the same woman who managed to survive the burning fires of a hellish nightmare, despite the fact that I was alone and scared to death. I will be resilient and strong, and I will bring my newborn baby into this world! Samuel and I will start a wonderful new life with our precious child and we will be blessed. Good always prevails over evil.

Suddenly, another powerful pain came back, becoming decisively worse, unmanageable; like trying to prevent the hot flow of volcanic lava after an eruption. Gripping her body tightly, as if able to prevent the pains from gathering force, Louisa began screaming in her native Polish tongue, "Please somebody help me. Stop the contractions! Make them go away! I cannot take this anymore!"

Sitting across from her bed were three stoic nuns, their faces ashen, looking as if they had been deprived of sunlight for ages. They sat upright on high-backed wooden chairs. All of them knitting peacefully, deliberately avoiding even the slightest glance in Louisa's direction. With each ripping contraction, they ignored her fitful tossing, as she lay on the starched white bed linens that were tightly wrapped around the narrow hospital bed. The nuns remained non-plussed, poised rigidly on the chairs, holding their spines erect. Occasionally, one of them would look up at the wall clock while keeping time with each contraction before deeming it necessary to call for a doctor.

Feeling all alone, Louisa was plagued with worry: What is happening? Should the pains be so hurtful? Is something wrong with me or the baby? Is this the way I am to face my own death? I wish I could ask my precious mother. My 'mammala' didn't live long enough to tell me about any of this torture. I wish my dear Samuel was here to comfort me! How foolish I was to come here alone.

As Louisa's labor steadily progressed, her own fervent screams joined with the discordant chorus of moaning from the other laboring women in the maternity ward. Thankfully, every time a contraction had subsided, there was a moment's relief. It was the only time she was able to soothe herself, listening to the clock's ticking in tune with the synchronized clicking of knitting needles.

Louisa thought how curious it was how the nuns knew, instinctively without ever having experienced giving birth, when she was nearing the final stage of childbirth. Somehow, they did know exactly when it was time to put down their knitting and call for the doctor. Finally, when the doctor did arrive, Louisa's body was ready to push out a new life into the cruel, war-torn and overturned world.

Precisely at 4:11am, Louisa gave birth to a free spirit, a beautiful and healthy baby girl. The birth came at a time when she might have doubted the existence of miracles, after a time when there was only doom, humiliation, pain and suffering. Throughout her pregnancy, Louisa imagined the fetus growing inside, comparing it to the slow bloom of a flower; a tiny bud ripening with time. When finally ready to burst open and greet the world, it will bloom gloriously and give joy to the world. She wondered in a state of awe at the glory of nature and she felt as if she had given birth to a miracle.

It seemed like an eternity while Louisa waited for the nuns to finish examining, weighing, sponge bathing and wrapping the newborn in a clean, soft cloth. When a nun finally placed the tiny, feather-like bundle on Louisa's chest, she gasped at the sight of her daughter's face. As she inhaled the fresh intoxicating scent of her newborn, their eyes met for the first time. At that moment, Louisa became a mother. As Samuel lay sleeping in his bed, little did he know that he became a father again.

Louisa held her daughter swaddled in her arms, she ̠elirious with feelings of long-lost happiness. Her first words to her precious daughter were, "Welcome, my sweet angel. You are a miracle from God and without his mercy and grace, you would not be here. There is so much I want to show you, but first I want to tell you the truth about what happened to me and your father. You must know it all before we start our new journey together as mother, father, and daughter."

Just then, one of the nuns entered the room, stopping to watch the Louisa and her daughter wrapped together in the bed, mesmerized by the bond of love between them. She continued to speak to her daughter. "I was only 18 years old; a carefree teenager living a normal family life. My teenage years seemed perfect and happy, but in the blink of an eye, my life was turned upside down. I lost my youth and my whole family was wiped out; gone ablaze, like an out-of-control forest fire leaving behind only ashes of despair. I almost lost my mind. Always remember how fast life can change and go astray. But you must always remember to fight. Don't ever give in to hatred and always fight for fairness. With God by our sides, I will be here all the days of your life to protect you and to love you with all of my heart.

The infant remained curiously silent, wriggling her little body against Louisa's breast as if to encourage her to continue her story. Louisa smiled at her precious bundle of joy, a gift from the heavens whose eyes seemed to sparkle, twinkling with anticipation like shining stars amidst the dark sky. How could such a tiny life force be strong enough to lift away Louisa's looming past that hung like heavy cumulous clouds? This baby was the sunshine that brightened the view on the horizon. Louisa's flow of heartfelt tears began cascading onto her baby's face. After living a life of disconnect from everyone else in the world, Louisa imagined how her tears formed their own pathway, connecting two souls; uniting them in mind, body and spirit.

Ours is a country built more on people than on territory. The Jews will come from everywhere: from France, from Russia, from America, from Yemen... Their faith is their passport. -David Ben Gurion

Land of the Free

Samuel was pacing impatiently back and forth in the waiting area of the maternity ward. He was thinking about what it would be like to be a father again; to feel the strong, fast heartbeat of an infant against his chest, to be able to care for and love another human being even more than himself. The promise of a new life was beckoning to him. Little did he know that in nine months, thanks to President Harry Truman's efforts to lift the quotas allowing displaced persons to emigrate to America, they would be granted their visas.

Suddenly, a tall, lanky nun energetically pushed open the hospital door, stopping to face Samuel. Her stone-faced expression revealed no information and her gray eyes that peered over tiny spectacles were cold as industrial steel. Samuel was eager to find out news. "Tell me, sister. Is everything alright? What has happened? Did my wife give birth yet? Any complications? A boy or a girl? Healthy? Is she awake? Can I go in and see her now? Is the doctor with her?" The nun responded painfully slow, employing a low voice, a deliberate tone that might be used to soothe an out-of-control mental patient. "Yes, she had a healthy baby girl," the nun informed him with no indication of a smile. "I am assuming you are the father. No obvious issues. Right now, she is resting and will be able to see you." Placing her right hand squarely on the door knob and pushing the door open to Louisa's room, she motioned for Samuel to enter. He sprinted inside towards Louisa, passing by several other beds filled with tired mothers. While other babies continued to wail, this baby remained strangely quiet, still intent on listening to her mother's story.

Samuel bent down to hug and kiss them both, while unstoppable tears drenched his face. In that moment they became a family and his once shattered heart felt whole again. Together they stared at their perfectly beautiful daughter, suspended in a state of joy and awe. "My darling Samuel, what should we call her?" Samuel thought for a second and said, "Please, she must be named after my beloved mother, Sarah. The Hebrew name for Sarah means princess, noblewoman." Louisa's eyes lit up with approval, adding another suggestion, "That's perfect for her Hebrew name, but we really just need a name that begins with an S. I have always loved the name Sylvia. It means "Spirit from the trees of the forest. In honor of all our people who survived by the shelter of the trees in the forest, I must choose this name for our daughter."

The baby responded with a soft gurgling sound and they both laughed. "I believe she likes her name!" Samuel smiled and then he bent over to whisper lovingly into the baby's ear. "Hello, my precious Sylvia." Samuel kissed Sylvia's tiny cheek, and then he bent over to give Louisa a long kiss filled with deep gratitude.

Louisa made a last suggestion. "You know, my beloved mother's Hebrew name was Anna, meaning grace. Don't you think we should honor her too? Let's give her a middle name, Anita, little Anna. It means that God is gracious, has shown favor upon her, upon us all. My mother will be smiling upon her with her blessings from above for the rest of her life. Sylvia Anita Rosenberg, welcome to the world!"

It was a warm spring evening in May 1949, aboard the General Holbrook Army ship approaching the Boston Harbor, USA. Standing anxiously on the deck of the ship, Samuel, Louisa, and Sylvia were squeezed together along with many other immigrant survivors. Blocking their ears from the roar of the ship engine, they watched as the crests of breaking waves topped by crystal-clear whitecaps reflected the ultramarine blueness of the ocean. They welcomed the splashing droplets of sea spray that rose up to greet their faces and soak their clothes. It was nature's way of cleansing their past and preparing them for a fresh, new start.

The journey across the ocean on the United States army ship was almost intolerable. They lived for long weeks in primitive conditions, along with many other survivors in the steerage section of the army ship. They had no choice but to eat the canned food saturated with salt, and seasickness was rampant throughout the trip. Once again, Louisa and Samuel endured grueling conditions and survived. Faith, hope and love were their constant companions, along with their precious baby Sylvia.

Swaying in the glorious air with their spirits flying high, they were about to build a new future in America. They had finally arrived. The ship docked at the shores of the glorious land of the free, the golden key of promise! In the far distance, they could see the glistening lights of the beautiful city of Boston. One by one, many of them dropped down to their knees to kiss the floor, thanking the lucky stars, singing their praises to the land of the free.

Afterword

Louisa, Samuel and their nine-month old baby Sylvia got off the US Navy ship in Boston Harbor, and then made their way to Binghamton, New York. Their original Visa assigned destination was Dallas, Texas. Louisa's only remaining family member, her brother Kalman, lived in Binghamton and he became their sponsor. Fortunately, they were able to change their Visa and went to live with Kalman until they got on their feet. Kalman survived the war since he was stationed in Siberia fighting against Russia before they became allies with the United States. Louisa kept in touch with the Kupferbergs, her friends from the root cellar, for many years after the war. Samuel and Louisa became United States citizens and they lived the remainder of their lives in Binghamton, New York.

Rosenberg Family Pictures:
Samuel, Louisa and Sylvia

Author Notes: Sylvia Epstein

I grew up in the countryside of upstate New York, the daughter of Louisa and Samuel Rosenberg. As an only child of Holocaust survivors, I was living proof that they had survived against all odds. I was the symbol of their ability to start over again. Throughout my childhood, my parents freely shared their personal Holocaust stories with me. I have always been inspired to write about my parents' true story and to leave a legacy for my children and grandchildren. This book is filled with my parents' experiences during one of the cruelest, saddest times in history. Since my mother and father are both no longer able to give more detail, I based this book upon their stories as I remember them. I connected the factual dots, colored in the spaces with fictional characters, and seasoned the story with heartfelt emotion, empathy and compassion.

Being raised by immigrant parents taught me many valuable lessons about human nature, which I have carried forward in my own life. I developed the ability to empathize with others who had to make their way through challenging times. I have always been mesmerized with reading books that told of determined women who fought to make a difference and who were able to triumph over humble beginnings. Strength, faith, fortitude and resilience became the boat on which I have navigated the storms of life. Just like what happened to my parents, no matter what, I knew I would always find a way to survive.

My parents often told me how my grandparents would have been so proud of me, how they would have adored me. I dreamed that maybe I even resembled or identified with one of them in some way. When blessed with my first grandchild, I was overjoyed. I had a new sense of gratitude, the joy of belonging to an extended family; a deep sense of unity within a larger family unit. My deepening family roots grounded me and fortified me in ways I had never imagined. I wanted to give them everything that my grandparents would have wished to give me. The role of Nana has been the pinnacle of my life and it became the impetus that offered me the soulful purpose to tell the story of my mother and father.

During the writing of this book, my seven-year experience evolved into a proverbial sanctuary, a catharsis of pent-up, underlying emotions and an unearthing of buried treasures in my mind. The task of telling my parents' truths helped me assert the courage to bare my soul and innermost thoughts. I am the only one alive who holds this information and I feel a deep responsibility to preserve it, as one would preserve history in a book. This book is a portal, a window into the lives of those who lived on this earth. I feel compelled to be a voice to share their story, to leave a legacy that will ensure that future generations remember what took place. At this time in history, most Holocaust survivors have passed into the heavenly realm and can no longer share their stories. I want this book to be a testament to their lives and the many lives that were lost.

I write this as a reminder to keep your eyes open and to stand up for what is wrong, so we can prevent anything like this from happening again. It is my hope that readers might find a sense of solace as they read about the importance of having faith in the good, risk-taking actions of others. My life now has deep meaning, knowing that this story will be available to my children and grandchildren, citizens of the world, and future generations to come.

Author Biography

Sylvia Epstein began her thirty-two-year career teaching students in all K-12 levels in education. guiding teachers and families by means of her leadership. She retired after a successful and rewarding forty-year career in education. During that time, she worked as an elementary teacher and as an English teacher at the middle school level. Her first leadership position was as vice principal at a middle school before becoming an elementary school principal, a position she maintained for twenty years.

Among her accomplishments: In 2005, Sylvia Epstein was awarded Woman of the Year in Dutchess County, New York. She wrote articles for the Together Magazine for Holocaust Survivors, and presented motivational speeches designed for teachers, parents and students. Under her leadership, her school was honored with winning the New York State Character Education Award.

She holds two master's degrees in teaching K-12 and in educational administration and leadership, as well as having earned an ABD degree from the doctoral program at Northcentral University. She has served as a college mentor for student interns in the CITE leadership program at the College at St. Rose, Long Island, New York. Among her special interests: traveling around the world, practicing yoga and meditation, classical piano, watercolor painting, sketching, gifting her own hand-painted children's rockers to her friends, knitting, reading classic literature, historical fiction novels, leadership, and self-enhancement books.

Married for 52 years, Sylvia and her husband Harold have lived mostly in New York's Hudson Valley region. Aside from having two accomplished sons, two daughters-in law, this book is dedicated to her three adored grandchildren. Currently, Sylvia and her husband share their time primarily at residences in Rhode Island and Florida.

Acknowledgements

Many special thanks to the editing efforts of my devoted best friend and brilliant husband of the past 52 years, Harold Epstein, as well to my dear and cherished friends who volunteered to become additional edit readers: Ellen Wishner Koppelman, Cathy Meicklem, and Carole Marchese whose love and steadfast encouragement and inspiration helped me stay on track for the past seven years it has taken me to write my first book. Special heartfelt thanks to Romana Gould, who completed the final editing process, designed the cover, and whose expertise prompted me to self-publish through Kindle Direct Publishing on Amazon.

True wealth is a collection of treasured moments

This is a heart locket with Samuel and Louisa's pictures inside, along with important religious symbols. These treasures were recently found, tucked inside a tiny silver box.

Made in United States
Orlando, FL
29 February 2024

44195258R00163